Christ, the African King
New Testament Christology

STUDIEN ZUR INTERKULTURELLEN GESCHICHTE DES CHRISTENTUMS
ETUDES D´HISTOIRE INTERCULTURELLE DU CHRISTIANISME
STUDIES IN THE INTERCULTURAL HISTORY OF CHRISTIANITY

begründet von/fondé par/founded by
Hans Jochen Margull †, Hamburg

herausgegeben von/édité par/edited by

<table>
<tr><td>Richard Friedli
Université de Fribourg</td><td>Walter J. Hollenweger
University of Birmingham</td><td>Theo Sundermeier
Universität Heidelberg</td></tr>
<tr><td></td><td>Jan A. B. Jongeneel
Rijksuniversiteit Utrecht</td><td></td></tr>
</table>

Band 82

PETER LANG
Frankfurt am Main · Berlin · Bern · New York · Paris · Wien

Ukachukwu Chris Manus

Christ, the African King
New Testament Christology

PETER LANG
Frankfurt am Main · Berlin · Bern · New York · Paris · Wien

Die Deutsche Bibliothek - CIP-Einheitsaufnahme

Manus, Ukachukwu Chris:

Christ, the African king : New Testament christology /
Ukachukwu Chris Manus. - Frankfurt am Main ; Berlin ; Bern ;
New York ; Paris ; Wien : Lang, 1993
  (Studien zur interkulturellen Geschichte des Christentums ;
  Bd. 82)
  ISBN 3-631-45211-X

NE: GT

BT
270
. M36
1993

Published with the aid of the Institute of
Missiology Missio, Aachen, Germany

ISSN 0170-9240
ISBN 3-631-45211-X

© Verlag Peter Lang GmbH, Frankfurt am Main 1993
All rights reserved.

Printed in Germany 1 2 3 4 6 7

Through Christ, Our King, the door of life
is opened to us. Through the cross of the
Messiah-King and His Resurrection, the gates
of hell are shattered.

Cover photo: A Madonna carved on a door of an African local
Church in North Cameroun.

Source: Missio, Aachen, Germany, Adventbild (1991).

DEDICATION

To Mama Dora who first taught me that Jesus

Nwa Chukwu, bu EZE

TABLES OF CONTENTS

CHAPTER FOUR
KINGSHIP IN PRECOLONIAL AFRICA : EAST - WEST
THE YORUBA AND THE BAGANDA KINGDOMS

CHAPTER FIVE
THE SHILLUK AND THE ZULU KINGS

CHAPTER SIX
JESUS OF NAZARETH

CHAPTER SEVEN
THE KINGDOM OF GOD

4

CHAPTER EIGHT
THE KINGSHIP OF JESUS : SOME TEXTS AND THEIR EXEGESIS

CHAPTER NINE
KINGSHIP : AFRICAN AND NEW TESTAMENTS IDEAS

CHAPTER TEN
GENERAL CONCLUSIONS
KING-CHRISTOLOGY. IMPLICATIONS

6

ACKNOWLEDGEMENTS

My interest in the area of New Testament Christology has its inception in a research essay I published in the *Bulletin of African Theology*, Volume 7, (Kinshasa, 1985). In that study, I examined the confession of Jesus' divine Sonship by the Roman Centurion who supervised his crucifixion (Mk 15,39) and the import of Markan Christology of the text in the African context. Since the appearance of that study, my predilection for research in New Testament Christology for Africa and the world has more than doubled. *King Christology* which is the central manifesto of the present volume has, in recent times, attracted much more my time and attention. My article, *Jesu Kristi Oba ...*, the end-result of a research on the Christology of the *Aladura* Christians in Yorubaland, Nigeria, published in *Asia Journal of Theology*, Volume 5, (Singapore, 1991) provided richer insights and further impetus. For that study, I am indebted to my 1990 Part IV students of *Rel 412: Biblical Theology* at the Department of Religious Studies, Obafemi Awolowo University, Ile-Ife, Nigeria who assisted and cooperated in the field-research. Their stimulating and vigorous discussion helped me as a non Yoruba speaking Nigerian to re-align my original vision to the actual facts of the case.

I remain fully grateful to the Alexander von Humboldt-Stiftung, Bonn whose Fellowship enabled me to undertake research for this work in the Federal Republic of Germany from April 1990 to April 1992. I am thankful to the authorities of the Philosophisch-Theologishe Hochschule Sankt Georgen, Frankfurt am Main, my host Institute and the entire Jesuit Community of the College for their hospitality throughout the period of my research and for the use of the institution's library facilities. My academic host and good friend, Prof. Dr. Johannes Beutler SJ, who has shown a continuing interest in the pertinency of New Testament studies in the context of African Christian Theology provided much helpful guidance and encouragement. To him, I am specially indebted. I lack words enough to express my thankfulness to the staff and Herr Siegfried Seyfarth, the Chief Librarian of the Leo Frobenius Institute of Historical Ethnology of the Wolfgang Goethe University, Liebigstraße, Frankfurt am Main who were ever ready to help locate books and other literature I needed in a jampacked Library as theirs.

I also wish to express my unreserved gratitude to De Heer Etién D'Hont, the chief librairan at the Leuven University's Faculty of Theology, my *Alma Mater*'s Library, Louvain, Belgium, and his staff who helped me in their friendly and usual manner to make use of the Library as an AvH Europe Fellow during the months of November and December, 1991. I am ever grateful to the Rector and Vice Rector, of the American College, The Catholic University of Louvain, Belgium, Rev. John Griesbach, friend and course-mate in the Faculty during the 1974-1977 academic years for providing me with decent accommodation at their College. Thanks also go to De Heer Jaak en Mevrouw Monique Dacosse-Bekkers, my Belgian family friends in whose house I constantly made my port of call during my stay at Louvain.

There are many other people whose friendship, love and warmth contributed in no small measure towards the timely completion of this work. In this regard, I cannot fail to mention the Nigerian priest-students at St. Georgen, namely Jude Ike, Austin Echema, James Okpalaonwuka, Fortune Nwachukwu and the other brethren during the academic years 1990/1991-1991/1992 with whom I often entered into heated but intriguing arguments on the significance of African cultural values for New Testament studies, Traditional Christology and my *King-Christology* programme. Their criticisms and contentions, no doubt, helped broaden the focus of this work. For that I give them my grateful thanks. There are others who, on the social level, brightened up my stay in Frankfurt: Mr. & Mrs Bright Ebulue, Mr. & Mrs. Theo. Ninikanwa, Mr. & Mrs. Goddy Nwogwugwu, Mr. & Mrs. Morgan Oparaugo, Mr. Zeph Chiekezi Abara, my only townsman in the Rhine-Main area during the period.

My great thanks go to my German family friends, Familie Frohmaier-Schukow (Mainhardt), especially to Cecilia, who as my Tandem Patnerin during my Language course at the Goethe Institute in Schwäbisch Hall in Baden- Württemberg, made their home a haven for me. Both Dr. med. Emma. and Dr. med. Frau Umana who were my family doctors, I remember with thanks. I also register my deep appreciation to Rev. Fr. Edgar Behac, the pastor of St. Bonifatius Catholic Parish, Bonames, Frankfurt and the parishioners in whose Parish House I lived during the composition of the larger portion of this work. I do not forget Familie Bertsch for their generosity. I remain fully indebted to my neighbour, Herr Frank Biberger, Part II theological student at St. Georgen for his friendship and the assistance he rendered me in my Computer learning and practice; and for the time he put in on the lay-out of this work.

As could be noticed from above, research for this work was done during my sabbatical year and Leave of Absence from my home university. I am indebted to the

8

Obafemi Awolowo University, Ile-Ife, Nigeria for granting me leave for the two years of study abroad; and to the colleagues who covered my courses and assignments while absent, I am thankful. Lastly, but not the least, I ever remain grateful to my wife, Mrs. Mercy Chinyere Manus who lavished so much care on me during her stay with me in Frankfurt. To my daughters who endured patiently and sacrificed gladly as they were forced to miss the closeness of *Daddie* during the period, I remorsefully ask for their pardon.

I.   PREFACE

When the Jesus phenomenon erupted into our human world in the first century AD in Palestine; and as S. Neill instructively remarks:

> and struck human life, the fragments flew off in every direction. No single mind could encompass the whole, no single hand could draw the definitive portrait of him. Each took what he was able to grasp and recorded it in this way or in that; but each writer was sure that what was being recorded was not a matter of personal invention and creativity.[1]

Thus in the narratives of the New Testament, we discover what the early Christians believed about the person of Jesus. New Testament evidence supposes that different christologies can be distinguished already during the time of the New Testament church. It appears that from the very beginning, there occured divergent interpretations of faith in the Christ event. There is a conscious effort to incluturate the event in the Jewish/Gentile religiosity and piety of the time using the OT scriptures as proof-texts.[2] Certainly there is a clear variation in emphasis. The central theme of Jesus' message is anchored on the theme: *God in Search of Man*. Jesus proclaims this message in his parables whose main thrust is usually on the lost condition of man and the possibility of his allowing himself to be *re-discovered* by God. The way and means of realizing God's will is what Jesus proclaims in his message and demonstrates in his actions as he breaks through certain religious and ethnic barriers regarding tax-collectors, sinners and the socially despised people.

The kernel of Jesus' message, no doubt, preserved in the New Testament has altogether been assumed into a new vision of faith. This faith vision can be summed up as follows: Jesus of Nazareth has been able to bring God nearer to man because he is divine. The whole concern of the earliest church mission was to confess and proclaim the transcendence of Jesus. Cross and resurrection had been central in the Church's primitive kerygma; especially by St. Paul, whose teaching and preaching virtually focused and

---

[1] S. Neill, Jesus Through Many Eyes. Introduction to the Theology of the New Testament, Philadelphia, Fortress, 1976, p. 4.

[2] Cf. M. Czajkowski, "Die Inkulturation des Evangeliums Jesu im Neuen Testament und Heute" *Collectanea Theologica* 58(1988)29-38.

revolved on the death and resurrection of Jesus. For Paul and those earliest Christians, they had maintained that the divine character of Jesus was established by the doctrines of the cross and the resurrection. Thus, as the oldest and the most revered Christology, the death of Jesus on the cross constituted the core of the Christian catechesis as well as the unique Christian ritual. However, it is crucial to recognize that even in the theology that first detailed out this "divine character" or the "transcendence" of Jesus, there was a gradual development in the thought-forms of the early Christians as is represented in the Synoptic gospels and John. Today, the phenomenon has continued to widen as Christianity has penetrated other cultures and is being expressed in autochthonous forms.

African Christology is one such arm of the current development. In recent times, it has become so hastily pursued and could be sufficiently misguided. There is therefore need for further thinking, elaboration and research apart from the prevalence of West European and North American christologies in our midst. This study is offered as an effort to fill this lacuna. It seeks to expose the NT texts associated with Jesus' kingship in order to translate them into local imageries in our receptor cultures so that an eventual hermeneutical task of re-stating the categories analogous to scriptural ones can become possible. Let me be permitted to sound this *caveat*: working in my area of expertise and interest, it is my desire to share my scholarship in a fairly non technical language. Thus, the Greek in the passages commented upon in this study, will be transliterated where necessary to enable you, perhaps, as a non expert read fluently "the things of which you have been informed" (Lk 1,4).

II.   ABBREVIATIONS

AAS	Acta Apostolicae Sedis
AB	Anchor Bible
ACNT	Augsburg Commentary on the New Testament
ATJ	African Theological Journal
AJBS	African Journal of Biblical Studies
AJT	Asian Journal Of Theology, Singapore
AnBib	Analecta Biblica
ANTJ	Arbeiten zum Neuen Testament und Judentum
AThANT	Abhandlungen zur Theologie des Alten und Neuen Testaments
AUSS	Andrews University Seminary Studies
AUS DDS	Andrews University Seminary Doctoral Dissertations Series
BAT	Bulletin of African Theology
BEThL	Bibliotheca Ephemeridum Theologicarum Lovaniensium
BEvTh	Beiträge zur Evangelischen Theologie
BhEvTh	Beihefte zur Evangelischen Theologie
BHTh	Beiträge zur Historischen Theologie
Bib	Biblica
BJRL	Bulletin of John Rylands Library
BTA	Bulletin de la Théologie Africaine, Kinshasa
BTB	Biblical Theology Bulletin
BWANT	Beiträge zur Wissenschaft vom Alten und Neuen Testament
BZ	Biblische Zeitschrift
BZNW	Beihefte zur Zeitschrift für die neutestamentliche Wissenschaft
CBAA	Catholic biblical Association of America
CBC	Cambridge Bible Commentaries
CBQ	Catholic Biblical Quarterly
CHIEA	Catholic Higher Institute of Eastern Africa
CUP	Cambridge University Press
EKKNT	Evangelisch-katholischer Kommentar zum Neuen Testament
ET	English Translation

12

ETL	Ephemerides Theologicae Lovanienses
EUS	European University Studies
ExpT	Expository Times
FRLANT	Forschungen zur Religion und Literatur des Alten und Neuen Testaments
Fs.	Festschrift
GS	Gospel of Thomas
HR	History of Religions
HThKNT	Supl. Herders Theologischer Kommentar zum Neuen Testament, Supl. Band
HTR	Harvard Theological Review
IBS	Irish Biblical Studies
ICC	International Critical Commentary
IDB	G. A. Buttrick, ed., Interpreter's Dictionary of the Bible
Interp.	Interpretation
ITQ	Irish Theological Quarterly
JASO	Journal of the Anthropological Society of Oxford
JBL	Journal of Biblical Literature
JHSN	Journal of the Historical Society of Nigeria
JMB	Japan Missionary Bulletin
JRA	Journal of Religion in Africa
JSNT SS	Journal for the Study of the New Testament Supplement Series
JTSA	Journal of Theology for Southern Africa
JTS	Journal of Theological Studies
LXX	Septuagint
MHUC	Monographs of the Hebrew Union College
MT	Masoretic Text
N.A	No Author
NB SSSc	New Babylon Studies in the Social Sciences
NCE	New Catholic Encyclopedia
N.D	No Date
NJTh	Nigerian Journal of Theology
NovT	Novum Testamentum
NovT Suppl	Novum Testamentum Supplements

NTA	New Testament Abstracts
NTS	New Testament Studies
OUP	Oxford University Press
PL	Patrologia Latina
RAT	Revue Africain de Théologie
RB	Revue Biblique
RSV	Revised Standard Version
SBL DS	Society of Biblical Literature Dissertation Series
SBT	Studies in Biblical Theology
SBS	Stuttgarter Biblische Studien
SNTS	Society for New Testament Studies
SNTS MS	Society for New Testament Studies, Monograph Series
SPCK	Society for the Promotion of Christian Knowledge
StUNT	Studien zur Umwelt des Neuen Testaments
TD	Theology Digest
TDNT	G. Kittel, Theological Dictionary of the New Testament
ThLZ	Theologische Literaturzeitung
ThQ	Theologische Quartalschrift
ThR	Theologische Rundschau
TrinJ	Trinity Journal
TS	Theological Studies
TWNT	Theologisches Wörterbuch zum Neuen Testament
URAM	Ultimate Reality And Meaning (The Journal of)
VJTR	Vidyajyoti Journal of Theological Reflection
WAJES	West African Journal of Ecclesial Studies
WMANT	Wissenschaftliche Monograpien zum Alten und Neuen Testament
WUNT	Wissenschaftliche Untersuchungen zum Neuen Testament
ZKTh	Zeitschrift für Katholische Theologie
ZNW	Zeitschrift für die neutestamentliche Wissenschaft und die Kunde der älteren Kirche
ZThK	Zeitschrift für Theologie und Kirche

14

III.   INTRODUCTION

Christ the African King, is a theological study. It is the result of a research undertaken from
the African cultural and the New Testament scriptural perspectives. As a work on theology,
its primary focus is a reflection on God, man and society. It is a reflection, in other words,
about the human condition in relation to God, the articulation of human finite situation
concerning the infinite that has incarnated Itself into our world. In this perspective, theology
is certainly a science of faith. Perhaps, it may best be understood in the Rahnerian terms.
According to Karl Rahner, theology is "the conscious and methodological explanation and
explicitation of the divine revelation received and grasped in faith";[1] and I would like to
add, by man. Revelation is God's gift of Himself in human history by an act of His self
disclosure to mankind. The task of theological reflection therefore is, among other things, to
explain and to explicitate the phenomenon of revelation in order to articulate its consequent
implications for the faith and morals of the faithful in their own concrete historical contexts.
Theology is not the object of revelation. God does not reveal theologies. As Wilfred
Cantwell Smith puts it:

> theology is one of many human responses to God and to His initiatives,
> responses decidedly human and fallible; always particularist .... Theology is
> an intellectual theorizing in words, by human beings, in the light of what they
> have received; about what God is, and has done for us and wills that we do.[2]

Throughout history, Christian scholars have established the fact that Christian revelation had
been expressed in various circumstances and in different cultural settings.[3] The deposit of
faith had often been articulated in hardware concepts and propositions. But the Risen Lord
charges his Church to go into the wide world to preach the gospel and to make disciples (Mt

---

[1] K. Rahner, *Encyclopedia of Theology,* London, Burns and Oates, 1975, p. 1687.

[2] W. C. Smith, "Christian-Muslim Relations: The Theological Dimension" *Studies in
Interreligious Dialogue* 1(1991)8-24, p. 21.

[3] Cf. J. Osei-Bonsu, "Biblically/theologically based inculturation" *AFER* 32(1990)346-
358.

28,16-20).[4] Thus, revealed truth must, of necessity, encounter other nations, their values and cultures. In Africa, this encounter generates its own problems given the vast number of African peoples embracing the Christian religion today. As S. Neill puts it,

> No power on earth seems able to stay the cataract in which literally millions of Africans are surging into the Christian church every year; there seems no limit, other than the ocean, to the possibilities of this expansion.[5]

Therefore, the content of the gospel demands reflection and re-interpretation in order to become meaningful to its host, the African soil. With Cantwell, I share the view that theological ideas are human constructs which are propounded, and accepted by fallible human beings doing their utmost to conceptualize their vision of the divine. Every vision of the divinity is, however God-given, limited and such expressions or verbalizations are "but an approximation even to that personal vision, and in every case the result is time-specific, culture-specific, group-specific, language-specific".[6]

In the African situation, and so in the Asian, the gospel message had, in the past, been employed as an instrument of the destruction of native worldviews and the installation of western cultural values and imperialistic ideas.[7] The nineteenth century missionaries who worked in Igboland of Nigeria had adopted this method in their evangelization praxis. On this subject J. P. C. Nzomiwu amplifies:

> The acceptance of the new faith was not easy for the Igbos. It meant in practice a profound revolution in their lives, beliefs, and customs. At this stage authentic Christianity was understood as throwing off the "old man". By this they meant everything that was connected with their lives prior to the advent of Christianity. The new converts, with the full support and encouragement of the white missionaries, often launched assaults upon

---

[4] Cf. C. U. Manus "'King-Christology': The result of a critical study of Matt 28:16-20 as an example of contextual exegesis in Africa" *Scriptura* 39(1991)25-42.

[5] Neill, Jesus Through Many Eyes, p. 3.

[6] Smith, "Christian-Muslim Relations", p. 18.

[7] Cf. A. Wessels, Images of Jesus. How Jesus is Perceived and Portrayed in Non-European Cultures, London, SCM, 1990, p. 162; esp. n. 5.

traditional customs, beliefs and institutions. Attacks on polygamy, the destruction of images and shrines were signs of genuine conversion.

A genuine convert viewed his culture as an undesirable and anti-christian superstition which should not only be discouraged but destroyed. The method of evangelization was designed in such a way as to ensure that the new convert was isolated from his corruptive cultural surroundings and indoctrinated in the new super-culture which was then regarded as genuine Christianity.[8]

Even perceptive foreigners have noted the drastic effects of the activities of some of the missionaries. Bill Rau, in his article, "Feast to Famine the Cause of Africa's Underdevelopment" states that:

> Missionaries denied the existence of African spiritual values and went a long way to undermine African concepts of self and worth.[9]

When as a result of the resurgence of traditionalism and the consequent rediscovery of the values of the indigenous culture the Christian message is castigated and branded 'imperialist' and 'foreign'; it becomes necessary to re-formulate the Christ event with autochthonous concepts and to re-interpret the Petrine response to the Dominical question (Mt 16,13-16) in the context of the cultural setting in which the Jesus phenomenon is being preached, explained and taught in the present. Early Christians employed the images and concepts of their own cultural tradition whose meaning was shaped by their experience of the historical Jesus. But later responses given in the attempt to answer the Lord's question had resulted in conflicts between orthodox and heterodox groups in Christianity. To provide answers today is still by no means an easy task.

However, here lies the background in which *Christ the African King* has to be received, read and comprehended. Even though I am aware of other efforts made by fellow

---

[8] J. P. C. Nzomiwu, "Inculturation: Its Meaning and Implication for the Nigerian Church" *Africana Marburgensia* 13(1989)11-23, p. 14; and also J. Aguwa, "Christianity and the Development of Igbo culture Today" *Bigard Theological Studies* 10(1990)26-37 who speaks rightly of the inconoclasm of African culture brought upon African traditional culture in her encounter with the West.

[9] B. Rau, Feast to Famine the Cause of Africa's Underdevelopment. A Document of the Afican Faith and Justice Network, Washington DC, p. 17.

Africans, it is in response to the need to further diversify our response that I propound a *King-Christology* to define the African conception of the sovereingty of Christ, the Messiah-King, as an important factor in contemporary African Christian theology. And since theology is both 'God-talk' and 'man-talk', which *in extenso* means that human experience should be at the centre of any theological discourse, I have purposefully elected to investigate African kingship systems. This is an institution which reveals how the pre-western African person actually was and the manner in which he experienced himself as a person in community-with-others, with the kings and with all the forces the sovereigns represented. Besides, *Christ the African King* is not only an elaboration of a New Testament doctrine in the African context, but a conscious effort to express in a theological way how Africans express their faith in, loyalty to and follwership of Christ, the King of their lives and total existence.

CHAPTER ONE

METHODOLOGICAL QUESTIONS

1.1   INTRODUCTION

In what follows, I will outline the methodological approaches which undergirds the composition of this work. To begin with, I will briefly highlight the scope of the work, the justifications of the study, the objectives of the study and the methodology I have adopted. Ideas may overlap here and there but I plead that they be not seen as flaws but as conscious effusions poured out in the interest of this novel approach in contextual Christology. My approach involves the presentation of full ethnographical and anthropological informations on the chosen four African kingship traditions and their people. The religious dimensions of traditional African kingships have for long been neglected in the study of African Religions. While scholars recognize the place of Oriental kingship traditions in biblical scholarship, the rich values of African court theologies have not been put at the service of theologians and New Testament exegetes in Africa. The conclusions will present in a coherent form the summary of the units comprising the chapter as well as the main thrust and vision of my working methodology.

1.2   SCOPE OF THE WORK

Since the early seventies, nearly two decades now, seeking to portray an image of Christ suitable for African Christian expression of faith in Jesus of Nazareth has, as I have hinted earlier on, been a challenging task; and one of much concern on the part of African Christian theologians. The increasing interest devoted to Christological studies reveal the burning desire of Africans to present a different horizon, of course, "not another Jesus ...," and "a different gospel ..." (2 Cor 11,4) from which Africans can perceive the figure of Christ already brought into the African continent. The interest of pioneer African theologians has, in general, been centred on the discussions about the historical Jesus typical of the nineteenth century *Leben-Jesu Forschung*; the search for paradigms with which one can glean from Jesus' life and mission lessons for urgent issues of liberation and adaptation (incarnation). Few had undertaken research into African traditional religious cultures to discover equivalent nomenclatures that suit the biblical titles of Jesus. In quite recent times, some notable African theologians mainly from the Central African regions have ventured deeper into the African socio-cultural traditions and have picked on such ideas as ancestor, healer, *nganga*, kinsman, chief, and *maitre d'initiation* in order to portray Christ's many-sidedness to the African Christians and the universal Church. Despite the appearance of these proposals, research has still not exhausted the vast cultural wealth of Africa for respectful and dynamic concepts. These efforts have however generated new and challenging questions while the insights have inspired further zeal towards the search for new options. There still remains however a general lack of some distinctive traits yet to be broached in the African Christological proposals. Africa needs a virile Christology which is responsive to African history and culture and at the same time biblically founded. Even though creative attempts have been made to offer responses to the perennial question: "Who do you say I am?" (Mt 16,16-17) with themes rooted and derived from African cultural setting; no known serious attempt has been made to give response to the same question from both the African background and the results of New Testament exegesis, nor has any indepth scientific exegetical approach representative of contemporary scholarship been employed to elaborate a Christology tailored for the African Christendom. We must remind ourselves that the raw data of divine revelation mediated through Jesus of Nazareth is a legacy of the early Church whose Books of Worship constitute what we know as the New Testament. In fact, the many approaches so far made, as we shall soon see in the next chapter, only skate over the New Testament materials to the extent that the value of New Testament theologies in elaborating Christological reflections in Africa often gets evaporated into thin air. John S. Mbiti's Cambridge Doctoral Dissertaion (1963) later published as a book made a good start in inculturational theology in Africa.[1] In the work, Mbiti explores the encounter between Christian theology and African religious concepts uncovered from research on African

---

[1] J.S. Mbiti, New Testament Eschatology in an African Background. A Study of the Encounter between New Testament Theology and African Traditional Concepts, Oxford University Press, 1971; London, SCM Press, 1978.

studies. Among other things, he examines the concepts of time and history, the meta-linguistic concepts of eschatology, the eschatology of the sacraments, and the proximity of the Spririt-world. Mbiti successfully articulates the Akamba, his own people's idea of the resurrection event as corporate eschatology. For me, he pioneers a work with an inter-disciplinary flavour still quite relevant for Africa. His work indeed represents the first effort to adopt the results of New Testament scholarship of that time to do African theology.

The scope of this work therefore is to elaborate a Christology faithful to Jesus and the gospel witness; rooted in African history and culture and made relevant to the experience of contemporary African Christians. The work has a twofold major focus: (a) it presents a comprehensive sketch of data distilled from the massive mine of anthropological literature dealing on the religious significance of African sacred kingship traditions in precolonial societies when separation between both politics and religion was yet unknown; (b) a thorough exegesis of New Testament stories about Jesus of Nazareth, his teaching on the Kingdom of God in the Gospels and the Pauline epistles, his Kingship and the salvific role he fulfills as the Messiah-King of the earliest Christian communities, the *Ekklesia*. Findings from this two-pronged approach will constitute the basis of my christological reflections; reflections whose basic task is to contemplate the Word of Life in order to show how the African regal cultures can provide us another horizon of recognizing who the Christ is. According to J.N.K Mugambi, earliest "followers of Jesus from all walks of life recognized and appreciated his power and authority, which they described in aristocratic terms".[2] My question is: how have

---

[2] J.N.K Mugambi, "Christological Paradigms in African Christianity" in J.N.K. Mugambi and L. Magesa (eds.), Jesus in African Christianity. Experimentation and Diversity in African Christology, Nairobi, Initiatives Publishers, 1989, pp. 136-164, p. 151. While I appreciate the efforts of my East African colleagues which led to the publication of this booklet, I take issue with a particular point in Mugambi's thesis. Based on authentic and accurate African historiography, and my research findings, I contest Mugambi's claim that "Monarchy is a rare political structure in traditional Africa", *ibid.*,p. 152. According to Mugambi, "The majority of African peoples lived within ascephalous socio-political structures (decentralized). Obedience to the 'king' or 'queen' was introduced to most African peoples by colonial authorities following the partition of Africa by the Berlin Treaty in the late nineteenth century", *ibid.*, p. 152. The situation is preposterously underestimated; an unhistorically corroborated statement to pass on to Africa's younger generations. Why would Mugambi not accept that except in a few states, kingship was the central means of rulership and administration in virtually all African communities in the precontact period; and up till the advent of the colonialists on the African shores, no matter their autonomy.

African Christians captured this countenance of Christ in the light of their own history, culture and experience of aristocratic rulership well known in their states for years? This is a question whose answers I will attempt to provide in many pages of this work.

As I have already stated, the complexion of my reflections will be shaped by anthropological and ethno-historical data; that is, by ideas, concepts, and notions derived from African regal heritage of the remote past. This is the cultural age from whose patrimony and legacy hails the material culture which is being revamped for the proposition of an autochthonous Christology. I am thus concerned with the exhumation of Africa's past ideologies; namely those inherent in traditional court theologies and religious cultures. The study will, in its first part, provide a disquisition of the history of four Africa's precolonial royal institutions. What is discovered will be related to the findings from my exegetical analysis of relevant New Testament passages. In one sentence, this work makes a contribution towards the realization of a comprehensive understanding of the value of the African peoples' kingship traditions and their implications for New Testament studies. It draws our attention to the urgent need for contextual exegesis in the service of a vigorous African Christology. Finally, it is my contention that findings which arise from a study of this scope have clear and important consequences for the future of the Church, her ecclesial praxis and leadership problems in the African continent.

1.3   JUSTIFICATIONS OF THE STUDY

In the precolonial period, the kingship systems of several African states had provided a calibre of leadership whose personality and authority still survive as symbols of the peoples' identity and unity. But relating regal patterns in Africa to Christology will induce a large number of conservative thinking Christians to ask: why a 'King Christology'? Must we have a Christology which draws from African royal traditions in order to be good Christians? Were African kings not afterall callously oppressive and blood-thirsty potentates? On their face value, these and many other yet unasked questions will ever appear well put. However, the critically erroneous mind must be disabused. The frivolities of kings are no new things. They are as old as humanity itself. Did Shimei ben Gera not curse King David, Israel's most cherished king and his entourage during the flight from Absolam's rebellion as "... men of blood" and the king himself as a "worthless fellow" (2 Sam 16,7-8)? The portrayal of African kings as tyrants must be re-assessed in the light of the colonialists' ignorance of and bias against the African culture-heroes and their propaganda to support why Africans must be 'civilized', christianized and ruled. Does Mark Twain's poetic utterance, "There are many humourous things in the world, among them the white man's notion that he is less savage than other savages", not ring this bell? [3] African Christians must be reminded of several Papal injunctions and the declarations of the Fathers of the Vatican Council II which recognize the symbiotic relationship between the message of salvation and cultures.[4] Even before the dawn of this aspect of the programme of *aggiornamento*, had the Hellenistic, the Roman, the Teutonic as well as the Anglo-saxon cultural life-styles not been employed, assimilated and handed down as customs of the Christian religion? Had the Church not turned these resources to the best of her advantage?[5] Our continued negligence to fully adapt Christianity to the African cultural forms and expressions may explain why some social scientists and critics have continued to chastize Christianity and regard it as a vestige of colonialism.[6] For these men and rightly too, western civilization and values were seen as part and parcel of the Christian religion.

Contemporary situation and the level of critical thinking in Africa is getting rather much too complex. As I have elsewhere attempted to show, the increasing interest being currently generated in the revival of traditional cultures and religion in many regions of Africa make it imperative for African Christian theologians to begin to stir a course towards a holistic theological revision which can enhance meaningful dialogue between Christianity

---

[3] Quote taken from Chinweizu, The West and the Rest of Us, London,Lagos, NOK Publishers, 1978, p. 26.

[4] *Gaudium et Spes*, n. 53; Vat. II, Ad Gentes, n. 6; see John Paul II, "Address to the Bishops of Zaire", in *AFER* 22(1980)223-224; also in John Paul II, Africa: Apostolic Pilgrimage, Boston, St Paul Editions, 1980, pp. 62-63; *Evangelii Nuntiandi*, n. 20; *AAS*, 58(1966)1075.

[5] Gaudium et Spes, Section II, No. 58.

[6] Chinwizu, The West and the Rest of Us, pp. xiv-xviii.

and African Religions.[7] Indeed, the resurgence of traditionalism in today's Africa is alarmingly getting on the increase. Is it not the baptized and the churched persons, in fact, Christians who are the vanguards of these re-awakenings in Africa today? It is well, at this point, to listen to what researchers in the area of religion and society are saying. Among many of these, Udobata Onunwa has this to say:

> The survival and study of the traditional religion are gaining ground inspite of several attempts by many agents of external change to obiliterate the faith. The religion is not only surviving but also acts as an important factor in determining, directing and dictating the life-style of many people. The African, irrespective of his status, is still attached to his traditional and ancestral past. He finds succour within the context of his society and unconsciously reclines on it for support.[8]

On the overarching influence of traditional religion in national life and outlook, Onunwa continues to amplify:

> Many countries' national constitutions have given enhanced status to their traditional culture. Some political leaders who advocate the 'secular state' and its ideologies, still avail themselves of the services of the traditional religious priests, medicinemen and diviners.[9]

This esteem given to traditional religion explains why the kings who represent the bridge between the society on the one hand, the ancestral spirits and the divinities on the other occupy reverent statuses in the communities that had culturally institutionalized kingship and even in those that still have them. Relating New Testament Christology to data deriving from the religious character of African kingship systems, one of the most widely diffused and revered institutions in Africa, is a fruitful enterprise, at least, from the academic theological

---

[7] Cf. C.U. Manus, "The Areopagus Speech (Acts 17,16-34): A Study on Luke's Approach to Evangelism and its Significance in the African Context" *RAT* 13(1989)155-170, p. 169.

[8] U. Onunwa, "The Concept of Secularization and the Study of West African Traditional Religion" *Africana Marburgensia* 13(1989)3-10, pp. 7-8; also cf. C.I. Ejizu, "Religion and Politics in Nigeria: The Perspective of the Indegenous Religion" *NJTh* 1(1991)72-86, p. 72.

[9] *Ibid.*

level of thinking in so far as it provides insight into the inculturation of the Gospel message in the African cultures. A New Testament Christology which is constructed on the person, teaching and the salvific role of Christ in the Kingdom of God and how these facts are analogically related to one of the principal concepts derived from the value-system of traditional African kingships is in no way bizarre. The effort, among other things, is to inspire African Christians to rediscover the image of Christ as the *Rex Communio* (the King of the Community), the 'hidden' Christ, and the Jesus of faith who is fully alive in the African royal theologies. Besides, the idea that Christ is King is quite commonplace in the New Testament. The evangelists show that he is born King in Bethelhem; a fact documented as having been witnessed by the Magi (Mt 2,1-2/Lk 2,8-11). With an intimidating crowd, Jesus rides into Jerusalem on a donkey's back as King (Lk 19,37-38 par.). Jesus uses Palestinian idioms, proverbs and parables to explain to his audience the nature of God's Kingdom and his messianic role in it. He is arrested, accused and crucified as 'the King of the Jews' (Mk 15/Mt 27). God raised him, installed and enthroned him as the heavenly King who shepherds his flock, the Church (Mt 28,16-20).[10] Evidence from the New Testament points up to Jesus' Kingship. It is Christ, God's Son, the Prince and the Divine Agent who reigns perpetually in Christian churches in Africa. He is King and the Lord over all African kings yesterday, today and forever. The Kingdom of God has been delivered to him. It has become his entitlement and prerogative to sustain his Kingdom and its citizens.

When Christ is thus presented to Africans as the King, the sum total of all the representative African kings; that is as the *Obakarenko*, there will have emerged a Christology derived from an Africa-wide culture and expressed in a category which evokes

---

[10] C. U. Manus, "'King-Christology': The Result of a Critical Study of Matt 28,16-20 as a Example of Contextual Exegesis in Africa", pp. 39-42. I am not unaware of the existence of the theology of "Christ the King", that idea and honorific festival in the Roman Catholic calendar which dates back to Pope Pius XI who, in the Encyclical, *Quas Primas* of December 11, 1925 declared that the triumph of the King of kings, the ascended Lord and the heavenly high-priest be recognized as a feast in the Universal Catholic Church. Cf.Acta PII PP. XI, "Litterae Encyclicae" in *AAS* 17(1925)593-610. See also W. J. O'Shea, "Feast of Christ the King" in New Catholic Encyclopedia, Vol 3, New York, McGraw-Hill, 1967, pp. 627-628.

the experience of the ordinary man and woman to adoration and loyalty.[11] Such a category would make it much simpler for our Christians to understand why Christ, his teaching and his Church should be worshipped, listened to and obeyed. This is because he is King for them. These and other reasons contained in this section, underscore my choice and disposition to promote a *King-Christology* from and for the African context. As I have always stressed, Christianity as a world-wide religion needs to be earthed in the African culture in order to retain her life in the continent and to attract African descendants in the diaspora. To inculturate Christianity and to make it live in African images and symbols, our festivals, our literature, our poetry and drama, our music and everyday rituals and worship; we need, among others, a *King-Christology*.

Questions may be raised as to why I have neither included in this study the rich and traditional *Eze-ship* (kingship) of the Igbo, the *Obong-ship* of the Efik nor the *Arki-ship* of the Hausa and Kanuri nor the Divine kingship of the Jukun of Taraba State of Nigeria.[12] Let it however be understood that this is not a work on kingships as such but a discussion of a few representative systems among so many. And with reference to the Igbo, let it be known that I am neither unaware of the immense and useful ethno-historical wealth of ideas which can be tapped from the great and powerful Igbo ritual kingship traditions such as the *Eze Nri* which M.A. Onwuejeogwu has spent so much energy to unravel;[13] nor the indomitable *Eze Aro* of Aro Chukwu in south-eastern Igboland in whose palatinate thrived the cult of the *Ibini Ukpabi* (the *Long Juju*) of Aro Chukwu till 1958; nor of L. U. Ejiofor's fine and penetrating scholarship on Umuezechima Clan of southwest Igboland;[14] nor am I ignorant of the cultural

---

[11] *Obakarenko* is an acronym which I have coined from the traditional titles of the four illustrious kings studied in this work. In this study, it is used to mean *King* as I ascribe it to Jesus in the African sense. Note well that the earliest christians devised an acronym, *ichthus* composed of the Greek prefixes to represent Christ.

[12] As are, for example, treated of in G. T. Stride & Caroline Ifeka, Peoples and Empires of West Africa. West Africa in History 1000-1800, Lagos, Nelson, 1971.

[13] M. A. Onwuejeogwu, An Igbo Civilization. Nri Kingdom and Hegemony, London, Ethnographica, 1981. For full details on Igbo civilization and ethnography, see *idem.*, "The Dawn of Igbo Civilization in the Igbo Culture Area", *Odinani, The Journal of the Odinani Museum, Nri*, 1(1972)15-56.

[14] See L. U. Ejiofor, Igbo Kingdoms. Power and Control, Onitsha (Nigeria), Africana Publishers, 1982.

richness of the principal kingdoms on the Niger like the great *Obi-ship* at Onitsha nor those of Western Igboland such as the *Obi* of Aboh; the *Obi* of Issele Uku; the *Obi* of Onicha Ugbo;[15] and others too numerous to mention here.

My omission of these monarchies is deliberate. It is deliberate in the sense that if traditions I have followed are correct as consensus of scholarly opinion indicates that they are, the Yoruba kingship which is my point of departure in the African kingship studies had had such a widespread dominion in the West African sub-region, the others might have had borrowings thereof. The culture of the Edo kingdom, an offshoot of Yoruba Royal ancestry is, for example, known to have had far-reaching impact on the towns on both banks of the River Niger.[16] On this issue, Olaudah Equiano informs us that as far back as the eighteenth century, the Benin Kingdom had subjugated parts of Igboland under its sway;[17] a period A.E. Afigbo zones into the Era of Bini-Igala hegemony of Igboland though believed to be restricted to the West Niger Igboland and the Northern fringes of Nsukka.[18] To my mind, there is little to doubt that those Igbo riverain communities which had had kingship systems had been influenced by the Benin social institutions which, of course, had been derived from the Yoruba traditions.[19] Thus a study of the Yoruba royal traditions as the representative of the the the kingship cultures of the southern coastal states of Nigeria and beyond is considered the 'mother' of all kingship studies in sub-Saharan Africa. And for the southern Igbo kingdoms, especially of the Aro, if the current hypothesis of Igbo dispersal from the Nsukka-Okigwe cuesta, and the Awka-Orlu uplands where the Isuama group from which the Aro Igbo descended as advanced by Afigbo and a host of Igbo historians, social anthropologists and ethnographers is anything to go by, Aro *Eze-ship* would have its roots deep in the Nri

---

[15] Cf. I. Nzimiro, Studies in Ibo Political Systems: Chieftaincy and Politics in Four Niger States, London, Frank Cass, 1972; Ejiofor, Igbo Kingdoms, pp. 137-181.

[16] A. E. Afigbo, Ropes of Sand. Studies of Igbo History and Culture, Nsukka, University Press Ltd with Oxford University Press, 1981, p. 19; L. U. Ejiofor, Igbo Kingdoms, p. 16 according to whom "The Benin empire once touched the Niger and even beyond".

[17] O. Equiano, The Interesting Narrative of the Life of Olaudah Equiano or Gustavus Vasa the African, Norwich, 1794, 8th Edition, pp. 3-4.

[18] Afigbo, Ropes of Sand, p. 16.

[19] Here also, see, Nzimiro, Studies in Ibo Political Systems, pp. 6-20.

ritual Kingship tradition which is Igbo in its fullest core. This could, perhaps, partially explain why the Aro claim to be agents of *Ibini Ukpabi*.[20] If this is a true position of the matter, it may then be concluded that the Aro, when they had settled in the midst of the Benue-Congo speaking peoples of the Cross River plain in south-east Nigeria and had encountered their local institutions, they must have borrowed other kingship traits from the host culture to enrich their *Eze-ship*.

1.4   OBJECTIVES OF THE STUDY

The central purpose of this work is to filter the New Testament perspectives on its royal portraiture of the historical Jesus, in his birth, life, work, death and resurrection stories with the aid of conceptual models deriving from the African cultural setting. This will be achieved, as has been stated, by way of analysing the data uncovered from the anthropological and ethno-historical narratives of African ancient regal systems.[21] I consider this necessary in view of the fact that most studies on Christology have continued to be expressed in Western theological categories of thought deriving remotely from the Chalcedonian formula of "true God and true man in one person" cast in Hellenic thought-form. Such Christologies interpreted and adapted with the assistance of existential philosophical worldviews have been at the service of the Euro-American Christianity whose favourites have oftentimes been the most powerful in society and its concomitant theology the preserve of the elitist class. The call for the liberation of theology from the "Constantinian captivity" by liberationists like Juan Luis Segundo gets wider impact and is being heeded in many regions of the Third World today.[22]

---

[20] Afigbo, Ropes of Sand, p. 7. Note: Afigbo describes his theory as "a popular working hypothesis", p. 231.

[21] My methodology must be differentiated from Karl Rahner's sort of anthropological approach within which "Christology is the absolute expression of anthropology, the study of man". Here, see, W. Kasper, Jesus the Christ, Kent, Burns & Oates, 1985, p. 18.

[22] See, J. L. Segundo, The Liberation of Theology, ET by J. Drury, New York, Maryknoll, Orbis, 1976.

Since "historical" study aims at the past as dead past, this living-dead past of the Africans must be retrieved and made relevant towards deepening African spirituality and faith in Jesus, the Christ. While liberation theology takes its starting-point from a critical reflection on the reality of the present and looks backwards; contextual Christology must start from the sacred traditions; namely the Scriptures, African traditions, and relate the two patterns in order to elicit the pure phenomena that is re-interpretable in the light of the gospel witness. Such is the task before me and on which I engage myself in this study.

The origin of the Christian faith is biblical. Christian religion appropriates what is sane in human cultures and re-interprets such in the light of the gospel message.[23] But the continuing and persistent transformations sweeping through present-day Africa and her under-privileged social political realities in Church and in the secular society oblige us to re-interpret the goodnews in new perspectives in order to re-shape the vision of Christ colonial and bourgeois theology has brought to the African continent. Thus, it is estimated that this study

(a)   explores one of Africa's principal social institutions rich in sacred symbols and rituals.

(b)   seeks out and re-habilitates holistic anthropological concepts, titles and nomenclatures from Africa's regal traditions such as the *Oba*, *(Kabiyesi)* (Yoruba), *Kabaka* (Ganda), *Reth* (Shilluk) and the *Nkosi* (Zulu) which the subjects had employed to revere their kings as divinely chosen leaders of vibrant and living communities.

(c)   re-asseses the image of Jesus of the Gospels in the light of African royal categories and integrates both into a virile Christology which can enhance faith development in the African Christianity.

(d)   contributes its own share of knowledge in the contemporary research on African Christology.

(e)   develops ideas that emanate from both the African and New Testament themes which can help update Christian catechisms so that converted Africans can

---

[23] Vat. II, *Gaudium et Spes*, Nos 58-59.

know better the Christ as revealed, *inter alia*, as God's Son, King and Lord of the Church.

(f)   interprets the gospel witness on the concept of the Kingdom of God and the Kingship of Jesus, his role and functions in the Reign of God for Church and society.

(g)   fills a vacuum in the African Christian theological discourse created by a yawning absence of an intelligent New Testament Christology formulated within the context of the African royal theology and symbolisms.

(h)   develops a Christology which is quite at home in the African soil and at the same time faithful to the New Testament witness of Jesus, the Messiah-King.

(i)   and demonstrates that autochthonous concepts have the advantage of assisting African Christians express in more meaningful manners and in their lifestyles eternal truths about the royal, kingly and priestly offices of Christ in the Church.

1.5   METHODOLOGY

There are a number of approaches for achieving these objectives. One such is that which methodologically raises the question or demands that African anthropological and ethno-historical data of precolonial period, that is to say, Africa's ancient cultural paradigms be employed to assist scientific theological reflections. Briefly put: the African-anthropologically-descriptive analysis is adopted. This, includes *inter alia*, a hermeneutics employing African socio-cultural and anthropological data in the service of New Testament exegesis. Ready to take the plunge, C. Taber's remark that:

> Cognitive anthropology, studies in mythology, and other types of anthropological studies are beginning to highlight the fact of quite divergent hermeneutical modes in different cultures. What is to prevent Africans, Asians, and others from using their culturally conditioned methodologies in the interpretation of biblical texts, just as we do?[24]

---

[24] C. Taber, "Is there More than One Way to Do Theology?" Gospel In Context 1(1978)2-10, p. 9.

has, for me, become quite appropriate and inspirative.

While some European critical scholars (H. Frankenmölle: 1983; W. Egger: 1987) influenced by the German communication theory of J. Habermas emphasize the 'pragmatics' of a given biblical text; and the New American critics (F. F. Segovia: 1991; R. Kysar: 1991; J. L. Staley: 1991) stress the values of the 'reader-response criticsm' in order to establish the meaning of the text, that is, the *intentio auctoris*, the message;[25] my task as an African exegete is to excarvate the past of our royal institutions by digging up the values inherent in our ancestral regal cultures and by projecting them before the gospel light in order to decode the meanings they have for African Christians today. This is realistic in so far as any peoples' past informs their present and determines to a large extent their future. Thus, implied are issues of contextualisation and inculturation. Therefore, my method includes a selectful assemblage of the deeply held values of African cultural groups; namely the culturally identifiable groups whose material culture include, among other things, the ancient kingship systems which are studied.[26] The enquiry espouses what Charles Nyamiti terms "the thematic approach".[27] It is thematic in so far as *King-Christology*, the central focus of this work is elaborated from specific symbolic themes or categories taken from African royal institutions; that is, from the African material culture, language, religious traditions, philosophical beliefs and the everyday activities and functions of the kings in society. Related ideas, facts of history, royal insignia and paraphernalia and the positive elements intrinsic to the African traditional kingship systems constitute the burden of the analysis and interpretations made towards the emergence of a King-Christology. And for the New Testament part of the study, the relevant Scripture passages are submitted to the scrutiny of critical but a balanced exegesis current with the most acceptable positions maintained in recent scholarship.

---

[25] Cf. J. Beutler, "Response from a European Perspective" in R. A. Culpepper, F.F. Segovia (eds.), The Fourth Gospel from a Literary Perspective (Semeia 53), Atlanta, Scholars Press, 1991, pp. 191-202; esp. pp. 192, 195-196.

[26] For a pertinent definition of the science of anthropology, see R. Olaniyan (ed.), African History and Culture, Lagos, Longman, 1982, p. 5.

[27] C. Nyamiti, "A Critical Assessment on some Issues in Today's African Theology", *African Christian Studies* 5(1989)5-18; *idem.*, "African Christologies Today" in J.N.K. Mugambi and L. Magesa (eds.), Jesus in African Christianity, pp. 18-39.

1.6   CONCLUSIONS

This introductory chapter attempts to situate the reader towards grasping the gist of this study. Aware of the fact that Christology is the centrepiece of theology, effort is made to plead the cause of a dynamic Christology which springs from African ethno-history and Jesus' story in the New Testament.

In the unit on the scope of the work, a delimitation of the focus of the study is sketched. The attempt to re-interpret Peter's answer (Mk 8,29 par.) remains the central issue. It is envisaged that the study proffers an answer derived from the African cultural setting and the data of scientific exegesis of the New Testament. The *raison d'etre* of engaging in the research for a *King-Christology* is outlined in the unit on the justification of the study. It is asserted that African Christian theology, especially King-Christology must arise from the African cultural setting in order to qualify for a dialogue of life with non-Christian influences which continue to errupt in various parts of Africa today.

The immediate purpose is to provide a conceptual basis of research with which I seek to re-interpret New Testament first Christological declaration (Mk 8,29) for the African audience. King-Christology is therefore another countenance of the mystery of Christ in the African context. I am however not unaware of the dangers inherent in a Royal Christology nor of the theology of glory reminiscent of the Constantinian and those of the late Medieval ages. It is important to stress that African royal theologies show no traces of triumphalism and are in no way authoritarian in the form of the *Kaiserherrschaft* mentality typical of European theology of the last few centuries. My idea of a King-Christology is meant to reflect Jesus' eschatological exaltation, his supremacy in the Kingdom of God and the humble Servant-Kingship he bears in the Christian community. Methodology adopted in this work has been discussed in details. As Jean Galot instructively remarks: "The divergences in method have found expression in the opposition between a Christology from above and a Christology from below";[28] a truism which is not far from positions maintained by many an African theologian as will be shown in the next chapter.

---

[28] J. Galot, Who is Christ. A Theology of Incarnation, Chicago, Franciscan Herald Press, 1989, p. 19.

My own approach, inspite of its stress on the value of African and native ideas, starts out with the historical Jesus and concludes with his divine Kingship. It appropriates the insights of both Historical and Redaction Criticisms. The purpose is to remain faithful to the criteria of rigorous exegesis and biblical confession. In the final part of the work, effort is made to discuss the principal motifs unveiled in the research and to isolate similarities and differences between the chosen African theme and its New Testament parallel ideologies. In the concluding section, a *perspectival* reading of the texts studied ties together the consequences of the study. The findings constitute the basis of the hermeneutic adjudged relative towards a *Service Christology* for contemporary Africa. The fresh vision on the person of Jesus as the *Messiah-King* the method uncovers boosts my christological reflections. Besides, the method helps us discover traits which emphasize Christian qualities of leadership in the spirit of Christ, the Messiah-King; a perspective I consider very relevant for Third World contexts where leadership is, more often than not, associated with oppression, tyranny, exploitation and corruption.

The approach to enquire into the socio-religious and regal traditions of African peoples unconditionally furnishes material which profit local expressions and verbalizations of the post-Easter image of Christ. Since African Christian theology is rooted in the experience, history and culture of all African peoples and the Black race everywhere, the cultural matrix of Africa is made my starting-point. African Christian theology does not consist solely in the interpretation or re-interpretation of traditional dogmatic formulas of belief, nor does it consist in quoting the scriptures alone. It is the vitality of African religio-cultural traditions that constitutes one important source of African Christian theology. But in this exercise, Jesus, the Christ remains the norm. Christology is the fountainhead of the Christian faith. As W. Kasper correctly states, Christology is nothing if not "the expression of the being and significance of the person and work of Jesus Christ".[29] If Christological profession, Kasper further says, "had no connexion with the historical Jesus, then belief in Christ would be no more than ideology; a general world-view without any historical basis".[30] It is in this light that *King-Christology* which arises from the historical image of Jesus in the New Testament and its portrayal in the light of the protective roles, benevolent

---

[29] Kasper, Jesus the Christ, p. 19.

[30] *Ibid.*

rulership and lordship typical of kings in the African communities is anchored. Jesus of Nazareth in whom God's revelation is, *par excellence* made manifest, is the divine ruler of believing African Christian congregations. Thus, I adopt the discipline of the *Religionsgeschichte* (History of Religioins) to find not only the relationship between African Traditional Religious values and Christianity but also to unearth parallel ideas in both the African and Christian religions.[31] My methodology is, therefore, in hot pursuit of a 'King-Christology' rooted in and for the African context.

---

[31] For an early articulation of the praxis of the History of Religions, see C. Colpe, Die religionsgeschichtliche Schule, Göttingen, Vandenhoeck und Ruprecht, 1961.

CHAPTER TWO

THE AFRICAN WORLDVIEW

2.1   INTRODUCTION

In this chapter, I wish to handle some pertinent topics without whose delineation the objectives of this work will not be fully realized. A brief exposition of the African worldview has been adjudged a necessary starting-point for this work. With its discussion and with those of other topics that follow, the chapter becomes a launch-pad into the rest of the contents of this study.

Africans had, throughout the ages, evolved a host of ideas about the world in which they live. I do not promise to cover all such ideas in this section. I rather wish to distil through few studies; especially the more popular ones which provide insight into the content of what determines, in essence, the thought-patterns of the social world in which Africans have all along lived their lives and have experienced the sense of the Ultimate Reality; and from which sacred kingship and its associated social institutions had originated and thrived. As J. S. Mbiti has correctly stated, "no thinking person can live without forming some views about life and the world" in which he or she lives.[1] According to Mbiti, "these views are expressed in myths, legends, proverbs, rituals, symbols, beliefs and wise sayings".[2] Researchers in the area of African Religions are unianimous on the pervasive hold religion has on the life of African peoples. The most outspoken of these has observed that "religious

---

[1] J. S. Mbiti, "African Views of the Universe" in Olaniyan (ed.), African History and Culture, Lagos, Longman, pp. 193-199.

[2] Ibid., p. 193; also cf. J. M. Schoffeleers, "Oral History and the Retrieval of the Distant Past: On the Use of the Legendary Chronicles as Sources of Historical Information" in W. van Binsbergen and J. M. Schoffeleers (eds.), Theoretical Explorations in African Religion, London, KPI, 1985, pp. 164-188.

beliefs affected every aspect of conduct in Africa".[3] This truism, as scholars have continued to maintain, can best be summed up in this way: the African is born religiously, he lives religiously and dies religiously. This state of affairs is vindicated by the fact that all over Africa, the universe is believed to be created and sustained by God. In most African languages, the name for God means 'Creator'.[4] In virtually all communities in Black Africa, even though one can today still find remnants of hunting-gathering societies, numerous nomadic groups, sedentary agricultural societies as well as developing urban industrial estates, belief in God as maker of all things is encountered in the names people bear, folktales and folkmusic. Thus, the African person sees the universe as a religious and sacred entity. Mbiti has put it rather concisely in this form: "the African view of the universe is profoundly religious".[5]

No Africanist worth his salt will today admit that African worldviews are structually homogenous. There is, of course, diversity. But within this pluriformity, there is an inherent distinctiveness which gives them their unique commonality; namely their African-*ness*. This basic underlying uniformity remains ever constant and still survives inspite of changes occasioned by agents of secularization, rapid westernization and modernity. An overview of some positions as they stand in historical, anthropological and sociological scientific literature is, at this stage, considered quite *ad rem*.

2.2   AMONG THE YORUBA

Among the Yoruba of Southwest Nigeria, whose kingship tradition opens my discussion on Africa's precolonial royal institutions, the cosmos is ruled by *Olorun*, a supreme deity more

---

[3] I refer the reader to the inaugural speech of the Chairman of the Review of the Scope of African Studies, Monsgr. M. Bakole of the Lovanium University, Kinshasa, Zaire, delivered at a conference organized by The International African Institute, London, in cooperation with the University of Ibadan, Nigeria, April 5-11, 1964 where E. B. Idowu, who is today associated with this opinion, acted as a rapporteur. On this, see D. Forde, "Tropical African Studies", *Africa* 35(1965)30-104, p. 43.

[4] Cf. G. O. Abe, "Theological Concepts of Jewish and African Names of God", AJT 4(1990)424-429.

[5] Mbiti, "African Views of the Universe", p. 194.

often called *Olodumare*[6] who had existed since "the beginning of things". This eternal God who is all-knowing has no cult attached to him. There is no direct worship made to him either in service or in liturgy as he has no shrine. He is the Creator of all things, including man whose destiny and fate remain in his hand. In the words of E. M. McClelland, "he is surrounded, assisted and advised by a company of deities who are thought to have derived from him" long time before man was created.[7] *Olodumare* is believed to be the King of the sky-kingdom. Here on earth, the *Oba* reigns over his people as the son of the Yoruba primordial progenitor, *Oduduwa*, sent down to earth by *Olorun* and as such the king is *Olorun*'s regent.

2.3 AMONG THE KALABARI

In an attempt to analyse the structure of African worldviews, R. Horton singles out the Kalabari people, a fishing village in today's Rivers State of Nigeria as a case study. Horton discovers a fourfold structure of the Kalabari cosmos which is made up of (a) the *tomi kiri*, "the place of people"; (b) the *teme*, the spirit-world in which the ancestors are part of the inhabitants; (c) the *am'oru*, the abode of the spirits of the village heroes; and (d) the *owuampu*, the domain of the water people - all "forming the corners of a triangle of forces"[8]. The third and fourth levels of Kalabari cosmology, Horton notes, relate to the observable world. This is only accessible through birth, life and death where the individual's *tamuno*, a personal creator which joins the individual's spirit to his body in the mother's womb operates. Death occurs when the Creator allows the two to separate.[9] *Tamuno,*

---

[6] E. B. Idowu, *Olodumare*. God in Yoruba Belief,London, Longmans, 1966. For a recent update of this view, see E. O. Babalola, "The Reality of African Traditional Religion: A Yoruba Case Study" *NJTh* 1(1991)50-63, p. 53.

[7] E. M. McClelland, The Cult of Ifá Among the Yoruba, Vol. 1, London, Ethnographica, 1982, pp. 11-12.

[8] R. Horton, "The Kalabari World-View: An Outline and Interpretation" *Africa* 32(1962)197-219, p. 203.

[9] See, *ibid.*, p. 205. Horton directs our attention to the active belief of Kalabari people in the destiny of the individual.

believed to be the creator of the entire world is at the fourth level. At this level, dwells *Opu Tamuno*, the Great Creator who is believed to have created all that there is in the world out of mud. This creator-being denoted as a female, and having a synonym, *so* (sky), is the author of everything in the cosmos.[10]

It is to placate these higher beings that Kalabari people, lineage and village groups collectively perform religious worships and duties. In sum, I agree with Horton that Kalabari belief system belongs to the African philosophico-religious worldview. In it, the people find their own answers to the questions "why" and "what" of human existence and being; questions which authentic human beings had been raising since time immemorial.

In 1971, Horton, this doyen of African cosmology, in a powerfully composed essay, narrowed down his understanding of African cosmology into a two-tier schema of observables: the microcosm where the lower spirits concern themselves with the affairs of the local community,[11] and the macrocosm where the Supreme Being minds himself with the whole world. The relationship between the two, according to Horton, consists in the fact that the Supreme Being is held as the ultimate controller and the existential ground of the lesser divinities.[12] The number and nature of such sorts of lower spirits and the manner in which they relate to the Supreme Being in African cosmologies vary from people to people. E. Smith and G. Parrinder have both demonstrated, with some measure of success, the differences which exist between the worldviews of some West African peoples and those of the Eastern and Central Africa.[13] According to Smith, in West Africa, prominent stress is laid on the place of nature spirits while among the Bantu, spirit entities are believed to hail from those of human beings who continue existence in the unseen world.[14] From this insight, it follows that in Bantu cosmology, there are four categories of spiritual beings: the Supreme Being, Spirits, Ancestors and magical forces and in the West African belief

---

[10] For further details on this principle, see *ibid.*, p. 206.

[11] For much of these ideas see his "Types of Spririt Possession in Kalabari Religion" in J. Beattie, J. Middleton (eds.) Spirit Mediumship and Society of Africa, London, Routeledge and Kegan, 1969.

[12] See *idem.*, "African Conversion" *Africa* 41(1971)85-108.

[13] E. W. Smith, African Ideas of God, Edinburgh, House Press, 1950.

[14] *Ibid.*, p. 23.

systems; especially in those of the Niger-Congo-Kwa linguistic group, perhaps with the exception of the Kalabari just surveyed and a few others, five categories of spiritual beings are recognized: the Supreme Being, the Divinities, the Spirits, the Ancestors and Magical forces (witchcraft).

2.4   AMONG THE IGBO

The Igbo of southeast Nigeria had maintained a non centralized, acephalous society based upon a democratic socio-religious system whose principal institution was not essentially political but religious. In this light, one can appreciate E. Uzukwu's analysis of the component structures of Igbo worldview. According to him, the Igbo conceive the universe as constituted of:

> Chi/Chukwu (source of life, giver of destiny), personal chi (personality emanating from Chi/Chukwu, the immediate carrier and embodiment of the particular individual destiny), ancestors (close to the source of life who became the immediate givers and guardians of the life of the community), spirits (forming or endangering the continuity of life).[15]

Elucidating further, Uzukwu relates that *Mmuo* (spirit) represents a generic concept which includes spirits that inhabit the Spirit-land (ani Mmuo) where ancestors, known and unknown, non local spirits (alusi), and the souls of human persons inhabit. For him, these spirits are at home in the world of man (ani Mmadu). These entities, Uzukwu notes, "are the two principal distinctions of worlds in Igbo universe (uwa)".[16] In this world, people settle on earth. The erath is thus the homeland of created things. It is treated with reverence as the Mother Earth. As E. I. Metuh would have us believe, among the Igbo, *Ala*, (the Mother-

---

[15] E. E. Uzukwu, "Igbo World and Ultimate Reality and Meaning" URAM 5(1982)188-209, p. 195; also S. N. Ezeanya, "God, Spirits and the Spirit World" in K. Dickson and P. Ellingworth (eds.), Biblical Revelation and African Beliefs, London, Lutterworth, 1969, pp. 38-39.

[16] *Ibid.*

Earth) is conceived in feminine terms.[17] On earth, there dwell both animate and inanimate objects usually held with religious awe and reverence, often amounting to veneration and worship. Uzukwu correctly points out that, "over and above man, his world and the world of the dead is the Lord of life and destiny variously called Chi, Chukwu, Chineke".[18] The place of *Mmadu*, (human being) is located in the centre of this universe created by *Chukwu*[19] and given meaning by human activities. On this point, J. S. Mbiti drops a useful hint on the situation. According to him:

> Man awakens the universe, he speaks to it, he listens to it, he tries to create harmony with the universe. It is man who turns parts of the universe into sacred objects ..."[20]

Even Olaudah Equiano, an Igbo, born in 1745, kidnapped and sold into slavery at the prime age of eleven about 1756, had, in his autobiography, left us a somewhat dependable ethnographic information on the religious culture of the eighteenth century Igboland.[21] Equiano tells us, among other things, that the Igbo believe in a Supreme Being which he described as 'one Creator'.[22] In describing the state of Igbo cosmology and religion in his days, Equiano states that the Supreme Deity, *Chukwu* "may never eat or drink".[23] On the sensitive matter of parallels between Igbo doctrine of eternity and that of Christianity, Equiano denies knowledge of such. But he admits that the the Igbo have a concept of eternity much like the Stoic philosophers' doctrine of cyclic return. According to him, there was no

---

[17] See E. I. Metuh, "Ritual Dirt and Purification among the Igbo" *JRA* 15(1985)3-23, p. 6; see also, E. B. Tengan, "The Sisala Universe: Its Composition and Structure". (An Essay in Cosmology) *JRA* 20(1990)2-19, esp. pp. 2-11.

[18] *Ibid.*

[19] *Ibid.*, p. 196.

[20] Mbiti, "African Views of the Universe" p. 195.

[21] Equiano, The Interesting Narrative; see also, P. Edwards & Rosalind Shaw, "The Invisible *Chi* in Equiano's *Interesting Narrative*" *JRA* 19(1989)146-156.

[22] Equiano, The Interesting Narrative, p. 18.

[23] *Ibid.*

serious demarcation in Igbo belief between the world of the living and that of the dead, after all, he observes, the Igbo believe that death is a process through which the human soul moves from the world of the living to the Spirit-world. This is what Equiano likely describes as transmigration.[24] In his own perspective, this is the means by which the soul returns from the Spirit-world to the human-world. Death and birth are the key aspects of this transition.

Indeed, Equiano pictures a view of existence which still reflects Igbo people's conception of eternity. The Spirit-world is conceived as the very replica of the village topography, everyday existence and life-style.[25] What the dead are believed to have in the hereafter are not dissimilar to what the living have on earth. As other classes of people live in their own ranks, the *Eze*, king or chief is believed to remain the leader of the community in the Spirit-world.[26] For the Igbo, there is a close contact between the two worlds, enhancing a two-way traffic. The access to the world-in-between is never blocked. Cast in theological language, it may be assumed that for the Igbo, the Kingdom of heaven would be realized in both places for *Uwa nkea* (this world) is considered good and the persons who do good and live righteously here on earth already live in the sphere of *Uwa Oma* (the good earth) and when they live this physical body they are strongly believed to go to *Ala-Eze Enigwe*, (the Land of the Sky-King) in the Spirit-world.[27] At this point, it is noteworthy to remark that the Igbo worldview presents some contrasts to the alternative Christian worldview. In Judeo-Christian tradition, the two realms are quite antithetical; one a place of eternal bliss (heaven), the other, a "valley of tears"; a pilgrim place . Unlike in the Igbo thought, in Judeo-Christian eschatology, there is no traffic between the other two eternal extremes: namely heaven/hell; but, for the Igbo, eternity is associational, dynamic, warm and humane.[28] The key to the understanding of this world and its totality is *ndu*, life. In

---

[24] *Ibid.*

[25] See even, F. A. Arinze, Sacrifice in Ibo Religion, Ibadan, Ibadan University Press, 1970, pp. 18-19.

[26] *Ibid.*, p. 22.

[27] Cf. C. U. Manus, "The Resurrection of Jesus: Some Critical and Exegetical Considerations in the Nigerian Context," *JMB* 41(1987)30-43.

[28] C. U. Manus, "The Concept of Death and the After-Life in the Old Testament and Igbo Traditional Religion: Some Reflections for Contemporary Missiology", *Mission Studies*,

Igbo world, man's life-long project is to preserve this life, to increase it and to relize it to the fullest.[29] To conclude the Igbo perspective, it seems to me that Metuh's careful observation sums it up well:

> The Igbo world-view shows a close bond as well as a degree of differentiation between the visible and the invisible, the divine and human beings.[30]

2.5   AMONG THE DINKA AND THE LUGBARA

Beyond West African states, other African peoples have impressive narratives about their peoples' philosophy of life. The land of the Dinka and the Lugbara peoples of Sudan had been made very prominent area-studies by the Oxford School of social anthropologists, represented by such men as J. Middleton and R.G. Lienhardt. These scholars had, since the sixties, exposed both peoples worldviews to the world of Africanists.[31] In the final chapters of his *Lugbara Religion*, Middleton presents a fascinating portrait of the Lugbara worldview. For him, the ancestors, the vehicles of the stability of the social order are antagonistic to the spirits, *adro*, the anti-social forces who wreck the labrynths of the society. In this light, the oppositions and the differences in the obseverable world are due to the overarching connexion between principles inherent in the apparent diversity.[32] These malevolent spirits represent forces contrasted with and indeed opposed to the benevolent ancestral spirits. In *Divinity and Experience*, Lienhardt argues that the Dinka worldview provides a basis for comprehending a cluster of observations such as intra-societal relationships, the connexion

---

Journal of the International Association for Mission Studies, 3(1986)41-56.

[29] See *ibid*.

[30] Metuh, "Ritual Dirt and Purification", p. 22.

[31] J. Middleton, "Some Social Aspects of Lugbara Myth", *Africa* 24(1954)189-198; idem., Lugbara Religion, Ritual and Authority among an East African People, London, Oxford University Press, 1960; R. G. Lienhardt, Divinity and Experience: The Religion of the Dinka, London, Oxford University Press, 1961.

[32] Cf. Middleton, Lugbara Religion, pp. 230-270.

existing between the established social order and the relative external forces that impinge on it; and the relationship between the individual, his life and the group. For me, the merit of Lienhardt's study resides in his ability to have pointed out the manner in which Dinka deities are believed to sustain the unity and harmony underlying the diverse realities of the Dinka spiritual world. And for Lienhardt, Dinka gods provide a model through which the people grasp easily the existence of various phenomena in the visible world as dependent on the operation of some unspecified principles.

Both works highlight, *inter alia*, the multi-levelled nature of Lugbara and Dinka worldviews. In both works, the authors have taken pains to show that ancestors and spirits are believed by these Africans as manifestations of the Supreme Being. In line with E.E. Evans Pritchard's *Nuer Religion*,[33] which, no doubt inspired their works, both men present the Supreme Being as the generator of the vital force which fills up the wider macrocosm in which the gods, spirits and ancestors exist and act in binary oppositions on the level of the more immediate world where people live and have their being.[34] Such worldviews have great impact on the myth of kingships which is redolent of the peoples' history and especially of their neighbours, the Shilluk whoe *Retship* is studied here.

2.6   AMONG THE GANDA

The Baganda of modern Uganda, as B. C. Ray observed, "live in a three-storey universe consisting of sky, earth, and underworld".[35] Each of the levels signifies a form of existence different from one to the other. The sky, *ggulu*, known as *olobaale* is the abode of the gods, the home of the divinities. The *ensi*, the earth which includes land and the country is the home of the people, the Baganda, the descendants of Kintu, or the *abazzukulu ba Kintu* who inhabit the kingdom established by Kintu himself, and where the *Kabaka*, the king reigns in

---

[33] E. E. Evans Pritchard, Nuer Religion, Oxford, University Press, 1956.

[34] On this specific view of reality, see H. Bucher, Spirits and Power: An Analysis of Shona Cosmology, London, Oxford University Press, 1980.

[35] B. C. Ray, "The Story of Kintu. Myth, Death and Ontology in Baganda" in Ivan Karp and Charles S. Bird (eds.), Explorations in African Systems of Thought, Bloomington, Indiana University Press, 1980, pp. 60-79, pp. 76-77.

his stead. The third level, the *magombe* is the home of the dead where *muzimu*, the spirits of the dead appear before *Walumbe*, the Chief of the underworld. It is believed, as Ray was informed, that from here the spirits re-enter into the earth where they hang around their graves.[36] This three-tier structure of Baganda cosmos expresses the integrated forum in which the Baganda live. In Kiganda social structure, the *Kabakaship* is regarded as the re-incarnation of Baganda primal father and the first Kabaka, Kintu who has even been accepted by Christian catechists as *Muntu wa Katonda*, the 'man of God'.[37] According to Ray, the ensemble "of Ganda cosmology was the division between the living and the dead";[38] a partition which is a reflection of two worlds: the "sacred world" and the human world; both founded by Kintu, Buganda's culture hero, who, at the end of his life on earth, was believed to have mysteriously disappeared.[39] This legend is still sustained and maintained in Kiganda royal theology. It affirms, among other things, that the *Kabakas* like the *Obas* in Yoruba court traditions and those of the *Reths* in Shillukland never die but "go away" from their people to the vault.

2.7   AMONG THE SHILLUK

The Shilluk of southern Sudan conceive their universe as an ordered and a meaningful whole. According to Lienhardt who had studied Shilluk cosmology, the people's spatial view of the world is tripertite; a division of the universe into earth, sky and river.[40] As known in Shilluk myths, *Nyikang*'s agnatic line of descent is traced from a man who descended

---

[36] For various cadres of spirits in Kiganda cosmology, see *idem.*, "Royal Shrines and Ceremonies of Buganda" *The Uganda Journal* 36(1972)35-48; pp. 45-47.

[37] See *idem.*, "The Story of Kintu", p. 66 who cites B. M. Zimbe (1939) as his authority.

[38] *Idem.*, "Sacred Space and Royal Shrines in Buganda" History of Religions 16(1977)368-373, p. 366.

[39] Cf. *ibid.*

[40] See Lienhardt, "The Shilluk of the Upper Nile" in D. Forde (ed.), African Worlds, Oxford, 1954, pp. 138-163, p. 145.

from the sky, the abode of *Juok*, God. *Juok* is believed to be the ancestor of Nyikang. Thus for the Shilluk, Nyikang is the bridge between human beings and the supra-human forces (spirits), between the below and the above; and between the earth, *piny* and the sky, *mal*. On account of Nyikang's mediational status, the shilluk venerate Nyikang under the title: *juok piny*, the spirit of the earth. From his maternal side, *Nyikaya* usually associated with riverain phenomena and beings, the genesis of Nyikang is traced to the river; especially in the crocodile stock. Thus Lienhardt asserts that all three regions of the Shilluk universe are nominally assimilated to Nyikang and he to them. According to him, it is "the single person of Nyikang which gives all three regions their coherence in a single world".[41]

2.8   AMONG THE ZULU

The Xhosa-Zulu are a significant part of the Bantu race. They however share common ideas and theories of the universe with the rest of African peoples. In Bantu cosmogony, for example, man is represented as the last work of *Umvel'nqanki*, First Appearer and Creator.[42] Among the Zulu, God is *Umkulu-nkulu*, the Great Great Ancestor; the Maker of man and the world; the First of Man.[43] In Bantu worldview, man, from the beginning and without any constraint, knew what was right; practised faith and executed justice. The world was a peaceful living place. There was no cause for fear, conflicts and punishment were unknown. The land yielded all kinds of fruits and plants in abundance. Man possessed joy and lived immortal life. Harmony prevailed but disorder, evil and death came as a consequence of God's wrath on the act of men who decided to poison a woman who bore a child, an event then misunderstood and considered an evil occurence.[44]

---

[41] *Ibid.*, pp. 149-150.

[42] H. Callaway, Divination As Existing Among the Amazulu in their own Words with English Translation, Natal, Blair, 1870, pp. 1-104.

[43] S. M. Molema, The Bantu. Past and Present, Cape Town, Struik, 1963, pp. 166; 173-176; D. M'Timkulu, "Some Aspects of Zulu Religion" in N. S. Booth (ed.), African Religions: A Symposium, New York, London, Lagos, NOK Publishers, 1977, p. 14.

[44] *Ibid.*, p. 174.

The Bantu believed in the existence of spirits and held the view that spirit entities could cause effects in the material world.[45] In fact, spirit beings constitute the most immediate object of Bantu religion. Spirits of the dead were believed to hover over the Bantu world and could be communicated with. Though fear of evil spirits prevailed as all diseases were believed by the Zulu to be the handwork of malevolent spirits and malicious men; the immortality of the soul and re-incarnation are highly defended. Ancestral spirits *Musimo*, whose effigies are housed in the *isiBoya*, cattle-fold, are believed to exercise much control over the living and even to shape their destinies. They are believed to create new life in yet unborn offsprings.[46] The Bantu conceive the hereafter in spatial terms. According to Molema, it is "a defined space on the other side of the firmament, and exclusively for the abode of the Supreme Being".[47]

Involved in Bantu religion is how man could obtain mastery of the secrets of Nature in order, "at least render himself impervious to their baneful influence".[48] It is in this context that one can evaluate the role of the Medicine-man, the *nganga* without whose presence and consent nothing that might affect individual or the people's wellbeing was carried out.[49] The *Nkosi* would not ascend the throne of his fathers without heeding his expert advice nor without availing himself of the assistance of the Zulu Medicine-man for protection from both seen and unseen forces.

2.9   CONCLUSIONS

The samples of African worldviews sketched here, reveal some intrinsic values fully inherent in the structure of African thought-forms and philosophy. They reflect how, among other

---

[45] H. Callaway, The Religious System of the Amazulu, Cape Town, Struik, 1970, pp. 417-419.

[46] A. T. Bryant, The Zulu People. As They Were Before The White Man Came, Pietermaritzburg, Shuter & Shooter, 1949, 1967 2nd Ed. p. 610.

[47] Molema, The Bantu, p. 175.

[48] *Ibid.*, p.164.

[49] *Ibid.*, p. 165.

things, Africans conceive the cosmos and how its various facets are mystically thought to have evolved over the ages. The three or four dimensional levels thought of the universe are not held to be separate entities in themselves but are believed to be linked one to another. The heavenly part of the universe, apart from being considered the home of the elemental beings, is believed to be the abode of the Supreme Being, God. This heavenly universe is also believed to have its own population; in other words, it is seen as a counterpart of this world though invisible to mortal men and women. For the majority of Africans the good ancestors live there among other beings in the vicinity of God. According to Igbo and Yoruba views, here, ancestors live as they were in their earthly existence.

One important insight arising from these philosophies of life is the fact that the social organisation of Africans is sustained by this sort of metaphysical views about life and the universe. African worldviews reflect a constellation of systems of thought-patterns which provide the basis for the understanding of a number of phenomena such as the genesis of a tribe, its migrations, its settlement on a given locale, the number of divinities the people venerate and worship and the bond of relationship between the leaders, oftentimes, the kings and their subjects. Common belief in the hierarchy of divinities, various spirit entities as titularies of the Supreme Being as well as the ancestors, in fact, demonstrate the unity in diversity which characterizes African worldviews. Such magico-religious perspectives on reality explains why African peoples regard both animate and inanimate beings as "spirited"; that is, as possessing mystical life. The possession of mystical quality of life makes certain objects and persons sacred. Such belief systems reflect decisive factors in a people's rapid adaptability to new religious ideas and concepts crystallizing into symbols which more often than not give vent to the metaphors with which they cast their object of worship in their own local images. Oftentimes such portraits become perceptible and tangible realities that permeate their liturgies, arts, music and sungs. As C. Geertz claims, such sacred symbols function to synthesize a people's ethos, and may consist of the tone, character and quality of their life with its own moral and aesthetic style as part and parcel of their worldview; namely "the picture they have of the way things in sheer actuality are, their most comprehensive ideas of order."[50]

---

[50] Cf. C. Geertz, The Interpretation of Cultures. Selected Essays, New York, Basic Books, 1973, p. 89.

The origin of royal lineages in Africa, especially kingships is usually related in mythic narratives shaped by these worldviews. Without doubt, such mythic "oraltures" provide character for African social institutions and the rationalizations of social previleges.[51] The account of the genesis, the sacred sonship of the office-bearers and their enstoolment which are strongly believed to put them into contact with their patriarchal forebears convince their subjects who had internalized such worldviews to revere them as divines and as "gods in the world of men".[52] This sacred status accorded the kings is believed to confer on them the singular right to relate to divine beings, to claim lordship over their subjects and territories and to possess the vitality and virility to guarantee fertility and prosperity in their kingdoms. In this sense, the royal figures are held as intermediaries and often as re-incarnations of their divine progenitors. They stand between the royal ancestors, the whole clan and the individual family ancestors, even though the later are still believed to remain loyal to the royal ones in the Spirit-world. Ideas as these culminate in the concept of an immortal "man-god-king", and among others, the "sacred Priest-King". In Frazerian terms, the phenomenon was typified as "divine kingship" then thought of as typical of some African kingship systems.

This understanding of the cosmos indicates how Africans relate to the world of things around them, and how they allow certain truths to shape and direct their lives. Such realities constitute the bedrock of their relationship with the sacred and the profane in everyday life and in the execution of their activities. It is in this light that the African lore had created the sapiential mythologies which etiologically explain the history of the intricate systems of kingships, the sacrosanctity of the kings, the divine nature of their lineages and dynasties and the authorities bequeathed to them as sovereigns. This worldview ensures itself that the sacral rulers represent all the powers in the Spirit-world; reign and administer their states with a divine mandate and and demonstrate same as masters of the fertility rites when they act as the first of the priests during regular ritual and ceremonial occasions. Given this insight, we

---

[51] *Ibid.*, p. 88.

[52] E. G. Parrinder, "Divine Kingship in West Africa" *Numen* 3(1956)111-121, p. 112; and also M. Godelier, "Economy and Religion, an Evolutionary Optical Illusion" in J. Friedman & M. J. Rowlands (eds.), The Evolution of Social Systems, London, Duckworth, 1977, pp. 3-12, p. 9.

48

may agree with C. K. Meek, that "the kings have an earthly image of the plurality of the gods".[53]

Finally, and in the light of what is found out in this section, I wish to submit that African worldviews reflect optimistic views of reality which support life and its wellbeing, industry and achievement-oriented goals in an equilibrated cosmos. As C. Geertz puts it,

> In religious belief and practice a group's ethos is rendered intellectually reasonable by being shown to represent a way of life ideally adapted to the actual state of affairs the world view describes, while the world view is rendered emotionally convincing by being presented as an image of an actual state of affairs peculiarly well arranged to accommodate such a way of life.[54]

The African world is, therefore, a universe in which, among other things, kingship remains a sacralized institution; and in which the incumbents fulfill their sacral duties in a specific territory as divine agents for the good of their subjects. In this respect, the religious dimension of kingship belongs to that aspect of religion which establishes powerful, over-arching and permanent moods and motivations in men and women because religion regulates a general order of existence. It is my view that without the exposition of the traits of such a *Weltanschauung*, the reality of African kingship systems which forms the *terminus a quo* of my elaboration of a King-Christology would not be fully grasped. This is because the African worldview indicates, *inter alia*, how the sacral notions embedded in the royal traditions can enlighten the mystery of Christ for the up-building of the Church and the relevancy of inculturational theology in Africa. From insights as these, can emerge a Christological anthropology in which Christ is both the *Basileus* (King); the *Kyrios* (Lord) and the *Doulos* (Servant) of God; the One who serves the living *qahal Yahweh* composed of persons created in the image of God (*imago Dei*).

---

[53] C. K. Meek, A Sudanese Kingdom. An Ethnographical Study of the Jukun-speaking Peoples of Nigeria, London, Paul Kegan, 1931, p. 122.

[54] Geertz, The Interpretation of Cultures, p. 90.

CHAPTER THREE

CONTEMPORARY IMAGES OF JESUS IN AFRICA

3.1   INTRODUCTION

W. Kasper, the German theologian (now Bishop of Rottenburg-Stuttgart) informs us that Karl Rahner's article on Chalcedon as the end or the beginning of Christological reflections marked the first wave of modern Christological thought in the second half of this century.[1] According to Kasper, this began twenty-five years ago; that is, fifteen centuries since after the Council of Chalcedon (451-1951). While Rahner's article set the tone in what is decidedly a Eurocentric Christological profession since the mid sixties;[2] African theologians had, within a period not too distant from the epoch-making essay, started to search for alternative expressions of the image of Christ that is not wrapped in the garb of Western European theology. For African theologians and the various congregations they represent, the question about who Christ is, is one that is biblically based. In the light of Africa's multifarious socio-political problems and negative experiences of oppression, exploitation, apartheid, injustice, hunger, bad governments and underdevelopment the question on the person of the Christ is being responded to in various forms. While among some critics, it is commonly agreed that, inspite of the rapid spread of Chritianity in Africa,[3] Christological

---

[1] K. Rahner, "Chalkedon - Ende oder Anfang?" in A. Grillmeier and H. Bacht (eds.), Das Konzil von Chalkedon, Vol. 3, Würzburg, 1954, pp. 3-49; see also Rahner, Theological Investigations, Vol 1, London, 1966.

[2] Kasper, Jesus the Christ, p. 17.

[3] According to Global Mission Report, out of 24 million world Christians, Africa has 6 million practicing Christians. However, one can compare figures with D. B. Barret (ed.), World Christian Encyclopedia. A Comparative Survey of Churches and Religions in the Modern World - AD 1900-2000, Oxford University Press, 1982, p. 782.

reflections and literature are quite scanty; C. Nyamiti is of the opinion that Christology is the most developed subject in contemporary African theology.[4]

In this section, views expressed by authors of previous studies on the subject; or may I say, a survey of the current trends in Christological thinking in Africa are chronologically surveyed. For the presentations, I will discuss the literature in two stages in order to encompass the two decades the review spans. Their positions will be discussed in a separate unit on observations. Perhaps, Nyamiti might have asserted rightly. Evidence before us will prove.

3.2   (a) 1972 - 1981 : THE FIRST DECADE

By the year, 1972, J. S. Mbiti had declared that there was barreness in African Christological concepts. This was, according to him, due to the fact that few Africans, no more than ten at that time, were engaged in actual theological research.[5] In this other pioneering effort, Mbiti's approach is, as usual, quite novel. He undertakes (a) to discover Christological titles which are well-known to Africans and (b) to apply the African traditional worldview to the person of Christ presented in the New Testament.[6] In the light of the miracles Jesus performed, especially his resurrection, the greatest miracle of all times, Jesus is, according to Mbiti, *Christus Victor* who is, for Africans the vanguisher of all evils in the African world and the beaqueather of immortality. In order to evolve a comprehensive Christology for Africa, Mbiti attempts to develop an anthropology based on African socialisation. He finds this in the popular rites of passage which is made up of birth, puberty, marriage and finally death, the gateway to the ancestral world. For him, these circles mark the incorporation of the individual into his society.

---

[4] Nyamiti, "African Christologies Today", in *Op. cit.*, p. 17.

[5] J. S. Mbiti, "Some African Concepts of Christology" in G. F. Vicedom (ed.), Christ and the Younger Churches, London, SPCK, 1972, p. 51.

[6] Here, see Mbiti, "Afrikanische Beiträge zur Christologie" in P. Beyerhaus et al., (eds.), Theologische Stimmen aus Asien, Afrika und Lateinamerika, Vol. 3, München, 1968, pp. 72-85.

What is the relationship between the puberty rite and the major events in the life of Jesus, one may ask? Mbiti finds the answer in the praxis of the *Aladura* Churches of the Yoruba of Nigeria. According to Mbiti, the theology of these churches endears itself to the birth, baptism and death of Jesus as circles in his life which establish him as a "perfect man".[7] Jesus is therefore a man who has fulfilled all the rites of life.[8] In his application of the NT teaching on the person of Jesus to the African worldview, Mbiti adopts the comparative method. This approach enables him to isolate parallel elements and the differences that exist in the New Testament and African traditional lore. With the approach, Mbiti is able to discover biblical themes which are similar to African trado-religious concepts such as, Son of God, well known among the Ndebele and the Shona of Zimbabwe, the Shilluk of Sudan and the Dogon of Benin; Servant of God, Redeemer, Conqueror and Lord - all quite familiar in many African societies. The advantage of Mbiti's Christology rests on its social implications and thus has bearing on the lives of many Africans who find succour in these values. Jesus' death on the Cross, Mbiti opines, is not regarded by Africans as a thing of shame and humiliation. It is neither a vicarious death nor an expiatory sacrifice, he argues. Jesus is, in his totality, a symbol of the perfect state in life. He died on the cross because he was a *perfect man*; fully grown and responsible to the Father.[9] The cross was therefore a means by which he realized his death, for as a full grown man he had necessarily to die.[10]

In a 1975 article, G. Setiloane, a black South African theologian, admits that Africans accept the primitive Christian confession of Jesus as the Messiah without question and have in various ways of deep faith expression responded to this title.[11] In Setiloane's perspective, the vision of Christ as the Messiah would not be unconnected with the South African black

---

[7] And so, see C. U. Manus, "'King-Christology': The Example of Some Aladura Churches in Nigeria", Ms. submitted for publication to *Africana Marburgensia*, Marburg University, Germany, 1990.

[8] Mbiti, "Some African Concepts of Christology", pp. 54-56.

[9] *Ibid.*, p. 57.

[10] For a balanced and positive view of the theology of the cross in Africa, see K. A. Dickson, Theology in Africa, New York, Maryknoll, Orbis, 1984, pp. 185-199.

[11] G. Setiloane, "Confessing Christ Today: From One African Perspective: Man and Community", *JTSA* 12(1975)35.

experience in the face of dehumanizing apartheid. In another study (1979), Setiloane re-stresses his views and challenges African theologians to define the task of African theology in the perspective of the Christological question: who is Jesus ...?, and what does Messiah or Christ mean in the African context?[12] These questions successfully spurred challenges to future researchers. K. Appiah-Kubi, a Ghanaian theologian (1977), like Mbiti before him, laments over the paucity of studies done by Africans on Christology in the African context. Following on Mbiti's foot-path, he discovers the image of Jesus as Mediator, the intermediary between God and African Christians; Saviour, Redeemer with Power, Liberator and Healer. His original insight and concepts have today become further developed in such works as those of Kabasele et *alii*.[13] Allan Boesak, the well known and abrasive South African black theologian, categorically states that the historical Jesus of the New Testament bears a peculiar significance for all persons who share the experience of the black man everywhere.[14] Boesak instructively shows that for people who are marginalized, dehumanized and deprived of their rights, dignity and freedom among other things, Jesus of Nazareth is for them a 'Black Messiah'.

In a well researched work, John S. Pobee, a Ghanaian theologian devotes a chapter of intensive enquiry on the doctrine of the person of Christ in the context of the Akan (a sub-tribe in Ghana) religious spirituality.[15] For him, the point of departure of Christology is the credo: *Christ is true God and true man*. In order to relate this article of faith to the Akan mentality, Pobee raises the question: "Why should an Akan relate to Jesus of Nazareth who does not belong to his clan, family, tribe and tradition?".[16] According to him, response to such a question will help African theologians pursue the inculturation of Christianity in

---

[12] *Idem.*, "Où est la theologie africaine?" in K. Appiah-Kubi et al (eds.), Liberation ou adaptation? La theologie africaine s'interroge. Le Colloque d'Accra, Paris, L'Hamattan, 1979, p. 81.

[13] F. Kabasele et al. (eds.), Chemins de la christologie africaine. Enraciner l'evangile, initiations africaines et pedagogie de la foi, Paris, 1986.

[14] A. A. Boesak, Farewell to Innocence: A Socio-ethical Study on Black Theology and Power, New York, Maryknoll, Orbis, 1977, pp. 41-43.

[15] J. S. Pobee, Toward an African Theology, Nashville, Abingdon, 1979, pp. 81-98.

[16] *Ibid.*, p. 81.

Africa rather urgently. It is Pobee's view that biblical faith should provide the plumb-line for measuring the validity of the Chalcedonian thought-form which is rather metaphysical than the biblically functional images of Jesus. Pobee opines that "functional terms in the discussion of Christology"[17] is the most suitable approach in the African society. What appears to me as the most instructive merit of Pobee's thought is the emphasis he places on the humanity of Jesus which, according to him, "the attempt to construct a Christology in an African theology cannot skirt".[18] Pobee is of the opinion that for the *homo Africanus* , the ideas of Jesus' humanity are far more meaningful than metaphysical ones. In the final analysis, Pobee proposes a *royal-priesthood Christology* by which Jesus is conceived as the *Okyeame* - the representative of the Chief who, in public matters, is himself the Chief".[19] Among some of the titles Pobee experiments with, is that of *Chief Nana*, "the Great and Greatest Ancestor" which stands for an ancestor who had led exemplary life and had inspired his followers. For Pobee, Christ is this *Nana* for he has power and authority to judge over his followers and to punish the wrong-doers in their midst.

S. O. Abogurin, a Nigerian New Testament scholar (1980), draws our attention to the urgent need for the creation of African Christology. According to Abogurin, the New Testament must remain the source for constructing African Christology.[20] Abogurin observes that the African Church is in dire need of biblical theologians who are methodologically equipped to evolve a relevant but biblically based Christology.[21] With reference to the much debated subject of the historical Jesus since Albert Schweitzer, Abogurin asks: has the discussion on the historical Jesus any meaning for Africans?.[22] For him, there must be a relationship between Christian faith and the New Testament. Western theologians, he opines, have not strictly understood the biblical worldview with its parallel

---

[17] *Ibid.*, p. 82.

[18] *Ibid.*, p. 84.

[19] *Ibid.*, p. 95.

[20] S. O. Abogurin, "La recherche moderne du Jesus historique et le christianisme en Afrique", *Journal Theologique del'Afrique* 1(1980), p. 36.

[21] *Ibid.*, pp. 36-37.

[22] *Ibid.*, p. 34.

identity with those of the Africans. Abogurin pertinently asserts that Jesus is the eternal word become flesh who now lives in the African milieu.[23] In the same year, another Nigerian, C. B. Okolo examines the meaning and the place of Christ in the wake of current interest in the "Africanisation" of the Christian religion. He insists that the crucial task before African theologians and Church leaders remains how to respond to the question Christ put to Peter at Caesarea Philippi: "But who do you say that I am?" (Mt 15,16). According to Okolo "growth in faith and in the life of the Church is for Africans to see Christ more and more as *Emmanuel* dwelling in us and in our midst".[24] He rightly argues that for the incarnation of Christianity in the African soil, Africans have to see Christ as African, that is, through the eyes and aspirations of Africans.[25] This change of attitude, Okolo maintains, implies seeing both Christ and his Church as African. Okolo vehemently declares that African cultures must be uplifted by Christianity in order that "the Christ of faith can be seen authentically by an African only through his culture and thinking categories"[26]. On this issue, I allow Okolo to speak for himself:

> To see Christ as African is, in short, to see Christ as African *Emmanuel*, one who dwells among Africans, in their world of meanings, of signs and symbols. The mystery of the incarnation expresses itself in the words, "And the Word was made flesh and dwelt among us".[27]

To lend weight to this observation, Okolo opines that "Christianity becomes rooted in Africa only when Christ and his Church dwell among Africans in the world of their values and meanings, not in alien signs and symbols".[28] In sum, then, Okolo's Christological concept is *Emmanuel*, God-with-us Africans.

---

[23] *Ibid.*, p. 36.

[24] C. B. Okolo, "'Emmanuel': An African Enquiry", *BAT* 2(1980)15-22, p. 16.

[25] *Ibid.*, p. 17.

[26] *Ibid.*

[27] *Ibid.*, p. 17.

[28] *Ibid.*, p. 18.

Bishop Emilio de Carvalho roots his Christological interpretation in the reality of the incarnation of God in Jesus Christ.[29] He notes that the Africans, first and foremost, see Jesus as a human person; in fact, as "the elder brother of Africans".[30] Jesus is regarded as the elder brother because in African cultural setting, the elder brother is the one who provides defence, mediation and protection to the rest of the family. With a somewhat different nuance, the Bishop restates some of the categories with which African theologians had, by the seventies, expressed the Jesus image, the most prominent being the view of Jesus as the liberator of Africans from oppression, colonial domination and all enemies of life.

In the light of the repression Africans in Angola from where the Bishop comes and those in South Africa had passed through, he opts for the search for a *Black Christ*;[31] especially as revealed through African charismatic figures and Messiahs such as Chimpa Vita (Angola, 18th c.), Simon Kimbangu (Zaire, 20th c.), Simon Mapadi (Zaire), Johana Owalo (Kenya), all who had seen the incarnation of Jesus as an event that happened in the Black situation and in the African context.

3.3   (b) 1982 - 1991 : THE SECOND DECADE

In an interesting study which appeared in *Spiritus* in 1982, E. J. Penoukou, highlights the salvific significance of Jesus in the form of a *Joto-Ancestor.*[32] Penoukou, a native of the Ewe-Mina of Togo elaborates his Christology from insights arising from his tribe's rituals of death and life. The rites, in their structure, reflect a cosmotheandric vision of the world in which occurs a symbiotic fusion of the Divine Presence, human beings and the cosmic order. In the hereafter, life is seen as a viable reality. Death is a gateway to life. Like the Igbo worldview described above, the successive circles of birth, death and rebirth are generative phases of the global process. Each phase has its own importance in so far as it is a moment

---

[29] E. de Carvalho, "What do the Africans say that Jesus Christ is?" *ATJ* 10(1,1981)27-36; and Vol. 10(2,1981)17-25.

[30] *Ibid.*, p. 17.

[31] *Ibid.*, p. 18.

[32] E.J. Penoukou, "Realité africaines et salut en Jesus Christ", *Spiritus* 23 (1992) 274 ff.

of "the being-there-with others" including God, spirits, other human beings and the universe itself. This openness implies Divine symbiosis with the socio-cosmic order.

Relating the mystery of the incarnation to this cosmotheandric *Weltanschauung*, Penoukou acclaims that the Christ event is a passage. He argues that notwithstanding Jesus' divine pre-existence, he suffered death as a necessary passage to a new status. Since everything was created through and for him, he is, in his new state of life, mediator between God and the rest of the created order. Through the circles of his incarnation, death and resurrection, Christ has become Lord of history and thus the fulfiller of the cosmotheandric relationality between God, humanity and the universe. By his death and resurrection, Jesus Christ has conquered evil and death and has given them a new value and significance. Penoukou goes on to demonstrate the consequences of his Christology in the practical life of the Ewe-Mina people and all Africans.

In his study, *Biblical Christologies* ..., K. Bediako, a Ghanaian evangelical missiologist reflects on what he terms the "Christological problem as it confronts us now".[32] He seeks the solution to this crux in the religious belief and worldview of the Akan, his own ethnic people as did Pobee before him. He reads the Scriptures within the context of Akan traditional religiosity in order to reach out to a Christology "which deals with the perceived reality of the ancestors".[33] Bediako firmly argues that due to the universal primacy of Christianity, Jesus Christ is not a stranger in the Akan heritage. He thus, explores the "Akan Spirit-world" and in line with my findings on general African worldview, Bediako highlights the cardinal role of the ancestors in the Akan thought and traditional religious piety.[34] In order to establish the significance of Jesus' salvific role in the life-experience of African Christians, Bediako relates Christology "to the realm of the ancestors" at which Africans can encounter the Christ event.[35] In his own words:

---

[32] K. Bediako, "Biblical Christologies in the Context of African Religions" in V. Samuel & C. Sugden (eds.), Sharing Jesus in the Two Thirds World, Bangalore, Brilliant Printers, 1983, pp. 115-175, p. 139.

[33] *Ibid.*, p. 143.

[34] *Ibid.*, p. 141.

[35] *Ibid.*, p. 142.

We need to apprehend God in the Lord Jesus Christ speaking immediately to us in our particular circumstances, in a way that assures our people that we can be authentic Africans and true Christians.[36]

Bediako achieves this feat in his effort to explicate the relationship of Christian faith to the African culture and tradition which he blamed early missionaries to have under-rated.

Like Setiloane and Boesak, Mofokeng, another South African, speaks out of the experience of Blacks in South Africa. In his work, *The Crucified Among the Crossbearers*[37], Mofokeng traces the genesis of black consciousness and makes it the axle on which his thoughts on Black Christology revolves. He interprets this philosophy in the light of scriptural texts from both the Old and the New Testaments. These three sources provide him data for the elaboration of his image of the 'Black Christ' in the South African context. In the same year, E. B. Udoh, a Nigerian proposed that Jesus Christ be recognized as a *Guest* to the religio-cultural home of Africans.[38] In his view, in the African cultures, Jesus is a stranger who is received with every respect, dignity, hospitality and honour customarily accorded strangers in African homes. But inspite of the hospitality accorded him, the guest has to conform to the manners and customs of the hosts. In other words, Jesus and his goodnews have to submit to a process of inculturation. Thus, in order to portray the strangeness to Africa of Christ and his gospel, Udoh styles his perception of the Christ event, *Guest Christology*.

The question of who Christ is and the consequences of his gospel message to African Christians represents a significant watershed among the questions African elites ask about the Christ event. In my study, *The Centurion's Confession of Faith (Mk 15:39) ...*[39], I have employed contemporary exegetical methods to uncover the Markan Christology implicated

---

[36] *Ibid.*, pp. 142-143; and also his n. 75.

[37] T. A. Mofokeng, The Crucified Among the Crossbearers. Towards a Black Christology, Kampen, 1983.

[38] E. B. Udoh, Guest Christology. An Interpretative View of the Christological Problem in Africa, Ph.D Dissertation, Princeton University, Princeton, 1983; also Frankfurt/Main, Peter Lang, Studies in Intercultural History of Christianity, No 59.

[39] C. U. Manus, "The Centurion's Confession of Faith (Mk 15:39): Reflections on Mark's Christology and its Significance in the Life of African Christians" *BTA* 7(1985)261-278.

58

in the *confession* of the Roman Officer who supervised the execution squad that nailed Jesus to the cross at calvary. The article suggests that in the mouth of the centurion, Mark's notion of Jesus' divine Sonship muted at the beginning of his gospel in the enigmatic expression, "the gospel of Jesus, son of Mary, son of God" (Mk 1,1) becomes fully clarified. Of cardinal importance for me is Mark' s conception of the person of Jesus, and "the mission and the soteriological significance of Jesus' life seen in the African christian experience"[40]

The meaning of the titles, *son of God* (Matt and Mk) and *dikaios,* (Lk) are exegetically studied as they are used by the Synoptists. Perhaps, Luke's term, *dikaios,* innocent, is much more primitive and most probably it was adopted as the pious equivalent to the title, *son* and stood for the quality of a man justified to claim God as his *father* in the Palestinian-Syrian region where the Q-community had thrived during the later part of the first Christian century. The title son of God adopted by both Matthew and Mark is quite a familiar title in those gospels. But put in the mouth of the centurion, it seems to carry with it pagan connotations associated with the concept of the *divus filius,* a term usually ascribed to men who were held as saviours, benefactors, emperors, rulers and great philosophers. Given its religio-historical background, the centurion's use of the term remains unclear. What interests Africans, I argue, is not so much the signification of the title as "what message Mark intends to convey via the centurion to a believer in contemporary times"[41] For me, "Jesus as the son of God is a confession of faith which Mark has so neatly contrived and let be uttered by a non-Jew in order to guarantee his gospel universal significance".[42]

The centurion's exclamation is cast in the form of a proclamation. For Mark, the crucified Jesus is the son of God and no longer the emperor as hitherto known in Greco-Roman religion. Son of God is therefore a high Christology in Mark. As a fundamental Christological category, it involves suffering, rejection and death. It is, as I claim, "the proof of Jesus' divine sonship" and Messiahship.[43] I quite agree with V. Taylor who posits that in the activities of the earthly Jesus, he was recognized by his contemporaries as a

---

[40] *Ibid.*, p. 262.

[41] *Ibid.*, p. 269.

[42] *Ibid.*

[43] *Ibid.*, p. 271.

Messiah and that everything he did was not kept secret as W. Wrede had much earlier told scholars.[44]

But what is the importance of Mark's Christology for African Christians? This is a question I have been asking myself as I composed the essay and which, in the present study, I have continued to seek the answer. For me, Mark proclaims a message of consolation through his Christology. He conveys a message of hope and faith to all those who are underprivileged and subjected to all forms of structural hardship and the resultant indiginity to humanity. Christian living is not a bed of roses. Jesus' life and mission had their moments of suffering and pain leading to death. However, through rejection and death Jesus becomes King of Glory and Judge of all. Mark's invitation to radical faith and hope remains the goodnews to all Christians including African rural and peasant Christians who are exposed to the manifold problems which can force "a believer to question the meaning of life afterall and the why of his faith in Jesus".[45]

The barrenness of the socio-political culture; the economic as well as spiritual bankruptcies in our societies are not without their own multifarious difficulties. Africans suffer from all forms of deprivations and injustices forced upon them and their families by conditions created by the maladministrations of local rulers and overlords and from the consequences of their collusions with the international financial institutions whose fiscal policies aggravate and impoverish the living condition of man in the African world. The spirit of heroism and fortitude which Jesus exhibited that baffled the centurion and made him utter his confession in Jesus' divinity are completely absent in the lifestyles of many an African ruler. For me, Mark says that:

> Christian leadership must reflect the examples set for us by Jesus himself. To follow him and to confess him as Son of God demands a living witness in our daily life however highly placed we may be.[46]

---

[44] *Ibid.*, p. 274.

[45] *Ibid.*, p. 276.

[46] *Ibid.*, p. 277.

In the conclusion of the article, I recommend that Africans, the leaders of their political and religious institutions should recognize the givenness of the human commonality; namely our humanity and brotherhood in God. The article challenges our men and women in authority to sink their ethnic and religious differences, to deepen their religiosity and to come "to realize that true religion has both vertical and horizontal dimensions binding man to God vertically and man to neighbour horizontally"[47] In our mutual and interpersonal relationships is our godliness expressed and our confession of Christ as the Son of God fully realized.

The conception of Jesus as Ancestor for African Christians has received greater prominence in recent times; especially from theologians of Eastern and Central Africa. In their works, they are urging the African Church to recognize, as Bénézet Bujo avers, *Ahnentheologie als Ansatzpunkt für eine neue Christologie* in the Church.[48] Hopefully Bishop John Onaiyekan of Nigeria would not be taken as being cynical when he avers that "it seems that in these parts, the veneration of ancestors plays a key role in traditional religious life".[49] Among East and Central African Catholic theologians, it is B. Bujo (Zaire) and C. Nyamiti (Tanzania) who are among the most prolific in the thought and development of African Christology. Others like Kabasele (Zaire) find the role of the African "elder" person in the African Ancestor concept.[50] And in his popular work, *The World in Betweeen*, the visionary Archbishop Millingo, formerly of the Archdiocese of Lusaka (Zambia) asserts that Jesus is the Ancestor. In his bid to marry Jesus with our ancestors, Millingo affirms that Jesus is One who is alive among Africans just as the ancestor. He cites his clients' experiences of relational rapport with their dead ancestors.[51] Both Bujo and Nyamiti have published, apart from other articles, monographs devoted to showing that the Christ event

---

[47] *Ibid.*

[48] See, B. Bujo, Afrikanische Theologie in ihrem gesellschaftlichen Kontext, Theologie Interkulturell, Band 1, Düsseldorf, Patmos Verlag, 1986, pp. 79-98.

[49] J. Onaiyekan, "Christological Trends in Contemporary African Theology. A Challenge to Nigerian Theologians" NJTh 1(1991)11-27, p. 19.

[50] F. Kabasele, "Le Christ comme Ancetre et Ainé" in *Chemins, op. cit.*, pp. 127-143.

[51] E. Millingo, The World in- Between. Christian Healing and the Struggle for Spiritual Survival, London, C. Hurst, 1984, p. 78; and in the Daystar Press edition, Ibadan, 1986, pp. 86-89.

assumes its greatest peak in the belief that Christ is Ancestor for all Africans. Bujo exposes the ritual structure of African ancestral beliefs and traditions in which is embedded a "commemorative narrative soteriology" which guarantees cosmic harmony. In the context of his Christocentric ethics, Bujo proclaims Christ as the *proto-Ancestor*, the unique Ancestor, Source of life and greatest model of ancestral archetype.[52] One of the best summaries of Bujo's position is done by Nyamiti. According to him, Bujo is of the opinion that:

> Through the incarnation Christ assumed the whole human history including the legitimate aspirations of our ancestors. This assumption of the future which the ancestors sought to guarantee is assured because our ancestors'experiences have been made efficacious in Jesus crucified and risen. Thus the incarnation enables Christ to be the unique and privileged locus of total encounter with our ancestors and allows them to be the locus where we encounter the God of salvation.[53]

Commenting further, Nyamiti says:

> ... Christ as proto-ancestor is, for Bujo, the foundation of a narrative ethic affirming that Christ is the proto-Source of life and accomplishment and the model of human conduct through the experience of His paschal mystery. Bujo believes that this Christocentric ethic confirms the positive elements in African anthropocentrism such as hospitality, family spirit, solicitude for parents. At the same time it corrects and completes African traditional and modern customs.[54]

In 1986, Bujo, in a work which appeared in *die Reihe, Theologie Interkulturell* of the Catholic Theological Faculty of the Unit, Religious Studies, of the Johan-Wolfgang-Goethe University, Frankfurt am Main, Germany, offers in full his novel Christological and ecclesiological implications of the role of the African ancestor (Ahnen).[55]

---

[52] Bujo, "Pour une ethique africano-christocentrique", *BTA* 3(1981)41-52. For the English resumé, see, *idem.*, "A Christocentric ethic for black Africa", *TD* 3(1982)143-146; also, see, *idem.*, Afrikanische Theologie, pp. 82-84.

[53] Nyamiti, "African Christologies Today" p. 25.

[54] *Ibid.*

[55] Bujo, Afrikanische Theologie, pp. 79-121.

In his own study, *Christ as Our Ancestor,* Nyamiti elaborates the theological significance of his assumption that Christ is our Ancestor in the context of African culture and belief in Brother-Ancestorship[56]. For Nyamiti, the concept of Ancestor implies five essential elements:

(I)   It affirms both consanguinal and religious significance.

(II)   Through death, the ancestor acquires a supernatural status in the hereafter, nearness to God, sacred power and other supernatural traits.

(III)   The ancestor is a model, an archetype to his living kinsmen. The life he led on earth represents a remarkable quality of examplary morality to the extent that posterity sees it as a model of refernce.

(IV)   The ancestor is a mediator; an intermediary between God and his kinsmen, the living whose wellbeing remains his concern. In Bantu conception, the ancestor is within the sight of God.

(V)   The commemoration of the ancestor is kept alife by the descendants through ritual contact and prayers. Negligence of this evokes the anger of the ancestor before God.

One may wish to ask: why does Nyamiti devise such elaborate equations in order to explain his Ancestor-Christology? According to him, his approach is merely analogical. Jesus fulfills all these roles in a special way and hence is a "Brother-Ancestor" to Africans. The five criteria of ancestrality applies to the Christ event, Nyamiti maintains. Thus, Christ is "Ancestor in the faith". He further argues that "our ancestors" are not only ancestors by reason of their participation in the ancestorship of Christ but because "our ancestors" are a reflection of the ancestrality of Christ. This status explains, as Nyamiti wants us to believe, quite naturally the sanctity of our ancestors, the just members of the families.[57].

In a recent study devoted to African Christology by a group of Eastern African theologians, Nyamiti presents an overview of the contemporary state of Christological studies

---

[56] C. Nyamiti, Christ as Our Ancestor. Christology from the African Perspective, Gweru, Mambo Press, 1988.

[57] For a balanced review and critic of Nyamiti's work, see, T. Okere's review of Charles Nyamiti's, Christ as Our Ancestor, in *NJTh* 1(2,1986)68-70.

in Africa.[58] He argues, among other things, that the emergence of the "hidden Christ" is becoming a reality. Besides, he sounds quite optimistic of the African sense and the social background out of which these Christological titles are being born.

J. M. Schoffeleers has, in 1989, done an article which I would be ill at ease to omit in this review.[59] His insight reveals that one Christological paradigm prevails over a large extent of the sub-Saharan Africa; namely that of the medicine-man, *nganga*. In traditional African societies, the nganga has been a vehicle "of fortune and the counteraction of misfortunes".[60] He is an individual to whom the villagers run to in times of difficulty. In the light of his roles, African churches in many parts of Africa consider Jesus as the real nganga, the Medicine-man and Healer in place of their healing priests and prophets.[61] The term nganga is also applied to Christian pastors in general, especially in many parts of the Kongo region. Ngangas however do not proclaim themselves to be Jesus Christ but in a number of cults, a mythical *nganga* is presented as the alternative Christ.[62]

In sum, one gets the impression that what Schoffeleers is saying is that in preference to "a westernized image of the Saviour", African folk Christology is inclined towards an Africanized version of the biblical Christ.[63] The merit of Schoffeleers essay lies in the fact that in many parts of Africa, the medicine-man (*Onisegun* in the Yoruba traditions; *Dibia Mgboro-ogwu*, among the Igbo) provides a conceptual framework in which the soteriological role of Christ through the pastors are understood. He insists that the nganga is a folk

---

[58] Nyamiti, "Africn Christologies Today", in J. N. K. Mugambi & L. Magesa, *Jesus in African Christianity*, pp. 17-39.

[59] J. M. Schoffeleers, "Folk Christology in Africa: The Dialectics of the Nganga Paradigm", *JRA* 19(1989)157-183.

[60] *Ibid.*, p. 160.

[61] Also see, *idem.*, "Christ as the Medicine-man and the medicine-man as Christ: A Tentative History of African Christological Thought" Man and Life, Journal of the Institute of Social Research and Applied Anthropology, Calcutta, 8(1982)11-28.

[62] *Ibid.*, pp. 169-170.

[63] *Ibid.*, p. 158.

paradigm and not the creation of professional theologians.[64] For him then, the nganga paradigm offers insight into African peoples' view of both Christ, his ministers and of evil and redemption. Among other things, Schoffeleers concludes that the *nganga*, in his capacity to heal and cure illnesses, is likened to the biblical Christ.

In an article titled *Jésus, le maître d'initiation initié*, N. Diatta, probes into the cultural heritage of the Joola of Senegal in order to decode its latent religious message and the meaning it bears in contemporary African Christianity.[65] In his view, the encounter of traditional Joola ideal with evangelical models of the modern age offers insight into the inevitability of the problem of convergence and divergence. In order to bridge the gap, Diatta proposes a Christology founded upon the Joola experience of *maitre d initiation initié* (the initiated master of the initiation rites) which from an African point of view, clarifies the reality of the incarnation. According to Diatta, for thirty years, Jesus, the Son of God let himself be *initiated* into a local human culture. From this experience, Diatta opines, Jesus, later on his own part, initiated man into the divine intimacy; thus achieving for the faithful the status of sons of God in their humanity.

Admittedly structural evils continue to dictate the tone of christological reflections corrently done in South Africa. M. P. Moila, himself a South African, attempts to confront the socio-political evils perpetrated by people in the South African society with the structural sins of Jesus' times. He proposes a *historical Christology* as a solution in the situation [66]. In Moila's definition, historical christology "compares the historical context of Jesus with the present historical context and then tries to find the siginificance of Jesus' responses to his context for the Christian's response to the present context".[67] In the perspective of Black Theology which sees man's predicament as one of oppression, Jesus is the liberator. Moila evaluates these historical perspectives in the context of his historical christology. In the effort to achieve these objectives, Moila reviews the christologies of some mainline Black

---

[64] For further reflections on 'Folk Christology 'and what is meant, see, A. Shorter, "Folk Christianity and Functional Christology" AFER 24(1982)133-137.

[65] N. Diatta, "Jésus, le maitre d'initiation initié", Telema 57(1989)49-72.

[66] M. P. Moila, "Christology in the context of oppression in South Africa", *ATJ* 19 (1990)223-231.

[67] *Ibid.*, p. 223.

theologians. In light of the oppression experienced in their midst, Black theologians should see the human predicament as one of oppression, inequality and bondage as moments in which Jesus is the dynamic liberator. For him, the oppressive socio-political climate of South Africa calls for a steady construction of this image of Jesus. In other words, it is in the situation where people are deprived by evil structures that Jesus emerges as the liberator.

Let me close this survey with two studies that have appeared in the last few months of the beginning of the nineties. The authors are incidentally fellow Nigerians. A.O. Nkwoka, my onetime student and now colleague at the Obafemi Awolowo University, Ile-Ife; an Igbo himself, in his article, *Jesus As Eldest Brother, (Okpara)*, takes his point of departure from the concept, *Okpara Chineke* which had been adopted as a translation term for *Son of God* in the Archdeacon Dennis Union Igbo Bible.[68] Nkwoka undertakes to explore the significance "of *Okpara* in Igbo life and culture and the great Christological significance of this title to Igbo Christians".[69] In Igbo culture, the Okpara is *Eze's* (the King's) arm of government, he notes. The Eze co-ordinates both priestly and social leadership roles through him. In the homestead, the Okpara is the confidant of the father and as a consequence, he alone knows the secrets and the landed property of the father. It is to the Okpara that the father confers all essential prerogatives of inheritance and possession.[70] It is his right to distribute the inheritance to his juniors as he wills. As Nkwoka rightly states, administratively, the Okpara acts as the "second father" and as his representative; religiously, he is the family priest, the link between the family members and the ancestors. On the socio-political arena, he executes his role as both the family's socialite and "traditional prime minister".[71]

Armed with these ideas, Nkwoka then traces the beneficient significance of Jesus as Elder Brother in the context of Igbo anthropology. According to him, "the brotherhood of Jesus with regenerated mankind is inseparably tied up with his Divine sonship"; consequently all those who do the will of God irrespective of colour, race, status or sex have Jesus as

---

[68] A. O. Nkwoka, "Jesus As Eldest Brother, (Okpara): An Igbo Paradigm for Christology in the African Context" *AJT* 5(1991)87-103.

[69] *Ibid.*, p. 87.

[70] *Ibid.*, p. 91.

[71] *Ibid.*, p. 93.

Eldest brother.[72] Christ was the first to rise. Through his resurrection, he is the Eldest-Born. In light of this, Nkwoka insists that *Okpara Chineke* should remain a valid Igbo rendering of the term, *Son of God*. He cites plentiful NT pericopes to support his thesis.[73] Jesus, *Okpara Chineke* is to the various Igbo family groups the only exemplary *Okpara* they know today. The Igbo Christians endear themselves so much to the "only begotten Son of God" theology as the concept is quite at home with their cultural values. To sum up, Nkwoka admirably states:

> The place of Okpara in Igbo cosmology has proved to be a very fertile ground for the contextualisation of Jesus as both the Son of God and a very loving 'big brother' to man irrespective of his lot in life. This we believe might have contributed in no small way to the massive embrace of Christianity by the Igbo.[74]

The second article is written by Bishop John Onaiyekan. It is a review of the Christological research trends in present-day African Christian theology which with Nyamiti's *"African Christologies Today"* complements this section of my work.[75] The focus of the article is on what some African theologians have written about "what our people are saying and thinking about Jesus Christ whom they have accepted as Lord and God".[76] According to him, the main trends in Christological studies in Africa are derived from the Bible, Classical Christology, African traditional culture and Contemporary African realities. In his effort to offer a model, Onaiyekan zeroes in from the perspective of the religious tradition of the Yoruba to which he belongs. He discovers a model which arises from the *Orisha* cult and belief system. In the light of their religious experience and confession of faith, Yoruba converts to Christianity see Jesus Christ as "the Great Orisha, superior to all others".[77]

---

[72] *Ibid.*, pp. 94-95.

[73] See *ibid.*, p. 96.

[74] *Ibid.*, p. 99.

[75] J. Onaiyekan, "Christological Trends".

[76] *Ibid.*, p. 11.

[77] *Ibid.*, p. 22.

Inspite however of "the gallery of Christological portraits" offered by Africans, Onaiyekan notes that "none of them claims to have found a comprehensive and perfect portrait of Jesus" just as R. Moloney has asserted in his article in the *Theological Studies*.[78] In any case, it is my humble view that due to the imperfections inherent in human thought and accretions, the articulation of autochthonous concepts which can express once and for all times African Christians experience of Christ must ever be varied and manifold. The search continues. This volume represents our effort in this quest.

3.4   OBSERVATIONS

Indeed the review keeps one quite *au courant* with the trends in research on Christology by Africans and non Africans who write from and for the African ambience within the last two decades. I do not claim to have exhausted all studies by Africans and others on the subject.[79] Effort has however been made to cover a wider spectrum. The purpose is to let readers come into contact with the methods being employed and the interpretations given by engaged African theologians and to let what is being done in Africa be recognized and be seen that the African world possesses adequate Christological analogues. Much as I remain indebted to the authors and the ideas they proffer, the fact that I am not alone in this quest patriotically encourages me.

As Bishop Onaiyekan correctly judges and Nyamiti also notes same, the material reviewed can conveniently be divided as J. Dupuis had done for Euro-American and Latin American Christologies into Biblical Christology, Traditional Christology, Systematic Christology and Liberation Christology.[80] My review shows that Africans, in their works,

---

[78] Cf. Onaiyekan, *Ibid.*, p. 19, and also R. Moloney, "African Christology", *TS* 48(1987)505-515.

[79] I could not, upon my visit to the Catholic Higher Institute of Eastern Africa, Nairobi in April, 1991, get access to S. Ssemanda, Christ our "Kabaka": A Christology from the Ganda Perspective, mimeographed thesis, CHIEA, Nairobi, 1988, which could have been useful to my present work.

[80] See, J. Dupuis, "On Some Recent Christological literature" Gregorianum 69(1988)713-740. I cannot imagine why Dupuis could not consider any study by African Christologists in his review. Could it be an oversight or segregation or a habit of selective myopia?

encompass all the four sections; and even interlope into one or two areas hence the difficulty one encounters in trying to classify the authors antheir works. One fact however remains to be stressed. Since 1972, when John S. Mbiti made his debut on African Christology from the Biblical perspective, a very negligible few had followed the trail he has blazed yet most agree that the Bible is the sole authentic source for Christology. Nyamiti whose work espouses both the New Testament, Classical and African Traditional ideas represents one of those hard to place well within a particular group. Perhaps, suffice it to state that he belongs to the Traditional Christologists as represented in the works of A. Grillmeier, the German historian of Christology. I say this because his works reflect a purposeful dialogue between culture, patristic and modern theology.

The review shows that efforts made by Africans to propound Christologies have shown little awareness of recent developements in New Testament exegesis and research. The approach of African biblical scholars must be allowed to produce a theology sympathetic with the social conditions of man in many regions of Africa today. The goodnews of the New Testament and the Bible as a whole is preferentially in favour of the poor. Nkwoka's utilization of the New Testament as a source to confront an African (Igbo) theme represents a further milestone in this direction of Biblical Christology. Okolo's *Emmanuel*, though biblical in origin, supports a Christology having its deep roots in Palestinian traditions. But one would wish to know exactly what familiar concepts in African tradition the title, Emmanuel evokes? The rest of the authors passed in review are engaged in rehabilitating systematic and classical Christologies with the aid of African religious concepts. This, in itself, is good as by their efforts Christology is made to enter into dialogue with African Traditional Religion.

The realities of oppression and exploitation dictate the tone of Christology done by South African theologians. For them, the starting-point of Christology is the existential situation. Thus one can see that our South African colleagues have practically been engaged in Liberation than in inculturational theology. More often than not, the question addressed is: how can faith in Jesus Christ empower black people who are engaged in the liberation struggle? The obvious answers yield themselves into reflections on Black Christology (Setiloane, Carvalho, Boesak, Mofokeng, Moila etc). Recent changes in the political history of South Africa may introduce another horison of theologizing in a multi-racial South Africa. We look with agog when this shall begin to blosom.

All these efforts reflect a beehive of activities within a theological community whose professionals engage their thoughts and talents in demonstrating to their kismen and kinswomen who Jesus Christ is to and where he is with them. Indeed, the review points towards the prevalence of a theological pluriformity. The many positions African theologians have maintaned remind us that theologians from St. Augustine to Karl Rahner (Barth to Tillich) have each been innovators who had had something novel and relevant to contribute to the knowledge of God. As W. C. Smith puts it, they had realized "that inherited formulations were to some degree inadequate ...".[81] Since the reality of the incarnation is a mystery, the images we devise and employ will ever remain opaque, yet as models they will continue to help generations of African faithfuls grasp good enough of the story of the Scriptures about the Christ.

3.5   CONCLUSIONS

This overview of major studies done on African Christology spans a full score years. The diversity of the views and conceptions reflect the inadequacy of human formulas to express the mystery of Christ. Hence, it becomes apropos to say that as at Pentecost, Parthians, Medes and Elamites ... heard the story of "the mighty works of God", every man in his own tongue wherein he was born (Acts 2,9-11); so from all corners of the continent, African theologians are expressing the Christ event, each in his own native idea and concept. Their efforts are indicative of the fact that Christology is the concern of every African person who has received the Gospel of Christ. It reflects a deeper response from the African Church. It demonstrates the corporate involvement of Africans in the mystery of the incarnation. As Teresa Okure has noted:

> Incarnation presupposes the existence of two distinct realities, the divine reality and the human reality, which then becomes united to form a new and unique reality in Jesus of Nazareth as the Christ. In this union, neither reality

---

[81] Smith, "Christian-Muslim Relations", p. 18.

is destroyed, down-graded or absorbed. Yet each is enriched and mysteriously transformed by the other.[82]

Certainly for Africans, participation in the reality of the incarnation is a symbiotic activity (Penoukou: 1982) a phenomenon which is already a way of life in which they are quite familiar; especially in their experience of the African flora and wild life. In the light of this experience, Christology must emphasize in the African audience the fact that the mystery of incarnation supposes, as Teresa asserts that:

> ... it is not only humanity that tends towards God in Christ and becomes one with God, but it is God also, who tends towards humanity and becomes one with humankind.[83]

---

[82] Teresa Okure, "Inculturation: biblical/theological basis" in T. Okure, P. van Thiel et alii (eds.), 32 Articles Evaluating Inculturation of Christianity in Africa, Eldoret, AMECEA, Gaba Publications, Spearhead, Nos 112-114, 1990, pp. 57-58.

[83] Ibid., p. 58.

CHAPTER FOUR

KINGSHIP IN PRECOLONIAL AFRICA: EAST - WEST
THE YORUBA AND THE BAGANDA KINGDOMS

4.1   INTRODUCTION

The nineteenth century *Aufklärung* heralded, among other things, a new era in Europe's awareness of the external world. Beside the shock of the French Revolution and the hectic Napoleonic era, romanticism became the order of the day. The African continent was seen almost as a virgin land to coast and to discover for Europe. Once explored, hordes of travellers, adventurers, traders, politicians, troops, envoys of mission institutes, among them, men of letters and the arts began to gravitate towards Africa, and to take contacts with its peoples. This golden age of exploration produced the brains who had documented most of the literature reviewed in the following chapters. I shall take the East-West belt as my starting-point where I will examine what I consider two representative kingship systems; namely the Yoruba *Obaship* and the Baganda *Kabakaship*. The purpose is not to offer any ethnological analysis. I find myself incompetent to handle such a task. I have rather chosen to probe the ethno-historical elements constitutive of these kingships as well as their religious dimensions. The North-South belt shall constitute the subject of the next chapter. These discussions shall attempt, unlike some previous theological studies employing African ethno-historical data, to explore in details the religious traits of kinships as well as the sacred status of the kings who occupied offices in these ancient kingdoms and the various aspects of their sovereignty. The approach is purposeful. Some African authors, without solid historical, anthropological, and ethnographical back up, have hastily concluded that African kingships and the titles "King" or "Chief" are unfit for Christological reflections.[1] Much as their views

---

[1] A. Shorter, African Christian Spirituality, New York, Maryknoll, Orbis, 1978, p. 66; J. S. Pobee, Toward an African Theology, p. 97; J. N. K. Mugambi, "Christological Paradigms", p. 152. For a rather positive view, see D. W. Waruta, "Who is Jesus Christ for Africans today? Prophet. Priest. Potentate." in J. N. K. Mugambi & L. Magesa (eds.), Jesus

may, speaking from the polity of the Early States sound correct, their researches have not, however, been able to uncover the deep socio-religious import of the phenomenon of rulership wielded by African kings as they reigned over their people as the "incarnate regents" of the gods of their lands and representatives of their progenitors; nor do they take count of the anthropological theory which upholds the view that *le roi régne, mais il ne gouverne pas* (the king reigns but does not administer) by which one can understand the intricacy of the "myth of society" which invests the kings with high statuses but with limited powers.[2] In other words, evils associated with kingship and its so-called *status remotus* derive not from the kings themselves, but from that aura of sacrality which is invidiously defended and guarded by powerful traditionalists and royalists and accorded to kingship by the society. These aspects of the social drama relative to African kingships and transmitted in legends, court histories and royal mythologies of the precontact period of the African civilization await constant re-assessment. Let me begin with some background information about the Yoruba and their kingship system. I will present my discussion of the Yoruba kingship in the English present tense when necessary as the institution still flourishes. The Buganda kingship will be narrated in the English past tense since that institution had been abolished in 1969 by Milton Obote.

4.2   THE *OBA* - THE YORUBA KING
4.2.1   THE YORUBA PEOPLE

The Yoruba speaking people of southwest Nigeria, one of Africa's most studied race; especially with regard to their history, religion, art and culture,[3] more than twenty million in population today, are the descendants of Oduduwa, a valiant son of Nimrod (Lamurudu)

---

in African Christianity, pp. 40-53; pp. 43-44.

[2] H. J. M Claessen, "Kingship in the Early State", *Bijdragen TLV* 142(1986)113-127, p. 114.

[3] Among others, see F. Anton et al.(eds.), Primitive Art, New York, H. N. Abrams, 1978, pp. 409-421; H. J. Drewal, P. John III with R. Abiodun, Yoruba: Nine Centuries of African Art and Thought, New York, Center for African Art in Association with H. N. Abrams, 1989.

described by Samuel Johnson as "of Phoenician origin".[4] Oduduwa and his followers had settled in Arabia where they had practised their own religion.[5] But expelled from Muslim Arabia, Oduduwa and his sons migrated south of the Sahara, towards the forest region until they arrived and settled at Ile-Ife, regarded in Yoruba mythology as the cradle of Yoruba civilization and the centre of the origin of man. Here, Oduduwa became the first king and the founder of the Ife line of *Obas* who were known to have been charged by him to disperse all over what was then geographically known as Yorubaland to set up their own kingdoms (*Obaship*).[6] As it stands in Ife court history, Oba Oduduwa initiated the wearing of the crown, *ade* with veil as the essential sign of kingship.[7] Since that time, there had originated among the Yoruba, a strong kingship organisation marked by the coroneted headgear.

The kingdom of Benin of the Edo state of Nigeria is known to have derived from the Yoruba stock and was for several years subject to the Yoruba kingdom.[8] But by 1485 when the Portuguese explorers had reached that part of the Nigerian coast, Benin was already a separate kingdom. Besides, the Yoruba were known to have "extended from the Niger in the east across most of south-western Nigeria and into Dahomey and Togoland in the west".[9] According to 'Biodun Adediran, "the town had for long occupied a central position in the traditions and religion of peoples inhabiting the area of West Africa encircled by the rivers

---

[4] S. Johnson, The History of the Yorubas, CMS Bookshops, Lagos, 1921, Repr. 1960, pp. 6-7.

[5] *Ibid.*

[6] C. Legum, Africa: A Handbook to the Continent, New York, 1966, p. 213; O. Gbadegesin, "Destiny, Personality and Ultimate Reality of Human Existence: A Yoruba Perspective", URAM 7(1984)173-188, p. 174; P. C. Lloyd, "Sacred Kingship and Government Among the Yoruba", Africa 30(1960)221-237, p. 223, especially n. 1. See also E. Isichei, A History of Nigeria, London, Longman, Lagos, 1983, pp. 131-132.

[7] W. F. Mellor, "Bead Embroidery of Remo" Nigeria 14(1932)154-155. Also see, E. G. Parrinder, "Divine Kingship in West Africa" Numen 3(1956)111-121, pp. 115-116; R. F. Thompson, "The Sign of the Divine King: An Essay on Yoruba Bead-Embroidered Crowns with Veil and Bird Decorations" African Arts 3(1969-70)8-17; 74-80, p. 8.

[8] Stride-Ifeka, Peoples and Empires of West Africa, pp. 305-310.

[9] Parrinder, "Divine Kingship in West Africa", p. 114. As Idowu puts it, the Yoruba "have been a great race", ... "the progeny of great war lords, efficient kingdom builders and astitute rulers". Idowu, *Olódùmarè. God in Yoruba Belief*, p. 5.

Volta and the Niger".[10] Today, the Yoruba speaking people of Nigeria are spread over Lagos, Ogun, Oyo, Osun, Ondo, Kongi and Kwara states of modern Nigeria. The Yoruba population in Nigeria does not include the *Anago-Yoruba* communities in Dahomey, the modern Republic of Benin and Togo. Besides, there is a surviving Yoruba population in Brazil, part of the African Brazilian group and those in the Caribbean and Cuban islands. In the West African sub-region, it is also known that an older crop of ethnic Yoruba thrives in Senegal and in the Nile valley where they are found around southern Sudan.[11]

4.2.2   YORUBA *OBASHIP*

Data from Yoruba history and religion reveal that in precolonial times, the *Obaship* (kingship) is one of such institutions which dominates the socio-political life of Yoruba communities.[12] Associated with Obaship is the town. As town-living people, each Yoruba group live under the rulership and protection of an Oba whose *Aafin*, palace, stands facing the major market-place, often known as the *Oja Oba*, the king's market. Here, the Oba dwells surrounded by his chiefs, court officials and priests. As Smith observes, the Yoruba Obaship is a sacred office. The reigning monarch is recognized as the state's high-priest; the celebrant of the most important religious rituals;[13] anthe protector of his people who naturally wish to live in his shadow.[14] The *Ooni*, the (King) of Ife, the ancient city described, as far back as 1910 by Leo Frobenius, the German explorer "as the spiritual

---

[10] B. Adediran, "Politics and Religion in Yorubaland: A Case Study of Ile-Ife c. 1850-1930" in *Islam And The Modern Age*, November 1986, pp. 217-240; p. 218; see also the same article in *Afrika Zamani*, Review of African History 16-17(1986)129-144.

[11] See, C. U. Manus, *"Jesu Kristi Oba*: A Christology of 'Christ the King' among the Indigenous Christian Churches in Yorubaland, Nigeria" AJT 5(1991)311-330; p. 316.

[12] R. S. Smith, Kingdoms of the Yoruba, London, James Currey, 3rd Ed. 1988, p. 87.

[13] Claessen, "Kingship in the Early State", p. 118.

[14] *Ibid.*, On the fact that Yoruba kingship system is the subject of innumerable ethnological studies in Black Africa's history, see D. D. Laitin, Hegemony and Culture: Politics and Religious Change among the Yoruba, The University of Chicago Press, 1986, p.x.

centre of the image of the West African universe";[15] commands much respect and prestige among the entire Yoruba people. He asserts his superiority over the other Obas in the land as the king who is in the most direct line of their father, Oduduwa. It is to his court that the other Obas and their chieftains in West Africa (except, perhaps, the Akan of Ghana) trace their roots.[16]

As regards status, the Yoruba Obaship is an elevated kingship. The king is himself identified with the sacredness of the institution. Even though his political power is limited when necessary by the *Imole,* a powerful cultic group in the case of Ife,[17] for example, the sacrosanctity of the office carry great reverence. He is conceived by his people as a divinity to whose wellbeing their own fortunes are attached. It is from him that many of his subjects receive such largess as titles and chieftainces. He gives lands to the state nobility; confirms privileges and oftentimes donates money for rebuilding national infrastructure and derelict ritual centres.

4.2.3   The Selection of an Oba

Respectable tradition maintains that candidates for dynastic elections could only be persons of the royal lineage. It is only one of them who could succeed a king on the Yoruba throne. In some kingdoms, the ruling houses are more than one and the Oba is alternatively selected from the houses. Among the Yoruba, filial succession is upheld over against adelphic succession. The aspirant must be a son born to an Oba while on the throne; and this son must be born to a free woman and not to a slave. He must be phyisically fit neither unduly over-sized nor unusually tall. Upon the accomplishment of funerary rites for a deseased Oba, the senior members of the royal houses submit to the Council of Chiefs a list of eligible

---

[15] L. Frobenius, The Voice of Africa, Vol. I, New York, Benjamin Blom, 1913, 1968 Reissue, p. 265.

[16] Smith, Kingdoms of the Yoruba, p. 87.

[17] Some authors have discussed the probability of conflicts between the king and some of the guilds. See, for example, P. C. Lloyd, "Conflict Theory and Yoruba Kingdom" in I. M. Lewis (ed.), History and Social Anthropology, ASA Monographs 7, London Tavistock Publications, 1968, pp. 25-62.

candidiates. The Chiefs representing the prominent non-royal houses most of whose representatives are in-charge of one religious cult or the other,[18] in turn, consider the merits of the candidates, consult *Ifa* oracle in order to ascertain the length and prosperity of the reign of each aspirant to the throne.[19] At this stage, the king-elect is chosen and proclaimed by the *Olori Marun* the most senior chiefs of the royal court.

4.2.4   THE INSTALLATION AND CORONATION OF AN OBA

It is the duty of the *Olori Marun*, to plan out the coronation and installation ceremonies which is usually long and complex. The ceremonies are performed with solemn and lengthy rituals required to make the king-elect a sacral ruler. By his installation, he is set apart and projected above the society as a living incarnation of kingship. According to Marc Abélés, such a king "is transferred to a superior level, a transcended position".[20] An interesting point in the ceremonials is the stage when the Oba-elect pretends to be unwilling to take office. Tradition has it that he hides away in his house and is sought after and when he is later found, he is taken by the town police, the *efa*. He is, as it were, *captured* and led into

---

[18] O. Oyediran, "The Position of *Oni* in the changing political system of the Ile-Ife" *JHSN* 6(1973)376-396. On the intricacies of "dynastic elections", see J. Goody (ed.), Succession to High Office, Cambridge, CUP, 1966, p. 13; also Lloyd, "The Traditional Political System of the Yoruba" in R. Cohen & J. Middleton (eds.), Comparative Political Systems, Garden City, Natural History Press, 1967, pp. 270-292.

[19] On the place of Ifa divination system in Yoruba traditional religion, see, W. Bascom, Ifá Divination: Communication Between Gods and Man in West Africa, Bloomington, Indiana University Press, 1969; W. Abimbola, Ifá: An Exposition of Ifá Literary Corpus, Ibadan, Oxford University Press, 1976; *idem.*, "The Literature of Ifá Cult" in S. O. Biobakun (ed.), Sources of Yoruba History, Clarendon, Oxford, 1973, pp. 41-45; Judith Gleason, A Recitation of Ifá, Oracle of the Yoruba, New York, Grossman Publishers, 1973; McClelland, The Cult of Ifá Among the Yoruba, pp. 9-40; P. M. Peek (ed.), African Divination Systems: Ways of Knowing, Bloomington/Indianapolis, Indiana University Press, 1991, pp. 230.

[20] M. Abélès, "'Sacred Kinship' and the Formation of the State", in H. J. M. Claessen & P. Skalník (eds.), The Study of the State, New Babylon. Studies in the Social Sciences 35, The Hague, Mouton, 1981, pp. 1-14, p. 3.

the forest where he receives preliminary tutoring on how to rule the state.[21] Among the Rukuba of Nigeria, the king is said to be arrested by the "men of the rope" who thereafter tie him to the kingship. Thus, the inauguration of a reign is dramatically marked by this process of integression.

Thereafter, the Oba-elect undertakes a journey through the ancient routes taken by the Patriarch or the progenitor of the race to the capital and at each shrine, he performs ritual ceremonies. Arriving at the ancestral court, he renews the progenitor's promise to rule his people well, in justice and peace. At this stage, he is dressed in rags, manhandled, beaten and ritually cleansed. Thus the installation consists of violence on the part of the community and a loss of identity on the part of the king-elect. Later on, he puts on a white cloth and proclaims his throne-name. All these ritual ceremonies is meant to symbolise his re-birth as Oba (king).

In a secret but colourful ritual, the Oba-elect eats the excised and preserved portion of the heart of his immediate predecessor (*je oba*). By this and other rites, he is consecrated the ruler of a sovereign state, receives his material insignia and is put into immediate contact with his ancestors. It is a strongly held belief among his subjects that by this "eating", all the sacral powers of the ancestors including those of the progenitor, Oduduwa are transferred to him. The consecration or ritual anointing confers on the Oba the wisdom to reign over his people.[22] For three months after his coronation, the Oba-elect lives in the house of one of the court chiefs whose estate is usually opposite the *Aafin*'s entrance. In this seclusion, he is only visited by his chiefs who must teach him all he requires to know about his reign and the myths of origin of the state. From here, he later settles in the palace where he has no more contact with all and sundry but those chiefs qualified by their status to enter the king's apartment and reception hall; namely the *Egarefe* and the *Agbafe* (prelates and patriarchs).[23] The truth of the matter finds its expression in the ritual axiom which proposes "that whatever

---

[21] For the significance of the wilderness experience as the locale where special figures and kings win their kingship after communion with the wilderness beings, see Nancy E. Falk, "Wilderness and Kingship in Ancient South Asia", *HR* 13(1974)1-15.

[22] Lloyd, "Sacred Kingship", pp. 227-228; also Parrinder, "Divine Kingship", pp. 115-116.

[23] G. J. A. Ojo, Yoruba Palaces, London, 1966, pp. 67-74.

is sacred is hidden from view and elevated in height".[24] In sum then, the enthronement of
the Oba is characterized by a veritable taking-into-possession of the elected individual.

4.2.5 THE SACRED NATURE OF THE OBA

Sacred kingship, as P. C. Lloyd rightly observes, is, among the Yoruba, an ancient
institution.[25] Yoruba kingship is truely an institution of state centred upon the personality of
the Oba generally regarded as *divine*. This belief is founded upon the king's status which is
confered on him at the rites of his installation. According to Abélès such a king is:

> ... the incarnation of divinity; he appears as the guarantor of the natural
> order, the only one who can restore the world after a catastrophy and the one
> whose weaknesses are sufficient to provoke tragedy.[26]

The *Oba* lives with the people but is rarely seen by them. He is approached through court
officials and accredited intermediaries. His "outing" is an *epiphaneia* allowed only on special
occasions; and according to local custom, the king must march out with all his subordinates.
His outing is heralded by boisterous music made from ivory and *kakaki* trumpets and the
ogidigbo drums (talking drums). All business is usually suspended throughout the whole city
on such occasions.[27] On this phenomenon Smith amplifies:

> The Yoruba Oba is usually described as a sacred or divine king. ... He lived
> a life ... of ordered ceremonial, secluded in his palace, subject to many ritual
> restraints and approached only with infinite respect and by designated persons
> of the court. He rarely appeared in public, and then always robed and, in the

---

[24] B. Ray, The Kabaka as the Symbolic Center of Buganda, a concluding portion (pro
manuscripto) of his forthcoming book: *Myth, Ritual and Kingship in Buganda*, New York,
Oxford University Press, sent to me by the author during my research period in Frankfurt,
1990-1992, p. 12.

[25] Lloyd, "Sacred Kingship", p. 222.

[26] Abélès, "'Sacred Kingship'", p. 2.

[27] Johnson, History, p. 48.

case of the great Oba, wearing a beaded crown whose fringe hid his face. He was not only the head of the town and kingdom but their personification, reincarnating also his ancestors back to the origin of the dynasty and he was titular head of all religious cults in the kingdom.[28]

Seeking to explain further what made Yoruba Obaship a sacred institution, authors proffer diverse rationalizations. As one who lives and has, for sometime now, observed the Ife tradition in Ile-Ife, a university town and the seat of a reigning Oba, the *Ooni* of Ife, Oba Okunade Sijwade, Olubuse II, it is pertinent for me to advise that to respond to this question, one must not fail to take count of the special nexus existing between the king and deity. As in the Ancient Orient, the Oba is the embodiment of the deity in his state. To fully elucidate this view, let me employ the observations and comments of some scholars. On the subject in question, Robert Farris Thompson writes: "the rulers of these ancient provinces all claim descent from Oduduwa. They are honoured as seconds of the gods (ekeji orisa)".[29] According to G. J. A. Ojo, "the Oba was the visible symbol of the deity among the Yorubas".[30] In the words of J. O. Awolalu, the Oba fulfills the role of the priest and "embodies the unity of the ethnic group and offers sacrifice on its behalf as its representative".[31] In the same vein, E. D. Adelowo's recent remark on the sacrality of the Oba is quite apposite:

> In the cultic activities of a town, the Oba is usually the head of the ritual leaders. He is the priest-king. In Ile-Ife, for example, the Ooni of Ife, *Alase Ekeji Orisa* is usually the *Pontifex Maximus*. He is the *Olori Awon Iworo* - the head of all the priests. He assumes this office in consequence of his sceptre, *are*, which is derived from the divinity to which he is viceregent.[32]

---

[28] Smith, Kingdoms of the Yoruba, p. 91.

[29] Thompson, "The Sign of the Divine King", p. 8.

[30] Ojo, Yoruba Palaces, p. 75.

[31] J. O. Awolalu, Yoruba Beliefs and Sacrificial Rites, London, Longman, 1979, p. 110.

[32] E. D. Adelowo, "Rituals, Symbolism and Symbols in Yoruba Traditional Religious Thought" *AJT* 4(1990)162-173, p. 164.

The sacred character of a Yoruba Oba is, besides, attested to in a number of extant oral traditions and in various euphemistic speech forms uttered by the people. The demise of a reigning Oba is not said to be a physical death but a passage into the vault of the sky - *O wo Aja*. Thus, the people would not say the Oba 'has died', but that he 'has gone away'. No one sees him eating his food. He does not walk bare-footed. When he ever appears to the public, he is hardly recognized as a person. He is clothed in voluminous spreading gowns and wears a conical beaded crown, the *ade*, which A. I. Asiwaju has rightly described as "the significant element in the whole regalia".[33] Even though the Oba officiates at state rituals, the Oba does not belong to the professional priesthood. He is only the spiritual head and the father of the state in cultic matters. The rituals he performs and his leadership in other religious activities are seen mainly as part of his service performed on behalf of his people to the divinities. This feature is confirmed by the accounts of local historians and anthropologists. Asiwaju, for example, says, "... the Oba normally assumes his role as the community's high-priest" at public religious ceremonies and festivals.[34] In the exercise of his religious duties, the Oyo Oba, the *Alafin*, appears in state on four festive occasions; namely during the festivals of *Ifá, Orun, Bere* and the worship day of *Ogun* - the Yoruba god of war. The Yoruba along with their kings are bounded by religious ideas in their everyday life. In short, as Abélès puts it, "the sacrificing king" becomes himself "the sacrificed king"; that is to say, the king becomes through his ritualistic acts the *leitourgos*, the celebrant of the state.[35]

4.2.6   THE OBA AS AN INTERMEDIARY OF HIS PEOPLE

The Yoruba king, though a sacred ruler is, as I have shown above, democratically elected to reign over his people. Both the secular and sacred status of the Oba combine to make him a man of the people and the intermediary between them and the unseen world; that is,

---

[33] A. I. Asiwaju, "Political Motivation and Oral Historical Traditions in Africa: The Case of Yoruba Crowns, 1900-1960", *Africa* 46(1976)113-127, p. 113.

[34] Asiwaju, *Ibid.*, p. 113.

[35] Abélès, "'Sacred kingship'", p. 3.

between those of the *Aiye* (this world) and those of the *Orun* (the spirit-world). He is the community's authority symbol and one who unites in himself the people in the worship services he leads. He re-enacts through the rythmic rituals he performs the cosmic harmony which ought to exist between heaven and earth in the Yoruba world. In such ritualistic acts, it is believed that the king is the guarantor of the fecundity of herds and humans through the blessings and powers he gains from the gods and the ancestral spirits. This potency materializes in the flow of abundant riches for the state, and in the spiritual wholeness of the people. Like the *lwembe* of the Nyakyusa, the Oba is an "instrument of prosperity".[36] In this light, the mediatory role of the Yoruba Oba finds parallel in the nature of other sacred kings in the general history of kingship. As C. Gottanelli points out, in the excerise of the functions of such kings, "the cultic relationships between the society and the supernatural sphere" is ensured.[37]

4.2.7   THE COMPONENT OF ROYALTY

The Oba's crown symbolizes his essence of royalty. The *ade* is ritually consecrated in an elaborate ceremony before it is worn by the king. He does not see the inside of the crown. It is forbidden him to as it is considered taboo for the king to behold the underlinings of the crown which is held to be the permanent abode of the spirits of previous crown-heads. The crown is always placed on and removed from the Oba's head by a court official designated to carry out this function. The great respect accorded the *ade* lies in the fact that, for the Yoruba, the crown is the symbol of the royal ancestral spirits and as Awolalu himself a Yoruba says, the king is divine because of his sceptre "which is derived from the divinity to whom he is vice-regent".[38] As an important object in the kingdom, the *ade* occupies a conspicuous place in the palace shrine. Among its other symbolic uses, the *ade* is placed on the throne during the absence of the king and the subjects were wont to do obeisance to it as

---

[36] Abélès, *Ibid.*, p. 5.

[37] C. Gottanelli, "Kingship" in M. Eliade et al (eds.), The Encyclopedia of Religion, Vol 8, New York, London, Macmillan, 1987, p. 314.

[38] Awolalu, Yoruba Beliefs and Sacrificial Rites, p. 110.

was respectfully done to the real monarch. In a perceptive comment on the importance of the beaded crown as a sign of the divine king among the Yoruba, R. F. Thompson has this to say:

> The bead-embroidered crown with beaded veil, foremost attribute of the traditional leaders (Oba) of the Yoruba people of West Africa symbolizes the aspirations of a civilization at the highest level of authority. The crown incarnates the intuition of royal ancestral force, the revelation of great moral insight in the person of the king and the glitter of aesthetic experience.[39]

commenting further, Thompson writes:

> The gods of the Yoruba long ago chose beaded strands as emblems. The fact that the crowns are embellished with bead embroidery immediately suggests godhead. Indeed, the prerogative of beaded objects is restricted to those who represent the gods, kings and priests; diviners and native doctors. The beaded crown therefore connotes power sustained by divine sanction.[40]

To conclude this unit, let me cite the filial respect and attitude of contemporary Nigerians towrds surviving royal institutions which I judge relevant to the spirit of the present discussion:

> In all communities with long history of *Obaship, Emirship, Obiship* and so on, traditional rulers are regarded as God's representatives on earth. There is a lot of mythology surrounding their origin. Hence they have that sacred aura that even the massive inroad of Western culture has not destroyed.[41]

---

[39] Thompson, "The Sign of the Divine King", p. 8.

[40] *Ibid*.

[41] The Editorial Column, The Daily Times, Lagos, October 12, 1982, p. 3.

4.2.8   THE RULERSHIP OF THE OBA

In precolonial Yoruba socio-political system, the Oba was, as has already been shown, the personification of his state and the people as well as the embodiment of law and order. The subjects believe that a kingdom without an Oba cannot exist. For the ancient Yoruba, kingship was an efficient mechanism for maintaining peace and for the enforcement of cooperation among the people as well as the means to ward off evil, confusion, disorder and anarchy in the state. The Oba is believed to take care of his kingdom and to exercise restraint to the inhabitants. The fortunes of the towns within the kingdom are improved under a good Oba or are perversed under a bad one. This reminds us of the well-known Confucian philosophy attributed to Mencius: "When the prince is committed to the common good, everyone else is committed to the common good".[42] The Oba headed a sovereign government. His policies are meant to concern themselves with the wellbeing of his subjects. He has, for example, unlimited power over land use and determines the size of land leaseable to refugees and peaceful immigrants in his domain. Political views expressed in lineage meetings are laid before the Oba's Palace Council by the Royal Chiefs.[43] As Asiwaju notes:

> In every kingdom, the king or Oba (distinguished by his use of the beaded crown) advised by a council of titled men representing diverse interests, ruled supreme.[44]

The authority the Oba exercises is dependent on the exalted nature of the kingship itself. By his installation, he assumes both temporal and spiritual powers. He is symbolically the centre of the society. He mediates between the many sectional interest-groups that compose the social structure of the state under his reign; and as has been noted, he also mediates between the human and the spirit-world. Thus, there is truth in the judgment of Grotannelli that such functional kings hold "the social cosmos together".[45] The idea found in most kingship

---

[42] Mencius IV, ii, v.

[43] Lloyd, "Sacred Kingship", p. 230.

[44] Asiwaju, "Political Motivation", p. 117.

[45] Grotannelli, "Kingship", p. 313.

traditions; namely that the king is "a cosmic giver of life"[46] readily finds full expression in Yoruba traditions. The king is spoken of as *Oba Aiye*, king terrestrial and *Oba Orun*, king celestial, His Supernatural Highness, the king whose reign endures forever. These features attest to the fact that the king's supremacy extends to virtually every facet of existence both seen and unseen. He is *Kabiyesi* - "the king who rules for as long as he lives".[47]

The Oba's royalty includes certain charismatic qualities of leadership such as those implicated in his praise-names by which the loyal subjects endear themselves to the him. Such loyalties entitle him to enforce obedience on all who inhabit his state.[48] Even though a Yoruba Oba could today attend to some private business outside his domain, the fact remains that the magico-religious aura which had engendered popular loyalty, reverence and allegiance to his predecessors are deep-rooted in traditions which had been evolved years before the incursion of Islam in the nineteenth century, the onslaught of the colonial rule and the advent of Christianity to Yorubaland in the twentieth century.

4.3   THE *KABAKA* -THE BAGANDA KING
4.3.1   INTRODUCTION

In his classic presidential address to members of the Royal Anthropological Institute of Great Britain and Ireland in 1967, Meyer Fortes states: "kings die, kingship remains, ...".[49] Indeed kingship perpetuates itself. This is also quite true of the *Kabakaship* of the Baganda, one of the most dynamic kingship systems which flourished east of the African continent since the 14th century AD. The Ganda kingdom with its ancient traditions and thousands of kilometres away from West Africa shows traces of 'likes' and 'unlikes' typical of the Yoruba

---

[46] *Ibid*.

[47] Oral communication from Pa Ijaodola, aged 60 years, *Logun Emese*, court messenger at the *Ooni's* Palace, Ile-Ife, April 6, 1990.

[48] Here, see B. Schnepel, "Max Weber's Theory of Charisma and its Applicability to Anthropological Research", *JASO* 17(1987)26-48, esp. pp. 22-45.

[49] M. Fortes, "Of Installation Ceremonies. Presidential Address 1967" in Proc. of the Roy. Anthrop. Inst. for 1969, pp. 5-20, p. 6.

and the Akan kingships. Here, I intend to expose for the benefit of this study the data which early ethnographers and recent research have uncovered for scholarship on the Baganda kingship.

4.3.2   THE BAGANDA

As B. Davidson states: "by 1750 the king of Buganda, whose title was *Kabaka*, was supreme in all the Lakeside country between the mouth of the Kagere river and the exit of the Nile".[50] And according to Benjamin Ray, "... Buganda was formerly the largest and most powerful of the kingdom-states in the area around Lake Victoria".[51] Further sketching the location of ancient Buganda, Ray states

> Situated on the northern shores of the lake, the kingdom was bordered on the east by the River Nile, on the west by the kingdoms of Nkore and Toro, and on the north by the kingdom of Bunyoro.[52]

During the middle of the eighteenth century, Buganda was divided into five political units: (a) *Kibuga*, the district in which was located the royal capital (*mbuga*); (b) *Kyagwe*, the eastern portion of the kingdom; (c) *Bulamezi*, the northwestern corner; (d) *Budu* in the west; and (e) *Singo* in the north.[53] Each of these regions was governed by the *Batongole*, titled chiefs crowned and installed by the king himself. There were other paramount chiefs, among whom were an admiral and captains of the guards. The Baganda were members of the Bantu family. According to reports of early European vistors to the shores of Buganda, the people were quite ahead of their neighbours in culture, manners and etiquette. The race shared community life in small basic kinships known as the *kika*, clan, having its origin from a

---

[50] B. Davidson, The Growth of African Civilization East and Central Africa to the Late Nineteenth Century, London, Longman, 1967, p. 57.

[51] B. Ray, "Sacred Space and Royal Shrines in Buganda", p. 366.

[52] *Ibid.*

[53] *Ibid.*, p. 367, n. 4.

common ancestor. In their social setting, the *Kabaka* was the father and owner of everything in the land and the guarantor of the wellbeing of the state and his people.[54]

4.3.3   THE *KABAKA*

In Buganda, *Kabaka* was a royal title borne by three persons; namely the king, the queen-mother, the *Namasole* and the queen-sister, the *Lubuga* who was often chosen from the rank of the princesses and condemned to perpetual virginity in the royal enclosure.[55] The *Kabaka*, a divine emperor who traced his pedigree to Kintu, the first *Kabaka* and Buganda nation-builder reigned over his state, subjects and the suzerain states as a sovereign.[56]

4.3.4   THE CHOICE OF THE KABAKA

In Ganda tradition, there was no prince in the line of succession who was debarred from acceeding to the throne. Selection to the *Kabakaship* was based on visible and smart leadership qualities. There were normally many male descendants of the royal family. The heir-apparent must be a son or grandson of a king. Grandsons were acceptable when there happened to be no son born to the king. The preliminary choice was made by three royal officials; namely the *Katikkiro,* the chancellor or Prime Minister, the *Kasuju,* the guardian of the heirs-apparent and the *Kimbugwe,* the curator of the royal deities and the chief in-charge of the king's umbilical cord.[57] The reigning king often made his wishes to this three-

---

[54] For some of the ideas here and in other sections of this part of my study, I remain indebted to B. Ray "The Kabaka as the Symbolic Center of Buganda", pp. 8ff.

[55] Claessen, "The Early African State" in H. J. M. Claeseen & P. Skalník (eds.), The Study of the State, The Hague, Mouton, 1981, pp. 66-67; also for similar views, see A.I. Richards, "African Kings and their Royal Relatives" *Journal of the Royal Anthropological Institute* 91(1961)136-148.

[56] See, Ray, "The Story of Kintu", pp. 61-62; 75.

[57] J. Roscoe, The Baganda. An Account of their Native Customs and Beliefs, London, Macmillan, 1911, p. 235; and also A. Kagawa, The Customs of the Baganda. Columbia

man committee before his death though the chiefs could override the king's choice by nominating a prince they considered would fare better as a national ruler.

As soon as the king breathed his last, the *Katikkiro* directed the *Kasuju* to gather all the princes, the *Balangira* - to the capital.[58] The three chiefs quickly decided which candidate could be appointed king. Latter, they invited all the other principal chiefs, the *Amasaza*, representing Baganda clans and laid before them their choice. When the election was accepted by this committee of nine great chiefs, there was peace. In the open space of the royal enclosure, before a motely crowd of subjects, the *Katikkiro* requested the *Kasuju* to present the king-elect. The Kasuju then led the candidate by the right hand and handed him over to the Katikkiro with the words: "This is the King". The *Walukaga* of the Genet Clan handed the Katikkiro a bundle of spears. The Katikkiro facing the people and the princes lined up before the crowd announced:

So and so is king, those who wish to fight let them do so now[59].

He was willing to offer the spears to anyone who wanted to contest the choice. When the transfer of power happened as planned, the *Kasuju* turned to the princes and said:

You are peasants, fight if you wish, and we will put you to death[60].

From here the king-elect was conducted to the dead body of his father upon which he laid a barkcloth, the preliminary duty of an heir. The appearance and identification of the mother of the new king followed; and in the enclosure of another chief, the Katikkiro ushered in the Queen, the *Lubuga* usually a sister of the king though never of the same mother.[61]

University Contributions to Anthropology 22, Columbia University Press.

[58] For descriptive details of Baganda capital, see Ray, "Sacred Space and Royal Shrines", p. 367.

[59] Roscoe, The Baganda, p. 190.

[60] During this event fights could break out and as such the chiefs and the Katikkiro, all came to the spot with standing armed guards. See Roscoe, *ibid.*

[61] Roscoe, p. 191.

4.3.5   BAGANDA ENTHRONEMENT CEREMONY

Later, the king-elect and the queen were carried by the royal bearers to the Buddo Hill, the Ganda sacred spot to receive their confirmation on the Baganda throne.[62] Here, *Semanobe*, the state high priest and curator of the shrine had to ensure the security of the king and his party. The enthronement ritual consisted of eating and drinking herbal mixtures purported to fortify the king against rebellion and to make him, "wiser and stronger than anyone in the kingdom"[63]

On the arrival of the king and the Katikkiro at the foot of the Buddo hill, Semanobe challenged them:

> Why are you coming in such numbers;
> what do you want?

The train replied:

> The fire is extinguished, and we have brought a prince who is the new king.

The priest and his retainers armed with sugar-cane sticks and shields of plantain-leaves engage the visitors in a sham fight. Semanobe and his party were defeated and retreated. The king and the queen with their entourage freely mounted the hill. At the hill-top, the royal party visited the temple of *Serutega* and lived in the house known as *Buganda*. From there, they visited the Buddo Temple. Semanobe fed the king and his entourage with baked goat meat and plantains. They drank water from *Nfunvwi*, a sacred spring on the hill. The party stayed close to both the king and the queen to ensure their security from unexpected attackers.

"Eating Buganda" was part of the ceremony that took place at the Buddo shrine the following day. The king's party, quite early the next day, led by the Katikkiro, met the priest who ushered them into the Temple. Here, Semanobe handed them the jawbone and the

---

[62] B. Ray, "Royal Shrines and Ceremonies of Buganda", p. 36.

[63] Roscoe, The Baganda, p. 192.

umbilical cord of king *Lumansi* with the words: "You are the king". He conducted the king to the top of the hill. There, the king knelt down before the enclosure and crawled through to meet Semanobe who stood on the other side of the fence. With a bunch of twigs cut from three special trees, the priest struck the mound signalling to the king to climb up. When he successfully got to the top of the mound, he was made to repeat after the priest the following:

"I am the king of Uganda".

In a hole on the mound, the king planted a branch of barkcloth-tree and recited:

I am the king, to live longer than my ancestors, to rule the nations, and to put down rebellion.

The priest next handed him the *kanuna*, the Royal Spear used only during this ceremony. At this stage, the priest removed the king-elect's mourning clothes and put on him two new barkcloths sewn together on the shoulder side. The queen was also vested. The old cloths of the royal couple were allowed to be deposited in the Buddo Temple.

The royal couple were now carried down to the hill where the spear-shaft trees grew. The priest cut one and handed it over to the king with this prayer:

With this overcome your enemies.

The procession moved to a piece of land where creeper grass used for making baskets grew. The priest cut a handful and gave them to the king with this prayer:

May your life be like a basket which, when it falls down, does not break as an earthen vessel does.

The priest led the party further to a place where wild plantains grew. He plucked a few and handed them to the king with the prayer:

May you surpass your subjects in wisdom and understanding.

Finally, Semanobe led the king to the Sumba Hill and there handed him over to the priest, *Mainja*. At this point in the ceremony, Semanobe left the royal entourage and returned to the Buddo Hill. At the Temple of Mainja, the ceremony of "eating Buganda" was completed. From that time on, the king became the "legally appointed Sovereign" of Buganda.[64]

4.3.6 THE INSTALLATION OF THE KABAKA

In Baganda tradition, the installation of the Kabaka was marked by the sounding of the *Mujaguzo,* the royal drums in the evening. This happened after the royal hunt which usually marked the termination of the royal mourning had taken place. Next day, the chiefs and people assemble at Mulando's *massiro*, the shrine of one of the state deities. Mulando's sacred stool was displayed on a barkcloth mat covered with the royal rug, the *ekkiwu* woven together with a lion's, a leopard's and an eagle's skins. Both king and queen, borne on the shoulders of the carriers, were ceremoniously brought to the spot. The king was robed in two beautifully adorned barkcloths. With the help of the Katikkiro, the king mounted the stool. The *Mugema*, known as the father of the king, administered the oath of dedication to office on the king.[65] The liturgy of the ceremony was as follows:

Mugema :	You are king; rule over your people well, and always do what is right.
King :	I agree to do so.
Mugema :	Always give just judgment.
King :	I will.

Then the Mugema handed the king two spears and a shield. At this stage, the king swore an oath of fidelity to the nation. Directing the pointed end of the spear at the Mugema, he said:

I will never fear to rule Uganda, my country.

---

[64] Roscoe, The Baganda, pp. 195-196.

[65] For more details on the functions of this Chief, see Ray, "Sacred Space and Royal Shrines", p. 369.

At the king's response to each question put to him, he scattered some coffee-berries around and the crowd eagerly picked them up. The Mugema said to the people:

Never leave your king in difficulties, in the time of war and trouble.

The people replied:

We will never desert him, but will always honour him and stand by him.

The statues of the royal deities were displayed. The king beat the Royal Drum. The *Mujaguzo* drums were also brought in and he beat them. Then both the king and the queen were lifted up by two strong men from the Buffalo Clan with the assistance of Chief Kairo. The couple were conducted round the camp for all the people to pay their respects to them.[66] By this ceremonial, the Kabaka was officially installed.

4.3.7   KABAKA'S RULERSHIP

Ruling the Baganda kingdom was a one-man affair; namely that of the king though achieved through a hierarchical order of government. The king however sought advice from some of his Chiefs but much more often he acted upon his own wishes. Actual governmental affairs were run by a body of Chiefs, the *Aba-saza,* with the king at the head. The Lukiko, the highest court in the land met from time to time in the Palace Hall at the king's discretion. At the sound of the Royal Drums either in the evening or in the morning, the Chiefs, smartly and gorgeously dressed, gathered before the king.[67] Here, Buganda state business was discussed. The king entered into the *Blange,* the audience chamber, and took his place on a raised dias covered with a barkcloth and the royal rug, the *kituuti*. He was flanked on both sides by a retinue of intimates and favourites. The Chiefs sat in rows in the order of their

---

[66] All the interrogations and the answers given by the king were taken from Roscoe, The Baganda, pp. 197-199.

[67] Cf. R. P. Ashe, Two Kings of Uganda, London, Sampson-Low, 1889, pp. 84-99.

ranks. The Katikkiro and the Kimbugwe sat on either side in front of the king. On his entry into the hall, the Kabaka was greeted unianimously with the salutation: *Gusinze*: "May you overcome".[68] The Katikkiro as the Prime Minister and Chief Justice of the state directed the proceedings of the Lukiko.

Ganda kingdom was made up of twelve paramount chieftainships known as the *Bakungu* or the *Abamasaza*. The Katikkiro and the Kimbugwe (the number two strong-man in the kingdom) kept no personal districts but rather, in each district, estates were built for them to live during their working tours. Baganda was, in the period this study is interested in, divided into ten extensive districts known as the *Amasaza*. Each community was ruled by its own paramount Chief whose territory was demarcated from others by rivers, swamps, valleys and farmlands. The ten Chiefs were directly responsible to the Prime Minister, the man in-between the people and the king.[69] According to the account of an early European missionary, the Prime Minister was housed

> near the main entrance to the royal palace and in common with the Kimbugwe, he had the right of entrance to the inner courts in order to visit the king and to confer with him privately on State affairs.[70]

The rest of the chiefs could not see the king unless they had clearance from the Katikkiro to whom all matters of state and cases beyond the powers of the chiefs were referred. It was only in rare cases that such issues were sent to the king who was legitimately recognized as the *primus inter pares* with the clan chiefs.

The Kimbugwe was, as stated earlier on, both guardian and priest at the *Twin* Temple. As the state's Chief Curator, he regularly brought out before the king's presence the "Royal Twin"; a symbolic representation of the king's deceased father which, after

---

[68] Note that this sort of praise-greeting is quite typical with African subjects to their kings. It is *Kabiyesi* for the Yoruba, and *Bayede* for the Zulu king and so on. I however took notice of the variant title, *Businze* provided in B.Ray's article. Cf. Ray, "Royal Shrines", p. 42.

[69] A. I. Richards, "Authority Patterns in Traditional Buganda" in L. A. Fallers (ed.), *The Kings Men*, London, Oxford University Press, 1964, pp. 256-294.

[70] Roscoe, The Baganda, pp. 234-235.

inspection by the king, was returned to him for custody in the temple.[71] As a result of his sacred and religious functions in the kingdom, the Kimbugwe was a favourite of the king. He had the prerogative of entering the king's chamber at any time, and advised him on state and religious matters. Like the Katikkiro, he too had his enclosure adjacent to the royal palace and had estates kept and maintained for his use in every district. Among the state officers was the *Namasole*, the king's mother who exercised a much superior influence during the regime of the son, and who herself also held the title, *Kabaka*.[72]

4.3.8   THE RELIGIOUS ROLE OF THE KABAKA

As John Roscoe had correctly observed, "the Baganda have always been a religious nation".[73] The priests who ministered to the national gods had, among other functions, the duty to lay the national objects of worship and veneration before the king. The support for the upkeep of the national religion was the sole responsibility of the state. The king supervised the activities of the mediums and the priests who took charge of the temples of numerous minor deities scattered all over the land. The king himself allotted parcels of land for the construction of the temples of the national gods usually on hill-tops, hill-sides and valleys. He also authorized reconstruction work at any derelict temple; and such directives were usually passed through the *Kago*, the Chief who represented him in state religious affairs. Like in the Yoruba case, the Kabaka was the *Pontifex Maximus* of Baganda religion. Because of his self esteem as the deputy of the gods, the Kabaka reserved to himself the control of the worship of the state gods whose duty in turn was to protect the king and his sovereignty. After his accession, he returned the Royal Spear with gifts and fanfare to the

---

[71] Here, see Ray, "Royal Shrines", p. 39.

[72] Roscoe, The Baganda, pp. 236-237; Richards, "African Kings and their Relatives", pp. 136-148. A former student at CHIEA, Nairobi, Kenya had sought to demonstrate the parallel between the Kabaka and his mother and that between Christ, the King and his mother, Mary. Cf. S. Ssemanda, Christ our Kabaka. A Christology from the Ganda Perspective, CHIEA, Nairobi, 1988 cited by C. Nyamiti, "A Critical Assessment on some Issues in Today's African Theology", p. 14, n. 17.

[73] Roscoe, The Baganda, p. 271.

Buddo Temple, the sacred spot which fulfilled top sacral roles in the coronation of Ganda kings. In serious state affairs such as rebellion or disaster, the king believed the gods spoke to him and thus saw himself obliged to send the culprit to the sacrificial place or to offer the rightful propitiation.[74] Even though he consulted the deities, and from time to time sent his own offerings to each of the most important deities and obeyed their directives, the Kabaka did not hesitate to vandalize and desecrate the temple or shrine of any one and its priesthood that caused him trouble. The clan headman who could also be the local Chief Priest, the *Kabona*, appointed by the king presided over the temple and its property in his own territory.[75]

The reigning Kabaka believed in the power and listened to the promptings of the spirits of his predecessors, the *Bassekabaka*. He recieved from them advice on matters about the state; especially about the outbreak of war or disaster. To avert possible dangers, the king made periodical visits to the temples of previous kings, the *malalo* where he examined their jawbones and the umbilical cords in supplication for the welfare of the state.[76] As my exposée on African worldview shows, the Baganda, as well as other Africans believed that ancestral spirits could cause trouble to members of the clan to which they belonged if they were not well honoured and propitiated or render help when appeased. The king himself venerated "in great awe" the father's spirit and regularly made offerings to it. During the annual festival, the king who was usually the chief celebrant sent gifts to the god *Mukasa*, a benevolent god of the Baganda in order to secure his benediction on the people, crops and cattle. The early Ganda knew and worshipped *Katonda*, the Creator-God to whom the king sent a special animal offering. The victim was never killed as it was believed that *Katonda*, "the father of the gods" did not require bloody sacrifices. According to Ganda dynastic

---

[74] *Ibid.*, p. 273.

[75] On the functions of the *Kabona*, see Roscoe, *ibid.*, p. 274.

[76] See Ray, "Royal Shrines", p. 42. The *Malalo* was erected to house the Jawbone, the umbilical cord and those of the ex-Queen, the *Nalinya*. The Katikkiro appointed a Chief to take charge of the place and a Royal Spirit medium who regularly spoke the mind of the dead king in converse with the reigning Kabaka. On these ideas, see Roscoe, The Baganda, p. 111; Ray, "Royal Shrines", p. 38.

theology, it was *Katonda* who sent Kintu from heaven to found the Baganda kingdom.[77] Thus, as Roscoe stated, "the blood royal was held to be most sacred" in Ganda kingship.[78]

In discussing the sacred status of the Kabaka, it would be a serious omission not to recognize the importance of the Sacred Fire and the place of the Jawbone in Ganda Traditional Religion. The two elements contributed to the enhancement and the sacrosanctity of the Kabakaship. The Fire which was kept burning day and night at the main entrance to the king's palace was said to have originated in the period of Kintu; the Founding Father of Buganda. Wherever the king travelled to, Chief Senkole, the guardian of the Fire carried it with him in the royal entourage. The Royal Fire was kept burning throughout the reign of the king. The Ganda sacred Fire was a symbol of the life of the king. It was believed to provide strength to the virility the king reproduced in his benign powers.[79]

4.3.9   CONCLUSIONS

In the attempt to summarize the results of the foregoing surveys, I dare say that the narratives prove beyond reasonable doubt that the holders of the titles *Oba* and *Kabaka* in both the Yoruba and the Baganda early kingdoms were regarded as the most powerful of men, the omnipotents of their social and religious world. Their selection, installation, coronation and enthronement confered on them a distinct *status remotus*. In fact, the seclusions from their subjects formed part of the taboos inherent in kingship. In Abélès' words: "The constraints of avoidance define a potential danger and isolate not only the royal person, but also the royal function from the rest of society".[80] In their persons were lived out and experienced the binary aspects of kinship; namely the opposite terms of divine kingship for they reflected, on the one hand kings as social operators in the society yet agents impossible to control and on the other hand as palace prisoners for life yet the holders

---

[77] For these and similar ideas, see Ray, "Royal Shrines", p. 37.

[78] Roscoe, The Baganda, p. 87.

[79] Cf. Ray, "Royal Shrines", p. 36.

[80] Abélès, "Sacred Kingship", p. 7.

of powers of life and death. Both kings acted, as in other African kingship cultures, as the first of the priests during seasonal and national festivals. In the Frazerian terms, they were "divine kings" who exemplified the nexus between personal well-being and the fertility of their states.[81]

As close offsprings of the supernatural beings, the *Oba* and the *Kabaka* were believed to possess the power to influence the deities they represented in order to advance the fortunes of their kingdoms. Both "performed rituals to promote the fertility of land and people".[82] The offices they occupied and the rights they claimed were based upon a mythical charter and a genealogy traced to supernatural forces. They were nothing less than benevolent figures, sources of gifts, remunerators and donors of other largess. They were surrounded by a court of royalists and defended by teams of powerful bodyguards headed by ritual commanders such as the *Osiwefa* (Yoruba) and *Senkole* (Buganda). Thus, symbolic events and human agents constituted themselves into protective shields in defense of the kings against external forces.

The relationship of both the Yoruba and the Baganda kings with their subjects was based on reciprocity. All ranks of the subjects provided the kings with goods and services. The kings, on their own part, provided protection, represented the pinacle of law and order and granted spiritual and physical benevolences. In this manner, they fulfilled their functions as cosmic reproducers of the well-being of their communities. As was believed by their followers, they generated powers of fecundity and fertility and guaranteed social and natural order which enhanced communal stability and progress, an early image of Africa which had impressed many a goodwilled European explorers and travellers. Thus, in the light of their roles, statuses and sacrality, the evidence that kingship rises above society and acts directly with cosmic phenomena will ever remain an unshakable axiom.

---

[81] J. G. Frazer, The Golden Bough. A Study in Magic and Religion, London, Macmillan, 1890, 1911 3rd Ed., and in the Abridged Edition of 1922, see p. vi.

[82] Claessen, "The Early State", p. 63.

CHAPTER FIVE

KINGSHIP IN PRECOLONIAL AFRICA: NORTH-SOUTH
THE SHILLUK AND THE ZULU KINGS

5.1   THE *RETH* - THE SHILLUK KING

5.1.1   INTRODUCTION

Anthropological research over the years has unmasked immense data on Shilluk kingship. The ideology of the "divine kingship" associated with Frazer since the turn of the twentieth century, had received so much impetus to the extent that several anthropologists have striven to relate their findings on kingships in Africa to the concept. C. G. Seligman, among others, had since 1934 documented and described this peculiar trait of the African regal tradition.[1] And since after Frazer's pioneering ethnographical study of the Shilluk, social anthropolgists have continued to focus much attention on this Nilothic people of southern Sudan.[2] Be they of the evolutionary, the ecological[3] or the diffusionist schools of thought,[4] one thing clear is that Shilluk's institution of "divine kingship" has continued to hold a fascinating admiration for modern scholars[5] as it had done for travellers, missionaries and colonial administrators. Consequent upon the trail blazed by social anthropologists in Nilothic studies;

---

[1] C. G. Seligman, Egypt and Negro-Africa. A Study in Ddivine kingship, The Frazer Lecture for 1933, London, 1934.

[2] J. G. Frazer, The Golden Bough.

[3] See L. Wall, "Anuak Politics, Ecology and the Origins of Shilluk Kingship", *Ethnology* 15(1976)151-162.

[4] See for one, M. Riad, "The Divine Kingship of the Shilluk and its Origin", *Archiv für Völkerkunde* 14(1959)141-284.

[5] W. Arens, "The Divine Kingship of the Shilluk: A Contemporary Re-evaluation", *Ethnos* 14(1979)167-181.

ethnographers such as E. E. Evans Pritchard[6] and R. G. Lienhardt[7] had, as I have shown much earlier on, gone on their own ways to investigate the genesis and the royal traditions of the other southern neighbours of the Shilluk such as the Dinka and the Lugbara. Much as their findings on the history and religion of the Shilluk and their neighbours have been fruitful for the advancement of knowledge on and the understanding of Nilothic African cultures, the symbolic and religious significance of the *Reth*, Shilluk's divine king remains the main focus of this chapter.

5.1.2   THE SHILLUK

The Shilluk are initially the most northernmost Nilothic ethnic people of Africa. They are descendants of the mythological heroes, Nyikango and Dimo who had travelled eastwards across the Nile from Wipac, now known as Bahr el-Ghazal around 1500 AD.[8] Today, the Shilluk occupy the coastal plain of the Nile, and as Lienhardt states, settle like "beads on a string"[9]. The expanse of their territory is about 600 kilometres long on the west bank of the Nile, south of Khartoum, Sudan's capital city.[10]

Shilluk royal myths are quite versatile and mainly concentrate attention on narratives about the founding of their kingship. The Royal clan traces its origin from an early culture hero, *Nyikang*, the first leader and king who made Shilluk a nation state. Everything in the land is associated with Nyikang whose effigy is identified with each new king in the rites of installation.[11] The entire people accept the reign and primacy of the *Reth*, the king, who must always come from the Royal clan, the *kwareth*, a group quite dispersed and found in

---

[6] The Divine Kingship of the Shilluk.

[7] Lienhardt, "The Shilluk of the Upper Nile", pp. 138-163.

[8] Davidson, The Growth of African Civilization, p. 54.

[9] Lienhardt, "The Shilluk of the Upper Nile", p. 163.

[10] Riad, "The Divine Kingship of the Shilluk"; and also cf. Lienhardt, "Nilothic Kings and their Mothers' Kin", *Africa* 25(1955)29-42.

[11] Lienhardt, "Nilothic Kings", p. 30.

many lineages and families in Shillukland. The population, though dependent on crop production, are mainly composed of sedentary farmers and cattle raisers.[12]

5.1.3   THE *RETH*

The Shilluk *Reth* represents the very basis of existence for the land and people. Without a king the land is in crisis and nothing but anarchy reigns.[13] The full functions of the Reth can only be exercised when he is formerly installed. Among the royal insignia of *Rethship* are spears, drums, cattle and the *nyakwer*, the royal maiden. The several rites undergone by the reth-elect are, in many instances significant. When, for example, he is ritually compelled to tend the herd, he is being made to recognize his duty to serve rather than to rule in his position as king. The *Rethship* is a sacred possession of the Shilluk nation and no one occupies it on his own volition. It has to be bestowed upon a worthy prince by the responsible agents of society and ultimately with the approval of the nation as a whole. As Schnepel roundly puts it:

> During the ceremonies the *reth-ship* is entrusted to a chosen prince in a series of interconnected ritual acts through which these sections of Shilluk society who own these rites impress upon the tennant his accountability to society for the proper exercise of the office's functions, and through which they themselves come to terms with their own responsibility towards the new king.[14]

It is in the presence of the Reth that Nyikang's manifestation is 'graspable'. In Lienhardt's description, it is in their human king that the Shilluk "are able to see what they believe".[15]

The Reth's main function is to make Nyikang visible and palpable. The Reth is Nyikang's main human emblem. He stands and acts for Nyikang. In fact, he is himself

---

[12] Here, see B. Schnepel, "Shilluk Royal Ceremonies of Death and Installation", Anthropos 83(1988)433-452, p. 434.

[13] Riad, "The Divine Kingship of the Shilluk", p. 171.

[14] Schnepel, "Shilluk Royal Ceremonies", p. 446.

[15] Lienhardt, "The Shilluk of the Upper Nile" p. 163.

Nyikang. Shilluk royal theology affirms dual inter-relationship between Nyikang and the Reth. On one level, the Reth is only reth due to the benevolence of Nyikang, and on the other level, Nyikang can only become active when embodied by a Reth. For the Shilluk as well as in some other African systems, Schnepel is right to point out that "to have an emblem which is human and alive not only enables them to see and to grasp what they believe in, but also enables them to make what they believe in work for their good".[16]

5.1.4   THE CHOICE OF THE RETH-ELECT

The choice and installation of the Shilluk Reth is like in the two previous cases quite an elaborate activity. For my present purpose, I prefer to describe it rather briefly. In what follows, I shall depend on Riad's account and some ideas of Schnepel; of course, introducing the views of other authors and personal observations when necessary.

The king-elect must be chosen from the lineage of Nyikang through the male line. The candidate must be the son of a previous king[17] and must be a brave man, possessing a daring and charismatic personality. He must be in good health and be intelligent. An electoral committee of four to six men representing the paramount chiefs of the Shilluk tribe conduct the selection.[18] The council must satisfy itself of the Prince's moral integrity and ethical uprightness; his personal character and family life. They seek information through oral testimony of the Prince's village Chief. Soon after this, members of a sub-committee are despatched to the Prince's village who secretly observe him for several days. When satisfied with their findings, the committee returns to Debalo and summons a general meeting of all Shilluk Chiefs. It is at this occasion that the king-elect is proclaimed. He is invited to Debalo where he is put into seclusion in a special hut for some days. Here, he is expected to live in a state of contemplation and communion with Nyikang, the royal progenitor. Three fires are lit in front of his hut: one is donated by the royal family; the second is provided by the Ororo caste, the ritual clan, and the third is offered by the people. The fires which are

---

[16] Schnepel, "Shilluk Royal Ceremonies", p. 447.

[17] Arens, "The Divine Kingship of the Shilluk", p. 173.

[18] Riad, "The Divine Kingship of the Shilluk", pp. 185-186.

regarded as symbols of royalty are never extinguished through out the reign of the king. They are removed to Fashoda, the royal capital when the king settles there.[19]

The king-elect later proceeds with his retinue to Fashoda. While *en route*, he hears of the approach of Nyikang's army. He runs away and secretly returns to Debalo. Now he must wear the face of anxiety and fear. A combat awaits him, even though it is a sham battle. The Chief of Debalo accosts him before the village inspite of the unusual path taken by the king-elect and his retinue. He asks him:

What do you want here?

The king-elect answers:

I am the man whom god sends to govern the Shilluk.

After this encounter, he walks on a leopard skin which is laid out for him till the entry of the special house prepared for his forthcoming enthronement ceremony.[20]

5.1.5   THE RITE OF THE WATER ORDEAL

This right marks the beginning of the enthronement of the Shilluk king and heralds the descent of Nyikang from the North of the country to Fashoda in order to confer his blessings on the king-elect. Odang island, known also as the island of Nyikang on the eastern bank of the White Nile is the ritual centre. At Akurwa, the temple city of Nyikang, the priests produce a cow dressed with a white cloth and lead it to the bank of the river. Drums beat. The cow is led down into the water. The people sing and drums rend the air the more. Priests spear the cow. The blood is let to drain into the river. Two rams are tied in two boats driven by four men clad in Shilluk national dress, the white *Lauo*. One of the rams is wrapped in white cloth and tied to the centre of one boat together with the statue of Dak, the

---

[19] Cf. *ibid.*, p. 190.

[20] *Ibid.*, pp. 187-188.

son of Nyikang and the small drum, the *tom of Nyikang*. In this particular boat, three men decorated with Shilluk ornaments sit in. The second boat is rowed in escort. After the spearing of the cow, the boats begin their journey to the island of Nyikang. On arrival, the small drum is beaten, the statue of Dak watches the water at a spot where an eddy is to be found. The water eddy helps wheel the boat around. The men on board hurl the ornaments and the ram into the spot of the eddy, then a Moro diver jumps headlong into the eddy to seek out a cylindrical piece of whitish object and brings it to the boat. The material is wrapped up in white cloth and accompanied by the retinue, it is conveyed to Akurwa. The message is that Nyikang is found. The "body", as it is called, is brought to the temple where it is adorned by the priests with pearls and ostrich feathers and turned into the statue of Nyikang.[21]

In some reigns, this material is not found. Many attempts would be made to raise it. When non is picked up at the tenth occasion, the ceremony of installation is postponed for a year. This is a very precarious period for the king-elect and his loyalists. When "the body" is not found at all, it is a sign that Nyikang is not satisfied with the king-elect and if he dares mount the throne, his reign would spell disaster for himself and the entire people and Shillukland.

5.1.6   THE FIRST MOCK BATTLE

The first mock combat between the northern and the southern army, commanded respectively by the future sovereign and by the effigy of the nation founder, Nyikang and his son Dak takes place at Fashoda. The procession marches along from the north through the south towards Fashoda. On arrival news is brought to the king's camp. Here, a young black ox is dressed with a white cloth. The king rides on the back of this ox backwards. He is not allowed to look towards Fashoda. The two sides are by now ready to do battle and at the southern banks of the Khor Arepjur, the messengers of both sides meet. In the king's camp, a black bull is laid down on its back. Both king and his troops step and cross it. The forces later cross the Khor and engage themselves in a sharp battle with millet stalks and whips.

---

[21] Riad, pp. 189-190.

Bearers of the statues of Nyikang and Dak, with their guards rush towards the king-elect. They encircle him, *capture* him and hurtle him down to Fashoda. The battle continues to rage though the king is already taken prisoner by Nyikang.

5.1.7   THE ENTHRONEMENT OF THE RETH-ELECT

Shilluk enthronement ceremony happens with a momentous speed and haste. At Fashoda, the king is whisked of to the shrine of Nyikang where the throne of Nyikang stands outside and alredy decorated. Nyikang's statue is brought out and kept in an upright position on the throne by members of the Ororo clan. The king sits on a leopard skin beside the stool. He embraces a small drum placed before Nyikang. Prayers are uttered by the leading priests and the people. They ask for blessings on their new king and pray for his protection from the evil machinations of his enemies. There follows a display of songs and dances by the womenfolk. Later, the king stands up. Nyikang's statue is removed from the stool. The new king sits on it. He remains seated on it for some fifteen minutes in deep spiritual contemplation. He stands up, and directs an Ororo man towards his left-hand side where an ox is readily tethered. The Ororo man spears the ox. This is a crucial stage in the ceremony. It marks the incarnation of the soul of Nyikang in the body of the king-elect. Setting the figure of Nyikang on the stool and then removing it, implies that the soul is now in the stool and by sitting the new king upon it, the spirit enters the flesh and blood of the king. He is thus "anointed". Such anointing of kings have nothing to do with the anointment of the body with oil. According to G. von Rad, "anointing is the means by which a man is given the spirit"[22] By the anointing of the Reth, the entire life of the people, including temple and cult, is subordinated to his charism.

---

[22] G. von Rad, The Message of the Prophets, London, SCM, 1976.

5.1.8 THE RITE OF PURIFICATION

At this juncture, the king submits to a rite of purification. Upon his standing up from the great stool, water is brought in and the king's feet are cleansed with it. He is escorted into a hut opposite the temple. Here, he once again crosses the bull and is dressed in a new garment: the white Lauo and a leopard skin. He emerges from the hut holding the traditional weapons. On re-entry into the hut, he is fully bathed with the same warm water. On this same day, the Royal Fire is kindled at Fashoda by the friction method which is only contrived by the Ororo and the *Kwareth*, the members of the royal family.

5.1.9 THE KING'S SECLUSION

After these rites are performed, the king is subjected to a major period of seclusion in a hut opposite the shrine of Nyikang. For several days he communicates with no one but the Higher Beings and contemplates upon the tasks ahead. The Ororo clan-guards take responsibility of the security of the inmates of the hut by keeping night vigil. The king is accompanied in this seclusion by *Nyakwer*, a little girl of ten donated by the Jal clan. The girl's duty is to minister to the king during the period he remains in the hut. Upon completion of the stipulated period, the king is directed by the Ororo to another hut, this time much neater. This seclusion spot is located at the Mound of Athurwic at the other far end of Fashoda. He does not move into this place with Nyakwer, the little girl; but is enticed by a woman brought in by the Ororo. While here, he receives the news that Nyikang has abducted Nyakwer. Nyikang's reason is that the ten-year old girl had been betrothed to his herds and not to the yet unconfirmed king. On hearing this *bad* news, the king-elect becomes upset and infuriated. He rushes down from Athurwic to rescue Nyakwer from Nyikang, hence the cause of the second sham battle.

5.1.10   THE SECOND MOCK COMBAT

The Athurwic Mound, once again, provides the battleground. Drums of Nyikang beat high. The figures of Nyikang and Dak, their bearers and followers emerge from the shrine; enter a special hut and re-appear with an imposing statue of *Shal*, the first son of Nyikang, and the second king of Shillukland. In their company is the little girl, Nyakwer.

The battle begins. In a rage, Nyikang first attacks because the king has challenged him. Both sides move swiftly through and from, one attacking, the other side retreating. The scene is a hurly-burly. A bull is felled. The king steps upon its back. He plucks courage and charges. He recovers Nyakwer from Nyikang and returns with his guards to Athurwic amidst merriment and jubilation. Nyikang who is grossly vexed lashes out again. It is too late. This time, he is rebuffed. His drums beat faintly and in retreat, his army retires, roams around the shrine and unable to pick up more courage, returns to the shrine. The effigies of Dak and Shal remain outside. The company of men sing praises to Nyikang in order to appease him.

The battle ends with the victory of the king over Nyikang. He now becomes an embodiment of Nyikang himself. He now possesses the soul of Nyikang. The figures of Nyikang become merely souless effigies of the former hero and demi-god. The fights prove, *inter alia* that the king is now the total incarnation of the original king who was the guiding spirit of the nation. In his new status, he is the rightful heir of Nyikang and the lawful ruler of the Shilluk. He becomes a sacred king, a god-man, one with special charisma conferred by both his office and his god-given prerogatives.

The latter part of the ceremonies is punctuated by lengthy addresses by the chiefs. The king's response marks the close of the installation rites. Among other benign policies of his reign, according to Riad, the Reth

> promises to be a good ruler, to settle justice everywhere, to help the weak, and to punish evil-doers, to keep the unity of the nation and to preserve the tradition of Nyikang and the country, to pay attention to the advice of the elders, to keep loyal to the old customs and habits, ... [23]

---

[23] Riad, "The Divine Kingship of the Shilluk", p. 194.

5.1.11   THE REIGN OF THE RETH

The Reth exercises a threefold function in his capacity as king: the political, the judicial and the ritual. He reigns, as we have seen, over Schillukland and its peoples as the incarnation of Nyikang. It is precisely this aspect of the Reth phenomenon which makes him a divine personnage. Even though the Reth is the supreme authority in Schilluk socio-political affairs, he only regins in his kingdom while chiefs and other state functionaries administer the state.

The territorial organisation of Shillukland comprises (a) the hamlet composed of lineage-group homesteads with a chief at its head; (b) the settlement, made up of hamlets located in a large area and overseen by a Chief, the *Jago*; (c) the districts, about eleven in number. Each district is composed of a cluster of several settlements. The principal districts are Muomo in the far north and Tunga in the most southern tip of the nation. (d) The provinces form the most important political divisions of Shillukland. Two of such provinces, Gerr in the north and Luak in the south are organized and ruled by local chiefs on behalf of the king. Fashoda is the Royal Capital where the Reth lives and reigns as the paramount chief of the entire land. Elected by their lineage groups, the chiefs and the *Jagos* receive confirmation on their office from the king. These officials are, as Riad observes, responsible to the king for order, peace, welfare and the prosperity of the people.[24] The most important state functionaries in Shilluk administrative and regal structure are the *Jagos*, that is, the Chiefs of the settlements. They represent the chiefs of the dominant lineages in all the settlements. Besides, they act as agents "of the king whose duty it is to see that the king's orders are executed ..."[25]

5.1.12   THE RELIGIOUS FUNCTIONS OF THE RETH

In Shilluk kingship tradition, the religious role of the Reth occupies a central position in the scheme of things. It is the religious significance of kingship which confers importance to the political and judicial functions the Reth fulfills. Thus, the Reth reigns as a ritual chieftain.

---

[24] *Ibid.*, p. 203.

[25] *Ibid.*

His sacerdotal role rests on the fact that he is taken possession by Nyikang, the Shilluk patriarch and primary representative of *Juok*, God. By this rite he is invested with the right to perform rituals vital to the wellbeing of his people. As a "divine king", Evans Pritchard discovered that "his functions are primarily of a ritual order".[26]

It is in the performance of these ritual functions that his office as bearer of 'divine kingship' rests. In view of the fact that his office, as Arens contends, "was imbued with a sacred character", the Reth settles quarrels between two contending sections of his people, arbitrates and administers oaths on warring parties.[27] He is a peace-maker to his people. He can thus qualify as "both himself and Nyikang, both an individual and an institution".[28] Riad's research sums up the *opinio communis* rather eloquently:

> Butt says that "the identification of Nyikang with the king is the central point of the Shilluk political, ritual and moral system". Seligman ... considered the king as the absolute head - temporal and spiritual. Hofmayr also said that he was the highest priest of the country, and as thus he carried his holy spear with the blade pointing upwards, ...[29]

As the ritual father of the nation, the Reth is the only one who authorizes or rejects sacrifices during national festivals and ritual worships. He permits the sacrifices made to *Jouk*, the High God and to Nyikang, the demi-god. Since, like most Africans, the Shilluk believe that without sacrifices, ancestral spirits would not be appeased and the people's wishes not granted, the king stands in-between his people and the divinities. He is "the real power in religious matters, and sometimes he withholds his beneficial powers", especially if his people be disloyal.[30]

The king's permission for sacrificial rites to take place are granted during two occasions; namely during the rain-making ceremony and the celebration of victory in war.

---

[26] Evans Pritchard, The Divine Kingship of the Shilluk of the Nilothic Sudan. The Frazer Lecture for 1948, Cambridge, 1948, pp. 16-17.

[27] Arens, *art. cit.*, p. 177.

[28] *Ibid.*, and also Evans Pritchard, The Divine Kingship of the Shilluk, p. 21.

[29] Riad, *art. cit.*, p. 205.

[30] *Ibid.*

Once a year, and in the eleventh month, the king makes an annual pilgrimage to the Temple of Nyikang at Fanikang. At the rain-making ceremony, the Reth manifests his divine powers in public. As the custodian of public religion and worship, the Reth is responsible for the provision of cattle from the sacred herd needed for regular sacrifices at Nyikang's temples and shrines spread all over the land. When the Reth is in contemplative seclusion and in communion with Nyikang, he is often queried about the general condition of the people, their welfare and the manner in which the chiefs who serve under his regime look after the needs of the populace. The king usually reports that everything is under control and as well as ever.

5.2 THE *NKOSI* - THE ZULU KING
5.2.1 INTRODUCTION

The phenomenon of the sacred kingship was in precontact era quite versatile and generally widespread. As far as to the south of the African continent; and among the Swazi as the Xhosa-Zulu, kingship had remained, in pre-capitalist period, a paramount institution of ethnic pride. On the origin of the Zulu, A. T. Bryant had witfully noted: "the birthplace of the Zulu Nation" was in the *Makosini* valley otherwise known as the valley of the kings.[31] And C. T. Binns had supplied further information on this ancestral holy spot. According to him, there, lay buried "many of the early Zulu rulers": Nkosinkulu and Senzangakhona, the fathers of the famous trio: Chaka, Dingane and Mpande.[32]

Here as in the preceding sections, I wish to offer some ethnographical information on the Zulu royal tradition and the *Nkosiship* (kingship) of this "one of the noblest and most ancient branches of the great African Bantu family with one of the least altered types of prehistoric culture"[33] in such areas as the genesis of the people, the king's sacrality and sovereign functions.

---

[31] A. T. Bryant, Olden Times in Zululand and Natal, London, Longmans, 1929, p. 23.

[32] C. T. Binns, The Last Zulu King. The Life and Death of Cetshwayo, London, Longmans, 1963, p. 3.

[33] Bryant, *ibid*.

5.2.2   THE ZULU PEOPLE

The views of earliest authors and travellers on the origin of the Zulu sound discordant. Some have said that the race were initially a handful of people who had believed themselves to have descended from a single ancestor, the *Nkosikulu*; others have opined that they were not descendants of a common ancestor, but "a specie of localized people",[34] each having its own common ancestor. But as Max Gluckmann observed, "The Zulu nation ... consisted of members of some hundreds of clans, united by their allegiance to the king".[35] Inspite of the vagaries of ethnographic information on the tribe,[36] it is at the root of the peoples' regal tradition and their followership to their king, *Nkosi* that I invest my interest. Recent update in their ethnography suggests that the Zulu-Xhosa belong to the Nguni Bantu group of Southern Bantu. During late migratory periods, over some 3000 years ago, these hordes had reached South Africa possibly from the North of the continent.[37]

The fact remains that Zululand, in the last 20 years of the eighteenth century had most probably originated from the Umtetwa tribe, a group set in the coast-land between Rivers Umfolozi and Umhlatuzi. The Chief of the tribe by this time was king Jobe. Mawewe, his son hatched a plot to overthrow him. When Jobe discovered the secret, he ordered that Mawewe and his brother, Godongwana be executed. In the process, Mawewe died while Godongwana made good his escape and later returned to take the kingship after his father's death. The actual history and the unification of the Zulu began with this man, Gondongwana, later known as Dingiswayo whose triumphant return to to the capital still makes great history in Zululand.

The people had, under the hegemonies of their valiant kings, demonstrated a high sense of hospitality, generosity and mutual helpfulness. Quite early, they had a good sense

---

[34] A. T. Bryant, The Zulu People, p. 458.

[35] M. Gluckmann, "The Kingdom of the Zulu of South Africa" in M. Fortes, E. E. Evans Pritchard (eds.), African Political Systems, London, Oxford University Press, 1970, pp. 25-55, p. 29.

[36] D. M'Timkulu, "Some Aspects of Zulu Religion", in N. S. Booth (ed.), African Religions: A Symposium, pp. 13-30.

[37] Cf. J. Y. Gibson, The Story of the Zulus, London, Longmans, 1911 (A Reprint, New York, Negro Universities Press, 1970), p. 1.

of law and order and their society had well and ordered means of food supply, relevant tools and implements, weapons of defence and the maintenance of constituted authority, necessary revenue collection, and an established religion; a tribunal for justice and public care.[38]

There were four political units in the government of Zululand. The smallest was the *Kraal* (village), usually under the control of the *Umnumzane*, the Kraal headman. The Kraal leader was under an *isiGodi*, the District head in whose district the kraal was located. The District head, whose ancestors were known to have been rulers over the entire district was regarded as the father to all members of the kraals in his district. The *isiFunda*, a much larger area was usually under the care of an important *induna*, a hereditary Chief appointed by and subject to the king.[39]

5.2.3   THE ZULU *NKOSI*

In Zululand, the Nkosi was a paramount chieftain. Allegiance to his majesty was a necessary obligation. The members of the clan, the *abakwazulu* were unified by the kingship. The people's endearment to the prestige of the king united all the Zulu as members of one nation. The people belonged to the king and he took the responsibility to protect and to shelter them as his 'children'. He was spoken of as the *father* of the people. He alone owned the land and all the persons who migrated to Zululand had to accept his sovereinty.[40] The Nkosi (king), was greeted with inumerable praise-names and titles of respect such as "thou the awe-inspiring One"; "thou the Wild-Beast" and "thou the Lion of the Heavens"; "thou who art for ever"; "thou who art as high as heaven"; "thou who begettest men"; "The Black one"; "The peace-maker"; and "The bird who eats all other birds".[41] All such modes of address

---

[38] Cf. Gluckmann, "The Kingdom of the Zulu", *ibid*.

[39] Cf. E. J. Krige, The Social System of the Zulus, London, Longmans, 1936; 3rd Edition Pitermaritzburg, Shuter & Shooter, 1957. p. 217.

[40] Gluckman, "The Kingdom of the Zulu of South Africa", p. 30.

[41] See Krige, The Social System of the Zulus, p. 233; also cf. *idem.*, "Girls Puberty Songs and their Relation to Fertility, Health, Morality and Religion Among the Zulu", *Africa* 38(1968)173-185.

were coined in order to bolster the prestige and majesty of the king. He was equally addressed as the "nation" or as *Bayede*, the all-powerful ruler.

In all state affairs, the Nkosi's word was law. He controlled both powers of wellbeing and nothingness. The Nkosi ruled as a king in whom the subjects were expected to seek succour for all their material problems and difficulties especially in times of national disaster or calamity. He set as his goal the advancement and welfare of the people over whom he ruled.[42] Krige has drawn attention to the fact that the Zulu king was to the tribe what the Umnumzane was to the *Kraal* (village); that is, the "father" of his people.[43] He joined hands with the ancestors to regulate the welfare of the whole tribe. The Zulu king was described as "the personification of the law, and as the representative of the tribal ancestors, and the centre of ritual".[44] Against his judgment there was no appeal. In civil matters, he was guided by a council of specially selected *indunas*. In matters concerned with national defense and security, the Nkosi assumed undisputed leadership.

Zulu kingship, the *ubuKosi* was hereditary, and thus the birth-right of the clan family which had held its most direct descent in the male line from the person who founded the clan. The crown was very much retained within this hereditary royal family. Such kings were never figureheads. Bryant had described the Zulu king in ambivalent terms. According to him, he is a "captain of the ship and *paterfamilias* of the clan, absolute monarch both in fact and name" whose reign was "one of benevolent despotism".[45]

5.2.4   SELECTION AND CORONATION OF THE NKOSI

As among other Bantu tribes, the death of a Zulu king was regarded as a departure to the Spiritland. On his death-bed, he whispered to the clan Prime Minister the name of the prince he wanted to succeed him if not, the sons fought for the throne or the clan elders appointed

---

[42] See Gibson, The Story of the Zulus, p. 14.

[43] Krige, The Social System of the Zulus, p. 217.

[44] *Ibid.*, p. 218.

[45] Bryant, The Zulu People, p. 460.

a man of their choice. The candidate must come from the direct line of the royal house. As in the case of the Yoruba, this was usually carried out on "selective nomination". As soon as the funeral ceremonies of the late king was over, the date of the coronation of the new king was fixed by the Prime Minister as the *Katikkiro* did in Ganda installation ceremonies.

The event was begun with a public hunt in a selected bush within the vicinity of the Royal Kraal. Hunters were expected to display their skill to the best of their ability as the event marked their last respect to the deceased king. After the chase, all clansmen assembled, roasted and feasted on the game. This incident represented a preliminary purificatory rite which was believed to wash all the clan spears clean from all *umMnyama*, evil influences arising from the death of the king. The most senior members of the clan were assembled in the Royal Kraal. Here, the most prominent medicine-man, the *iNyanga* performed the rite of the *ukuMisa* by which the king was confirmed in office. The priest kindled the new fire with the tribal fire-sticks, the *uZwati lomuZi*. By this rite, he inaugurated a new "day"; that is, a new reign in the life of the clan. Thereafter, he roled up some twids to form the *ubuLawu* from which he produced the king's grass-ring. With ash collected from various burnt herbal items, he smeared the new king. This anointing known as the *ukuOunga* was part of the ritual aimed at strenghtening the new king against all sorts of external harm and from evil machinations by the opponents of the clan and the *abaTakati*, secret evil doers. At this point, the king had to drink a special concoction made from vegetables, herbs, some charms and the back of the *isEngama* tree in order to ensure his *imposingness*.

It was in the coronation ceremony that the sacrality of the Zulu Nkosi became fully achieved. The peak of this "sanctifying" ceremony was his submission to the rite of the great *Animal Charm*. In this rite, the face of the new king and his body were smeared with a mixture prepared from animal fat (oil) obtained from the great Mamba Snake, the most fearsome wild beast in the land. The main objective of the ritual was to grant the king superhuman powers and to make him become possessed of all supra-human virtues.[46] In these rituals, the sovereign was believed to have become "fortified" against all odds. He took

---

[46] On the ritual fortification of the king-elect, see Krige, The Social System of the Zulus, pp. 241-242; Gluckman, The Kingdom of the Zulus, p. 30.

possession of certain material objects inherited from the ancestors and upon which it was believed the fortunes of the nation depended.

The next important stage in the coronation ceremonies was the king-elect's entry into the national temple to pray and to commune with the ancestral spirits. The king's entourage to the temple included all his clansmen, the principal representatives of the Zulu nation and the *amaKosi*, that is, the ancestral clan gods who were supposed to guard Zulu social ethos. The troupe marched round the royal ancestral tombs with a herd of black oxen. The purpose of this rite was to 'wash the king clean' over the graves of his ancestors. Among the graves visited during the tour was the grave of his grand-father and father at which spots a halt was made, bullocks sacrificed and the blessing of the ancestors invoked in a cocncluding solemn chant, the *iHuba*.

The entourage returned soon after this part of the ceremony to the Great Place, that is the Hall of the Royal Kraal. The new king surrounded by the most prominent elders of the Zulu clan and its junior warriors was brought to stand on the national sacred-coil, the *inKata ye Zwe*. Here, he held the Royal Spear, the *isiJulo* (the hurling spear), believed to stand for ever in hand in an upright form and was officially proclaimed king by the Prime Minister.[47] The crowd roared with jubilation and hailed him with the praise-name: *Bayede*: hail Majesty. The *iNyanga* later prepared the new king's private *inKata* which symbolized his power to "bind together" the nation.[48]

5.2.5   THE SACRAL NATURE AND FUNCTIONS OF THE ZULU NKOSI

As Bryant had rightly witnessed, the heart-throbbing installation ceremony of the Zulu king confirmed "the aweful sacredness of the royal person".[49] He became after the ceremonies as Bryant had also put it the clan's "high tribal priest as well as tribal king and a

---

[47] On the importance of the *inKata* as a revered symbol of the unity of the Zulu tribe, see Krige, The Social System of the Zulus, pp. 243-294.

[48] *Ibid.*, p. 476.

[49] Bryant, Olden Times in Zululand, p. 471.

114

'prospective' god" [50] And according to Gluckman, he performed religious ceremonies and ritual acts on behalf of the nation.[51] He was solely in-charge of and responsible for all national rituals. He alone possessed certain therapeutic powers and employed his art to heal his diseased headmen. He alone judged cases of sorcery upon confirmation by his medicine-men. As Gluckman had stated, all these religious duties "... were invested in the office of kingship".[52]

The sacred nature of the king is manifest in the many forms in which obeisance was paid to him in the land. The king was the medicine-man of the tribe; the centre of all agricultural and war rituals. A. Krige had confirmed this. He reported that "the king collects to himself all medicines of known powers".[53] All information about the sick was passed to him and from his capital medicines were forwarded to patients. His medicines were believed to be more powerful than any in the land because his medicinal powers derived from the 'underground beings', the *Uzimose*. He was the only one who could approach the ancestral spirits for their blessings on the tribe. He alone was the *Umthakathi*, the wizard. With his "vessel", the king could divine the fortune of the nation especially in war-times and whether enemies, personal or tribal were working for the downfall of his kingdom.

Zulu religion, as has been noted in their worldview, recognized the existence of *Unkulunkulu*, the Lord of heaven and Creator of all things. The king usually prayed his ancestors to interceed for the nation with the "Lord of Heaven" during periods of drought. He also participated on behalf of the tribe in the First Fruits Festival when in a colourful liturgy, he was believed to drive away all evil forces and their agents from his kingdom as he spat out brewed medicines towards the sun.[54]

The sacred instruments of his office; namely the tribal *inKata* and the *isiJulo* represented symbols of his divine kingship, the *ius divinum*. The Nkosi was regarded inviolate and anybody who killed the king was himself doomed as the shedding of royal

---

[50] *Ibid.*

[51] Gluckman, The Kingdom of the Zulus, p. 30.

[52] *Ibid.*, p. 31.

[53] Krige, The Scial System of the Zulus, p. 242.

[54] Here, see Krige, The Social System of the Zulus, p. 247, n. 2.

blood was considered a heinous crime. His name was sacred, all people swore by it and reverenced it. As father of all and usually the richest person in the land, Gluckman's observation that "he was generous to his subjects, using his wealth for them; gave them justice; protected their interests ..."[55] becomes quite obvious as this was a typical character of most African kings. The Nkosi offered, from time to time, handsome rewards to distinguised members of the guild of skilled workmen who fabricated Zulu ornaments of war and furniture.

5.2.6   THE REIGN OF THE NKOSI

The *Nkosi* ruled his kingdom from his Great Kraal, the *k'omkulu*. As has been shown above, he was supreme and possessed every power and privilege within the clan. All the *Abakwazulu* were subject to him and none contradicted his word. As the 'high' father of the clan, every person and beast were at his command. Though guided by a council, he was the principal exponent and interpreter of Zulu legal system such as those concerned with the prosecution of wars and land tenure. He took upon himself the task of cleansing the state of all malefactors.[56]

The king's Council was traditionally composed of elder clansmen of distinction and proven moral ability. Prior to taking any decisive action on matters affecting the common welfare of the clan, he consulted his Council. Even though he listened to the consensus of opinion of the members, the *isinDuna*, the Zulu people were known to be ruled more by custom and usage. According to the study of Gluckman, the Nkosi suffered the consequences of his actions alone were he to fail to heed the advice of his councillors.[57] In the administration of justice and in the peace policies of the state, the *Nkosi* alone took decisions himself. And in times of national distress, for example, during times of invasion from other clans, he made sure that the unity of his people was guaranteed through effective mobilisation of all able-bodied young warriors. In matters affecting the internal affairs of the

---

[55] Gluckman, "The Kingdom of the Zulu of South Africa", p. 34.

[56] Bryant, The Zulu People, p. 472.

[57] Gluckman, "The Kingdom of the Zulus", p. 35.

state, the king as the supreme proprietor of all persons and property was both administrator and judge. He was the Court of Final Appeal at which all the clansmen could approach for redress and fair-hearing. He therefore reigned as a sovereign, that is, at once as king, law-giver and judge.[58]

Nevertheless, the Zulu king had a subordinate, a co-equal in power, usually the Army War-Lord. From among the councillors the king usually appointed the Great *inDuna*, Prime Minister as head over the assembly. Resident at the Royal Kraal, he executed his function as the king's spokesman throughout the land. His office served as the Supreme Court of Justice to which cases from lower or district courts were heard. The Tribal *inDuna* as he was generally known, could be likened to the second king, that is, the grand vizier of the Egyptian Pharaohs. He managed matters of war, justice and internal affairs on behalf of the king.

5.2.7   CONCLUSIONS

The surveys on the North-South kingship systems have shown, among other traits, that the tradition of ritual kingship had, in pre-contact times, prevailed throughout the length and breadth of Africa. Both systems had enjoyed the *ius possessionis* of the African tribesmen; and their kings had, as guardians of the social charter, played vital roles in their peoples' socio-political development and the advancement of their spiritual tradition. Both systems provide full insight into the constitutive elements of kingship and the components of rulership which are altogether not unparalleled in biblical historiography and the Ancient Near East.[59] The notions that the kings were "fathers" to their peoples and sat in the thrones of their fore-fathers staunchly reflect consequences of the pre-eminent status accorded the culture-heros and the progenitors of those early African states whom the kings represented.

The genealogies of the kings and their rooting in sacred ancestrality speak eloquently of their sacral status. The roles of both the *Reth* and the *Nkosi* as mediators who could

---

[58] *Ibid.*, pp. 30, 32.

[59] Cf. I. Engnell, Studies in Divine Kingship in the Ancient Near East, Uppsala, Almqvist, 1945.

approach and interact with the acestral spirits as well as the only intermediaries between their states and the spirit-world donate to their majesties an aura of mysticism and religion which the study of religion in Africa has hitherto not satisfactorily unravelled.

The subject of the kings' attachment and promotion of the well-being of their people is an interesting *locus theologicus* which African theologians must further wade into. As their tribe's chief medicine-men and as the ones who stood at the ritual apex of their society's socio-moral order, both kings lived not only as potentates of the secular order but also as aretologists mindful of both the physical and spiritual needs of their subjects. In both kings, the unity of their peoples and even those in the diaspora were epitomised. Exorcistic, therapeutic and cultic powers of the kings enhanced the quality of their sacred statuses. As in the Yoruba system, the kings functioned in such religious matters as no mean companions of the divinities and the ancestral spirits. Truly, these kings fulfilled significant sacramental roles on behalf of their peoples, land and cattle. The annual festivals through which they maintained harmony between society and its natural environment provided encounter between the communities and the Ultimate Reality; an event which is fully and best realized in Jesus, the Christ and our King as we shall soon see. The kings' festivals demonstrated that living was for ancient Africans not a dull or a one-man show, but that life was full of colour, community consciousness and ritual movement of body and soul.

CHAPTER SIX

JESUS OF NAZARETH

6.1   INTRODUCTION

The purpose of this chapter is based on the overall interest of this study; namely the 'Christology from below'. Since the historical and the human condition of Jesus in this world of ours is traceable according to the best in historical and exegetical methods, it is therefore made the starting-point of the following chapters. Scripture makes it clear that Christology takes off from the man, Jesus of Nazareth and reflects on his divine transcendence; thus, in "an endeavour to understand the true human being of Jesus the Christ" and some symbolic actions he perfomed,[1] I wish to present the story of Jesus in such a way that African Christians see that they themselves and their problems are addressed in his person and mission. That is to say, Jesus will be portrayed as a *Person* in whose image Africans see their own circumstances.[2] Put concisely, the question is, what does it mean to say that the man, Jesus of Nazareth is our King, Lord and Saviour: *Obakarenko*? In this light, could John Taylor's fundamental remark (1963) on the Euro-American image of Christ still be considered quite apposite in the African context? According to him:

> Christ has been presented as the answers to the questions a white man would ask, the solution to the needs that Western man would feel, the saviour of the world of the European world-view, the object of adoration and prayer of historic Christendom.[3]

---

[1] J. P. Mackey, Jesus the Man and the Myth. A Contemporary Christology, London, SCM Press, 1969, p. 8; and also R. Leivestad, Jesus in His own Perspective. An Examination of His Sayings, Actions and Eschatological Titles, ET by David E. Aune, Augusburg, 1987.

[2] R. J. Shreiter, Constructing Local Theologies, New York, Maryknoll, Orbis, 1985, p. 1.

[3] J. V. Taylor, The Primal Vision, London, SCM Press, 1963, p. 24.

For over a century of missionary work and intensive evangelization, this image of Christ had been planted in Africa. But with most Africans as astute kingdom-builders, devoted royalists and craft state administrators, as we have seen shortly, has such a countenance of Christ been the answer to the questions Africans had been asking from time immemorial and which are still asked by newly converted African adults to Christianity today? Their questions, among others, can be summed up as follows:

> Since there are kings everywhere in this world, is there one who is the greatest of all?

When I tabled the issue of the inculturation of Christianity in Africa before a group of African students at Leuven in December, 1991, and to find out if this query had bugged Africans as such, all acknowledged the fact that the question, among many others, are structurally rooted in African ontology. The chapters above indicate that kingship was a versatile and ubiquitous institution in all Africa, though few acephalous communities thrived. The fact that the question above reflects an African-wide problem found itself readily expressed in five African languages represented by the respondents as follows:

> Nigba ti Oba wa kakiri agbaye,
> n je Okan wa to ga ju awon ti o ku bi?   (Yoruba)

> nga bwewaliwo Bakabaka buli wantu mu nsi munno,
> waliwo omu kubo asinga kubanne?   (Ganda)

> Njengoba ku na makhosi e mhlabeni wonke,
> u khona na o phezu kwabo bonke?   (Zulu)

> Lokola Bakonzi batondi na mokili oyo,
> wapi moye aleki bango banso?   (Lingala)

> Ka ndi-eze juputara ebe nine n'uwa nkea,
> onwere Eze kacha ibe ya?[4]   (Igbo)

---

[4] These questions formulated in African languages as the translations of the English version above were communicated to me during an interview with five African philosophical and theological students at Leuven University, Belgium during the research visit to my *Alma Mater* in November-December 1991/92 academic year: Yoruba text by Tejumola Emmanuel Ayobami (Nigeria), STB III student; Ganda text by Joseph Wasswa (Uganda), 1st year STD

In the light of their own cultural and spiritual traditions, Africans had naturally answered that such a King was *Olorun* (Yoruba), *Katonda* (Ganda), *Juok* (Shilluk), *Unkulunkulu* (Zulu), *Chineke* (Igbo), and *Ntita* (Luba). But as Africans have massively embraced Christianity, the question continues to be asked, in its new forms. If African christians understand Christ as their *Obakarenko*, would he thus be acceptable to the rest of the church universal? To answer these questions, the source for the clues is the New Testament. Let us therefore probe, however brief, into who Jesus of Nazareth was and how he was experienced by the earliest disciples and the New Testament church and how their experience can lead us to a rightful recognition of his Kingship in our times.

While methodological questions about the "historical Jesus", "the earthly Jesus" or "the Christ of Faith"[5] usually raised by Jesus scholars in *Leben-Jesu Forschung* (Jesus research) have become so involuted since the 18th-19th centuries,[6] African and Third world christians do not question about who Jesus was or is. The real Jesus for them is God, the second person of the Trinity. This is what missionary catechism had handed down to African converts and the local evangelizers continue to pass it on to our people. And in faith African people do not doubt it.[7] But as more and more African theologians explore the doctrines about the person of Jesus and his abiding significance in the African churches and recognize Christology "as the highly significant source and centre of Christian thought and life",[8] it has become pertinent to provide a biblical view of the "the earthly Jesus", the man from Nazareth as he existed within this world of time and space and was experienced in principle

---

candidate; Zulu text by Maphala Tshepo G. T. (Xhosa-Zulu), (MA Phil.) Leuven University; Lingala text by Loba Mkole Jean Claude (Zaire), 1st year STD and the Igbo text originated from my conversations with Rev. Fr. Tim Njoku (Nigeria), 1st year STD, himself an Igbo from my local Government area, Ikeduru, Imo State, and a onetime local Pastor for ten years at Orifite in Anambra State, Nigeria where he ministered to both traditional religious devotees still in large numbers in the area and Catholics.

[5] For a critical rejection of these terms, cf. J. P. Meier, "The Historical Jesus: Rethinking some Concepts", *TS* 51(1990)3-24.

[6] J. Galot, Who is Christ?, *op. cit.*; K. Stendahl, "Quis et Unde? An Analysis of Mt 1-2" in W. Eltester (ed.), Judentum, Urchristentum, Kirche, Berlin, Töpelmann, 1960, 94-105.

[7] Meier, "The Historical Jesus", p. 21.

[8] *Ibid.*, p. 5.

by other humans. This chapter will "present ... a picture, ... of Jesus during his life on earth".[9] The New Testament portrait will be considered a necessary step towards the understanding of the stages in Jesus' life-project at which the divine inhered in him and through which he was 'anointed', and 'crowned' the Christos, the Messiah, King and Lord of Life. To do justce to this portrayal, I shall draw on the rich construals of Jesus by major European and North American Jesus scholars in recent scholarship. The purpose is to highlight what recent research has uncovered concerning the centrality of Jesus himself; who he was, his message and what he did and the direct challenges he posed to the men and women of his age in his social stance, his response to the political leaders, and to the Jewish crowds.[10]

Truely speaking, there is today an increasing re-awakening of interest on the person of Jesus in recent New Testament research; in fact, a renaissance as some of the authors describe the phenomenon.[11] A flurry of these recent studies concentrate attention on Jesus as a historical figure who acted in his time as a social radical in one form or the other. While B. F. Meyer avers that Jesus consciously set himself out to critique the religiosity of his age, and to reform the temple in order to achieve a restoration of true Israel,[12] Elizabeth Schüssler Fiorenza, in her own contribution, portrays Jesus as a wisdom prophet, a spokesperson of Sophia and the founder of a Jewish renewal movement whose aspirations

---

[9] Ibid., p. 20.

[10] For a detailed treatment of Jesus' socio-political involvement, see R.J. Cassidy, Jesus, Politics, and Society. A Study of Luke's Gospel, New York, Maryknoll, Orbis, 1978.

[11] For example, M. J. Borge, "A Renaissance in Jesus Studies", Theology Today 45(1988)280-292; idem., "Portraits of Jesus in Contemporary North American Scholarship", HTR 84(1991)1-22; J. Reumann, "Jesus and Christology", in E. J. Epp & W. MacRae (eds.), The New Testament and its Modern Interpreters, Philadelphia, Fortress, Atlanta, Scholars Press, 1989, pp. 501-564; S. Neil & T. Wright, The Intererpretation of the New Testament 1861-1986, Oxford, New York, Oxford University Press, 1988, pp. 379-403; J. H. Charlesworth, "From Barren Mazes to Gentle Rappings: The Emergence of Jesus Research", Princeton Seminary Bulletin 7(1986)225-230; idem., Jesus Within Judaism: New Light from Exciting Archaelogical Discoveries, New York, Doubleday, 1988, pp. 9-29; 187-207; 223-243.

[12] B. F. Meyer, The Aims of Jesus, London, SCM Press, 1979.

were targetted at a socially radical vision and praxis.[13] In the interest of her feminist hermeneutics, Borg informs us that Fiorenza argues that Jesus challenged "both the ideology and praxis of the dominant ethos of the Jewish social world".[14] In her best and strongest feminist stance, Fiorenza maintains that Jesus' main objective was to establish a community made up of *a discipleship of equals* based on "a vision of inclusive wholeness" in order to renew the Israelite society of his day.

E. P. Sanders furthers our knowledge on the renewal tendency of Jesus. He holds the view that Jesus is an eschatological prophet in the tradition of Jewish restoration theology. For him, Jesus sees the fulfillment of the promises to Israel quite at hand and the eschatological renewal of Israel fully begun in his life and work of Jesus. For Sanders, Jesus calls into question the social institution of the law in Judaism and warns of the dramatic intervention by God which shall involve the destruction of the Jerusalem temple and the coming of the new one. In saying these things, Jesus offends the priestly establishment and the temple authorities, Sanders would have us believe.[15] In two important books, Marcus J. Borg offers a sketch of Jesus which share much in common with the portraits of his colleagues but differs in his History of Religions approach.[16] For Borg, Jesus is an ancient Palestinian *holy person* who, in light of his spiritual insight opposes the increasing Jewish nationalism under the Roman colonial domination. In his view, Jesus was political in sofar as he was concerned with the status of the historical community of Israel. Interestingly enough, at least for the African Christians' mental disabusement, Borg sees Jesus as a subversive sage who undermined conventional wisdom and taught an alternative wisdom, a social prophet and an initiator of a movement aimed at the revitalization of Israel. To summarize his position Borg states:

---

[13] Elizabeth S. Fiorenza, In Memory of Her: A Feminist Theological Reconstruction of Christian Origins, New York, Crossroad, 1983, pp. 72-159.

[14] Borg, "Portraits of Jesus", p. 9.

[15] E. P. Sanders, Jesus and Judaism, Philadelphia, Fortress Press, 1985.

[16] M. J. Borg, Conflict, Holiness and Politics in the Teachings of Jesus, New York, E. Mellen, 1984; *idem.*, Jesus: A New Vision, San Francisco, Harper & Row, 1988,

With the images of holy person and the sage added to prophet and movement founder, a fairly full portrait of Jesus results, an image that integrates much of the Jesus tradition. He was a charismatic healer who also felt called to a public mission that included radical criticism of the dominant ethos of his social world and affirmation of another way.[17]

Jesus' pre-occupation with his social world still remains the central focus of R. Horsley's reconstruction of the image of Jesus. In the same line of thinking as Borg, Horsley presents Jesus as a social prophet taking his cue in the line of the radical prophetic tradition of Israel.[18] Somewhat like what I am doing in this study, Horsley applies the findings from his inquiry on pre-industrial peasant societies and the social dynamics operating between rural peasants and urban ruling elites to ancient New Testament data in order to allow the picture of the first century Palestine emerge. For him, the picture is that of a colonial situation where class struggle and conflict between the economically oppressive urban, ruling elites and the economically oppressed rural peasants exist. According to him, this state of affairs engineered all sorts of social upheavals in which bandits, popular prophets and violence upon violence was the order of the day. It is within this context, namely of colonial domination and oppression between the Jewish, Herodian and Roman ruling groups and the majority of the people, a teeming ninety per cent of the population, that the Jesus traditions must be located. The picture of Jesus that emerges out of this context, opines Horsley, is that of a social revolutionary who was on the side of the peasant population.[19] According to Horsley, standing in the convenantal-prophetic tradition of Israel, Jesus stood on the side of the poor and indicted the ruling classes. He refuted the importance of the temple which at that time stood as Israel's symbol of economic activities and the social world. He criticized the national priesthood who had used the temple as an "an instrument of imperial legitimation and control of a subjected people".[20] For Horsley, as for Borg and Fiorenza, Jesus stood for a social revolution and the renewal of Israelite village communities in terms of the egalitarian

---

[17] Borg, "Portraits of Jesus", p. 15

[18] R. Horsley, Jesus and the Spiral of Violence: Popular Jewish Resistance in Roman Palestine, San Francisco, Harper & Row, 1987.

[19] *Idem.*, Sociology of the Jesus Movement, New York, Crossroad, 1989.

[20] *Idem.*, Jesus and the Spiral of Violence, p. 287.

conventual tradition of Israel. Turning to the significance of Jesus' use of apocalyptic language, Horsley is of the view that Jesus' apocalyptic language has socio-political implications. Jesus was a proto-revolutionary figure opposed to the Roman occupation of Palestine and the native social institutions which colluded with Rome such as the temple, priesthood and Jerusalem to rape the land and people. B. L. Mack is one scholar who, on his own part, has spoken of a "softly characterization of Jesus".[21] In Mack's view, Jesus was a "Cynic sage" or a "Cynic teacher" whose background in a largely hellenized Galilee is doubtless. The parallels to Hellnistic Cynic tradition enhances, for Mack, the suggestion that Jesus was a wandering Cynic sage. The proposal that Jesus had taught his followers and his audience as a Cynic wise man has also received the attention of New Testament scholars in Great Britain.[22] Cynic wisdom presupposed the reversal of fortunes on behalf of the downdrodden.

These portrayals, much as they are illuminating, stand to advance our knowledge on the period in which Jesus lived and the possible major activities of his mission and perhaps, how his contemporaries viewed him and his ambitions. To my mind, it is in light of these reconstructions that we may be able to perceive the impression Jesus' self claim as King or as soon-to-be king of the coming Kingdom of God made on his followers; a claim that perhaps spurred them on to proclaim him King.[23] Commenting on E. P. Sanders' work, *Jesus and Judaism*, Seán P. Kealy, in this line of reasoning, states that for Sanders, Jesus:

> Expecting an eschatological miracle, the destruction and rebuilding of the temple, ... saw himself in the role of king or at least the agent chosen by God to usher in the kingdom.[24]

---

[21] B. L. Mack, A Myth of Innocence: Mark and Christian Origins, Philadelphia, Fortress Press, 1988.

[22] In England, F. G. Downing has, a year before Mack's study appeared, discovered the Cynic portrait of Jesus. Cf. his, Jesus and the Threat of Freedom, London, SCM Press, 1987; also *idem.*, The Christ and the Cynics, Sheffield Academic Press, 1988.

[23] Here see, Sanders, Jesus and Judaism, pp. 307, 321-322, 324.

[24] S. P. Kealy, "Gospel Studies Since 1970 (2)", *Irish Theological Quarterly* 57(1991)93-104, p. 98.

This particular role of Jesus shall be fully explored in chapter eight of this study.

6.2   THE NEW TESTAMENT LITERATURE
6.2.1   THE GOSPELS

Like other great founders of religion and teachers such as Gautama Buddha, Socrates, Muhammad, Jesus left nothing in writing.[25] What we know of him, though limited, comes essentially from the accounts of the Synoptic gospels. In the four gospels, the statistics of the references with the name "Jesus Christ" or "Jesus" are as follows: Matthew 152, Mark 82, Luke 86 and John 252. Meier is thus right to assert that, "to be sure, the Gospels serve as the chief sources for our reconstruction of the historical Jesus".[26] However, the material about Jesus is made much more scantier by the probable dates of the authorship of the gospels and the distance in time of what they narrate. Among scholars, the following dates are generally agreed: Mark c. 70 AD; Matthew and Luke c. 80 AD and John probably c. 90 AD.[27] We must also reckon with the fact that the gospel material passed through three well recognized stages of development: (a) the period of Jesus and what he said and did (the focus of historical criticism); (b) the period (c. 30-60 AD) when the preacher became preached as well as the existence and circulation of other strands of both oral and written traditions about Jesus (the storm-centre of Form Criticism) and (c) the stage at which the evangelists collected, shaped, modified and embellished those disperate traditions in the form they are transmitted to us today (the storm-centre of Redaction-Composition criticism).

In any case, the accounts of Jesus' early life and work transmitted in the gospels of Mark, Matthew and Luke and the references they make to first century Palestine and Judaism of that period and to such figures as king Herod, his family and the Herodians; the religious groups: the Sadducees, the Pharisees and Pilate are also attested to in extra biblical sources. The works of Josephus (37-100 AD); Philo Judaeus who died between 45-50 AD and several

---

[25] Neill, Jesus Through Many Eyes, p. 164.

[26] Meier, "The Historical Jesus".

[27] For further approximations, see J. P. Meier, The Vision of Matthew: Christ, Church and Morality in the First Gospel, New York, Paulist Press, 1978, p. 11.

other non Christian historical sources such as Pliny the Younger confirm the historicity of their accounts. Thus, apart from each evangelists' theological insight on the person of Jesus, the historical accuracy of the synoptists and fidelty to their sources and facts must be upheld.[28] For Mark, whom the other two Synoptists might have followed closely, Jesus is human and behind his fully human life, Deity is concealed.[29] To sum up this section, I agree with Sanders' view that any construal of Jesus' life which claims to be historically authentic must not ignore to take count of eight salient facts stressed in the gospels; namely that

(I)   Jesus was baptised by John the Baptist[30]

(II)   Jesus was a Galilean who preached and performed healing miracles

(III)   Jesus chose disciples and made twelve the leaders

(IV)   Jesus limited his activity to Israel

(V)   Jesus engaged in controversy about the temple

(VI)   Jesus was crucified outside Jerusalem by the Roman authorities

(VII) After his death, his followers congregated as a group with an identifiable movement

(VIII) At least some Jews persecuted some parts of the new movement.[31]

In what follows, I will discuss some of these facts which I consider closely relevant to my present study. The presentations will however be brief. The historic present is used throughout.

---

[28] Cf. G. O'Collins, "Jesus" in M. Eliade et al.(eds.), The Encyclopedia of Religion, Vol. 8, New York, Macmillan, 1987, pp. 15-28, p. 17; here, see also, J. Gnilka, Jesus von Nazaret. Botschaft und Geschichte, HThKNT. Suppl. 3, Freiburg-Basel-Wien, Herder, 1990.

[29] See my "The Centurion's Confession of Faith", p. 270.

[30] Peronally, I would make the fact that Jesus was born into a family the first issue.

[31] On these facts, I am indebted to Kealy, "Gospel Studies...", p. 98; and Borg, "Portraits of Jesus...", p. 3, n. 8. Both authors comment and summarize Sanders' Jesus and Judaism.

6.2.1.1   JESUS' BIRTH

Jesus is born a Galilean Jew about 7 or 6 BC and dies about AD 30 in the first century Palestine.[32] The mother's name is Mary, who is married to Joseph, a carpenter by profession. The Bethelhem traditions shared by the gospels of Matthew and Luke mince no words in establishing the fact of Jesus' birth stories as historical. Though Jesus is raised in the contemporary Jewish environment and is schooled in the basic religious education of his day, nothing is known of his teenage years. His public ministry, according to the records of the Synoptic gospels, lasted about a year. The Fourth gospel, however, gives the impression that Jesus worked for two to three years.[33] According to G.W. Buchanan, "Jesus was a human being who lived in history, where people live, become parts of their environments, and make human mistakes...".[34]

6.2.1.2   JESUS' BAPTISM

Among other people, Jesus is baptized by John, the baptizer in the River Jordan (Mk 1,9-11 par.)[35] According to the evangelists, it is at his baptism that God anoints him with the Holy Spirit. Thus he is elected God's son by the divine fiat: "Thou art my beloved son, with thee I am well pleased" (v. 11). The moment of Jesus' baptism is his calling, his choice. It is God's presentation and approval that Jesus' activities have the fullest divine support. He is sent in the same manner in which God sent John the baptizer though Jesus is empowered by

---

[32] Non-christian literature of the 1st and 2nd centuries AD such as those of Roman authors Tacitus, Suetonius and Pliny the Younger; the Jewish historian, Josephus Flavius, Lucian of Samosata, the Cynic philosopher and the Babylonian Talmud, a 5th century AD work speak of Jesus of Nazareth and his death during the time of Pontius Pilate, the Roman Procurator of Palestine in the reign of Emperor Tiberius.

[33] See Meier, "The Historical Jesus", p. 15 who reckons from this time-lag in his study.

[34] G. W. Buchanan, Jesus. The King and his Kingdom, Macon, Mercer University Press, 1984, p. 11.

[35] The fact that the story of the baptism of Jesus is attested to by more than one gospel lends weight to its historicity.

the Spirit and given fuller *exousia* in order to accomplish the task of inaugurating a new order: the Reign of God. This endowment with the Spirit of Power reflects an end-time activity which makes Jesus' baptism be seen as an end-time event.[36] The Spirit of power leads Jesus forth to operate on God's behalf. As Rhoads-Michie eloquently put it, "Everything he does and says seems to issue from a conviction that through him the rule of God has come near"[37] As the anointed Son of God, Jesus assumed full-fledged rights and powers for himself. In these lie the significance of Jesus' baptism.

6.2.1.3   JESUS' MINISTRY

Soon after his baptism, Jesus travels from place to place preaching. And as Rhoads-Michie remarks,

> pardoning sins, interpreting laws, appointing the twelve to share in his
> authority, exorcising demons, healing, commanding nature, prophesying,
> entering Jerusalem royally and occupying the temple.[38]

Jesus is quite benevolent. He uses his authority not to destroy but to build up and to renew the institutions of his day. He combats both human and non human forces which hold people under oppression. He cleanses the leprous by a single touch. He heals by words alone and commands both wind and sea. A touch of the hem of his garment lets off healing powers. He raises the dead and feeds thousands in a desert environment.

Jesus preaches "announcing to the nation that the time of release from captivity and of return to rest has arrived" (Mt 11,28-30).[39] He teaches on the same theme in the synagogue in his home-town (Lk 4,16-30. According to Buchanan, we have knowledge of

---

[36] See Joel 2; Enoch 42,2; Song of Solomon 17,2; Testament of Levi 18,6.

[37] D. M. Rhoads and D. M. Michie, Mark as Story. An Introduction to the Narrative of a Gospel, Philadelphia, Fortress Press, 1982, p. 105.

[38] *Ibid.*

[39] B. Charette, "'To Proclaim Liberty to the Captives'. Matthew 11.28-30 in the Light of OT Prophetic Expectation", *NTS* 38(1992)290-297, p. 294.

the period when "Jesus lived and the geographical territory with which he was familiar".[40] As he moves, from place to place and from city to city, he challenges all forms of oppression. The pages of the New Testament show that he takes much interest in the condition of public sinners, the down-trodden and the outcasts. Jesus choses disciples to follow him and from among them he nominates the Twelve. As V. K. Robbins admirably puts it, Jesus is "a disciple-gathering teacher".[41] He teaches his followers many things, among them, prayers especially, *The Our Father* in which he shows a special filial relationship between man and God.[42] Before any major event or crisis occured in his life, Jesus is shown to have entered into deep prayer either alone or on mountain-tops with a few of his disciples to communicate with God. In the Gethsemane, he, as any man of flesh and blood, dialogues with the Father in these moving words:

> Abba, Father, all things are possible to thee, remove this cup from me; yet
> not what I will, but what thou wilt (Mk 14,36 par.)

He so skillfully uses parables in his speeches that his illustration of God-man relationship becomes clear. Jesus performs miracles, and feeds the hungry. Crowds trooped after him. He invites the tax collectors, and attends dinner parties to the houses of some Publicans, members of a well-to-do class but generally despised.

In his ministry to the people, he challenges popular forms of piety and in his movement he calls people to action, and is opposed to certain traditions and legalisms (Mk 7,1-23), especially those that enslave man to the temple cult. For the wellbeing of man, he even violates some sabbath laws (Mk 2,23-27).[43] On occasions, he speaks what most Jews of his time considered irreverent to the Temple in Jerusalem (Mk 14,58; 15,29-30). Some

---

[40] *Ibid*, p. 13.

[41] V. K. Robbins, Jesus the Teacher. A Socio-Rhetorical Interpretation of Mark, Philadelphia, Fortress, 1984, p. 82.

[42] For the importance scholars have attached to the parayer, its history and interpretation, see W. M. Buchan, "Research on the Lord's Prayer" *ExpT* 100(1989)336-339.

[43] On Jesus and the Law, his criticism and fulfillemt of the Law in the rabbic Judaism of his day, see a review of the situation in G. Dautzenberg, "Jesus und die Tora", *Orientierung* 55(1991)229-232.

of the activities of Jesus bring him into conflict with the Jewish authorities.[44] When he arrives in Jerusalem to participate in the annual Passover celebration, he is betrayed by Judas, a close disciple, to the Chief priests of the Sadduccean party. He is arrested by the local police and is arraigned before the Sanhedrin where he is cross-examined on charges of despising the legal statutes. Later, he is sent to Pontius Pilate, the Governor and head of the Roman colonial administration stationed in Judea to oversee Palestine and its environs in the Eastern Mediterranean on a charge of high treason because he claims to be the rightful king of the Jews, the heir to the throne.[45] Pilate condemns him as a messanic pretender and "as a threat to public order"[46] and permits his execution on the cross. People mock and jeer at him. He dies on the cross and is later taken down and laid to rest on the same day.[47]

Is Jesus of Nazareth a political agitator? Opinions differ. Some biblical scholars find no basis to deny that he is; others spiritualise the Jesus phenomenon. But the fact most authors forget to take serious count of is that the Jews of the first century AD made no sharp distinction between politics and religion as is still today maintained in Islam in most states of the Middle East. All matters about politics, economics, social or religious activities were defined in terms of God and his law. There were no pure ideas about secularity among the Jews of the time. So Jesus' involvement in the events of his day could be perceived in either way depending on who or which institution had thought its interest most jeopardized.

6.2.2 THE PAULINE EPISTLES

The major epistles of the Pauline corpus composed between 50 and 67 AD, that is, much earlier than the four gospels provide us some reliable information on the historicity of Jesus

---

[44] C. U. Manus, "Jesus And the Jewish Authorities in the Fourth Gospel" in W. Amewowo et al (eds.), Communautés Johanniques, Johannine Communities, Actes du Quatrième Congrès des Biblistes Africains, Kinshasa, Saint Paul, 1991, pp. 135-155.

[45] See W. Hendriksen, New Testament Commentary. Exposition of the Gospel According to John, Vol. II, Michigan, Grand Rapids, Baker, 1954, p. 406.

[46] Cassidy, Jesus, p. 54.

[47] Here, see O'Collins, "Jesus", pp. 17-18.

of Nazareth and some of his traditions. In Paul's letters to the Galatians and the Romans; namely Gal 3,16; 4,4-5; Rom 1,3; 9,5, we are intimated of Jesus' pedigree. The letters tell us that Jesus is of a Jewish origin. He is a descendant of king David's family (Rom 1,3). In Rom 15,8, we learn that Jesus preaches to the Israelite audience. Among the things which he outlaws is divorce (1 Cor 7,10-11). Around him are gathered disciples, apostles and sympathizers.

Even the post-Apostolic epistles are not silent about the historical Jesus. The author of the Epistle, *Pros 'Ebraious* fosters one of the best in the ideology of Jesus' humanity in its historical terms. He discusses Jesus' temptations and his agony in Gethsemane as experiences which identifies him with suffering humanity (Heb 5,7-10). Hebrews conceives Jesus' humanity in functional terms. It discusses, among other things, Jesus' role in salvation history, the nature of his mission and his eternal priesthood. In 1 Tim 3,16 we read:

> Great indeed, we confess, is the mystery of our religion: He was manifested
> in the flesh, vindicated in the spirit ...

and as well in 1 Pet 3,18 it is written :

> For Christ also died for sins once for all, the righteous for the unrighteous,
> that he might bring us to God, being put to death in the flesh but made alive
> in the spirit; ...

Even in the context of their resurrectional discourses, these patronymous authors employ contemporary anthropology in which both the flesh and the spirit stand for and constitute a pair to refer to Jesus as a full-blooded historical personality. Already in Mt 27,50 we read:

> *Ho de 'Iesous palin kraxas phone megale apheken to pneuma.*

> Jesus cried ... with a loud voice and yielded up his spirit.

Matthew shares in the tradition which knows that Jesus has a corporeality; and here he is saying that without the expiration of the spirit, Jesus' death could not have been certified. Like Matthew and the post-Apostolic writers, African anthropology is emphatic on the two elements as constitutive of a person. The Akan of Ghana recognize that every human being possesses an *okra*, the underlying divine element which, at death, is yielded up and returned to *Onyame*, God. This destiny soul, *mmuo*, as the Igbo also know it, or the *emi* in Yoruba anthropology is an essential constituent of the life-force of the living person.[48] Thus, by having body and spirit, Jesus is a living human being Africans could encounter. Flesh or body is the external and visible embodiment of a person. Jesus shares this physical feature with corporeal humanity. It is by his possession of *aru*, flesh, that he is subjected to temptation like any other human being. With spirit and flesh his whole self is body; that is to say that Jesus has a personality of his own about which the scriptures do not fail to inform us. It is in his personality that he moves and has his being (Acts 17,28) in the Jewish world of his day. The fact that the full humanity of Jesus is described in the Scriptures is noteworthy. We see this especially in his obedience to God, the Father (Lk 2,49; 23,46). In his show of filial obedience, Jesus proves himself a man created with reason and freewill. The Gospel of Mark, often considered crude in its language ascribes no omniscience to Jesus. In Mk 13,32, Jesus' lack of knowledge of the parousia speaks of his limitations as a human being. In the Passion stories, we are made to feel with Jesus the painful death on the cross. The reaction of the horrified centurion points, among other things, to the phenomenon of death as man's finitude. Let me now discuss Jesus' death fully below.

6.2.3   JESUS' DEATH

The four gospels, Paul and the Pastorals refer copiously to the death of Jesus. In Gal 2,20; 3,1; 1 Cor 1,23; Phil 2,8, Paul attests that Jesus died by crucifixion. While the scribes and the Pharisees represent Jesus' opponents in the earlier sections of the gospels, the chief priests and the elders, mostly of the sadduccean party are his main opponents in the passion stories.[49] Much as the gospel narratives are theological in their emphasis, one thing certain,

---

[48] Cf. E. I. Metuh, God and Man in African Religion: A Case Study of the Igbo of Nigeria, London, Chapman, 1981, p. 85. For further enquiries about the author's descriptive analysis of this concept in Igbo Religion, see *idem*, African Religions in Western Conceptual Schemes: The Problem of Interpretation, (Studies In Igbo Religion), Ibadan (Nigeria), Claverianum Press, 1985.

[49] Cf. J. P. Mackey, Jesus the Man and the Myth, p. 59.

and as has been stated much earlier on, is that Jesus meets his death in Jerusalem under Pontius Pilate. As Mackay puts it, "the death of Jesus at least brings him into contact with a known historical figure and with the great empire he represented".[50] His death on the cross is a renunciation of his own life. It represents "his final act of service".[51] He is betrayed by one of his dear disciples and on that night, he celebrates the Last Super. The only three who follow on quickly sleep off and leave him to his fate at Gethsemane. They could not keep vigil. He struggles alone with his fear. It is indeed an agonizing struggle. Like other humans, he does not want to die. He prays that it could pass away, yet he submits to God's will. The phyical anguish Jesus endured has been graphically portrayed by Rhoads-Michie:

> They put hands on him and led him off. Some of those convicting him spit on him, then cover his head and strike him. The guards beat him. He is bound and handed over to Pilate who has him whipped. The soldiers spit on him and beat him over the head with a reed pole. After these beatings, Jesus is so weak that they draft someone to take up his cross. The agonizing crucifixion lasts six hours. The intensity of Jesus' suffering results in his quick death, for Pilate is surprised that Jesus has died so soon.[52]

When he is captured, he refuses no arrest nor escapes his fate. His best friends desert him. Peter, upon whom he recently confers a title in the ranks, renounces him. Taken by the law enforcement agents of the state, and removed from his supporters he is put to trail, mocked, derided, judged and condemned by evidence established on false witnesses. At Pilate's court, the sympathetic crowd abandon him. He is later left alone and handed over to the local Jewish authorities who return him to the Roman authority who approve his execution by the colonial troops. He dies on the cross and is buried by a stranger.

---

[50] *Ibid.*, p. 63.

[51] Rhoads - Michie, Mark As Story, p. 112.

[52] *Ibid.*, p. 116.

6.3   JEWISH SOURCES

Information from Jewish sources about Jesus can be scanty and sometimes spurious. However, in recent times, some scholars are attempting to present a balanced image of Jesus of Nazareth and the age in which he lived through the spectacle of the Second Temple Judaism. J. H. Charlesworth in his prestigious study, *Jesus Within Judaism*,[53] has deepened our knowledge on Jesus and his environment. In summarizing Charlesworth work, the relevant data is as follows: Jesus has acquaintance with John the Baptist who, along with other people, baptizes him. His public ministry starts out from Capernaum. He calls men and women to follow him from whose number he nominates a group of Twelve. He perfoms healings. He is an itinerant preacher who proclaims the nearness of the reign of God. He teaches his followers to conceive God as a loving Father, *Abba* and no longer as a *Deus Otiosus* (a hidden God) who is solicited only at times of emergency.

According to Charlesworth, it appeared to Jesus that he was the *Messiah* in light of his self definition as *Son of God*. After his ministry in Galilee, he shifts his base to Jerusalem where he confronts the official priesthood and the corruption of the temple. There he suffers through the betrayal of Judas and the denial of Peter. He is arrested and dies on a cross outside the Western Wall of Jerusalem in the spring of 30 AD. From data as these, Charlesworth concludes that we now know more about Jesus than about any other Palestinian Jew before AD 70. For him, this is the picture we can get about Jesus within Judaism of his time; and I think, not even any different than the gospels give.[54]

6.4   CONCLUSIONS

This survey demonstrates that there is indeed a history of the earthly Jesus of Nazareth who really trod this earth, entered into a true human existence (incarnation) in the first century

---

[53] J. H. Charlesworth, Jesus Within Judaism.

[54] However, it is worthy of note to state that the prodigious acts of Jesus as reported in the narratives while they offer a historical picture of Jesus may only be seen as literary ploys which confirm the basic facts about Jesus.

AD and with whom many people came into contact.[55] He fascinated them and they decided to keep company with him for as long as he lived. As E. Schillebeeckx gives it expression:

> This encounter and what took place in Jesus' life and in connection with his death gave their own lives new meaning and significance. They felt that they were reborn, understood and cared for. Their new identity was expressed in a new enthusiasm for the kingdom of God and therefore in a special compassion for others, for their fellow-men, in a way that Jesus had already shown them.[56]

Besides, the New Testament, according to Kasper does not hide "the fact that Jesus Christ was a real human being"[57] As he sums it up neatly, Jesus experienced "hunger, thirst, weariness, joy, sorrow, love, anger, toil, pains, God-forsakenness and finally death".[58] While the corporeal life of Jesus is clearly described in the pages of the NT, the authors are unconcerned with the details of his daily and personal lifestyle. What bulks large in the minds of the authors is the central significance of Jesus' human existence for salvation. The NT rather emphasizes the fact that in Jesus and through him God has acted in human history "in an eschatological-definitive and historically surpassing way in order to reconcile the world to himself (2 Cor 5,18)".[59]

From these insights, one can readily see that the encounter with Jesus in his humanity transformed the lives of the first set of people who met him and compelled them to pass on the experience to others (1 Cor 15,17). They never hoarded their knowledge about and their

---

[55] If Jesus is this historical figure who lived and died in the first century Palestine, how can one explain his relationship as Messiah-King to God without actually compromising the uniqueness and kingship of God? This is a problem I will address myself to in Chapter Eight devoted to the exegesis of the texts concerned with the Kingship of Jesus.

[56] E. Schillebeeckx, Interim Report on the Books *Jesus* and *Christ*. ET by J. Bowden, London, SCM Press, 1980, p. 10. The rich and invaluable exegetical insights that characterize the two volumes are recognized. See *idem*, *Jesus* An Experiment in Christology, ET by Hubert Hoskins, William Collins, 1974; *Christ* The Christian Experience in the Modern World, Et by John Bowden, London, SCM Press, 2nd Impression, 1982.

[57] Kasper, Jesus the Christ, p. 197.

[58] *Ibid*.

[59] *Ibid*.

136

experience of Jesus, the Christ. The rapture experienced by the earliest followers as a result of the encounter with Jesus of Nazareth, "a man from their own race and religion"[60] becomes the *point de départ* of the entire NT Christology. What thereafter emerged was faith experience expressed in ordinary human thought-form yielding itself into the language of encounter and experience (William James) and usually uttered by man when gripped by the sense of the Ultimate Reality. In their encounter with Jesus, divine revelation was mediated. Let us now explore how the divine in-breaking into human history is given expression in Jesus' conception of the kingdom of God.

---

[60] Schillebeeckx, Interim Report, p. 10.

CHAPTER SEVEN

THE KINGDOM OF GOD

7.1   INTRODUCTION

Both the OT literature and Judaism of the period during which Jesus lived had a conscientious understanding of the concept of God's kingdom, as well as his kingship. The crowds who followed and heard Jesus, no doubt, belonged to that age and shared in the thought-forms of the period. Jesus takes it for granted that his audience is already conversant with the idea and looked forward to the arrival of the kingdom of God in human history. But one may ask: what is for them a "new teaching" in Jesus' use of the concept? Is *malkhut*, (kingdom) in the sense in which Jesus spoke about it readily understood by his contemporaries? Did they understand it as government, authority and power of God any more or any less than their ancestors had hitherto known? Did Jesus' regal theology depart significantly from traditional conceptions? If at all it did, in what ways? Can the criterion of dissimilarity help us reach the *Sitz im Leben* of Jesus' sayings on the subject? These are pertinent questions whose answers will be provided in this chapter. Firstly, before investigating the OT and contemporary Judaism, it is quite approriate to examine briefly the background of the idea of God's kingship (7.2). Kingship traditions in the Ancient Near East (ANE) have offered scholars the impetus to trace the *fons et origo* of the idea. Here, parallel structures with those of the African systems may be spotted where necessary. After the survey, there will then follow an investigation of the concept of the kingship of God in the OT, the early and late Judaism.

In the second part (7.3), I will attempt to establish as much as possible what Jesus' concept of the kingdom of God implies. In order to remain faithful to exegetical practice, I will take count of the phenomenon of "believing" on the part of Jesus' followers in order to construct meanings out of the texts relating to the concept of the *Basilea tou Theou* (Kingdom of God) as Jesus used it. The section will examine if Jesus' thought or his idea of the kingdom of God implies that God is conceived King as in Judaism or not. Finally, an attempt will be made to show whether the evangelists obliquely made use of the term, king (*Basileus*) or the verb, to 'reign', (*Basileuein*) in their narratives on Jesus' discourse on the kingdom of God.

7.2   THE OT AND JUDAISM: THE ANE BACKGROUND

It is now common knowledge among biblical scholars that there had long been developed in the Ancient Near East the myth of the kingship of God; an idea which the Israelites are believed to have borrowed from the Canaanites among whom they had sojourned for quite a long time.[1] According to S. Mowinckel, the Israelites, had received the idea from the usages of the vast kingdoms on the shores of the rivers Euphrates, Tigris and the Nile (in Africa, most probably the Egyptians whose culture must have influenced the Shilluk as much, perhaps, as the Yoruba) where regal institutions had long been well developed and had flourished quite earlier, in fact, since the ancient Sumerian Age.[2] The myth narrates the story of the creation of the world by the god who acted as the king just like among the Yoruba, *Oba Oduduwa* is beleived to have descended form heaven unto Ile-Ife and fashioned the Yoruba world. The Baylonian myth has a parallel account to a divine origin of the progenitor. J. B. Pritchard informs us that the Etana "kingship descended from heaven".[3] As the Oduduwa overcame chaos represented in *Okun*, the sea and the opposing line of *Obatala* rulers,[4] the Oriental god had overcome and slain the primeval monster. As Oduduwa enacted the *Edi* and the *Oramfe* annual festivals, so did the Oriental god-king set up an annual festivals through which the fertility of the earth was renewed. As Oduduwa ensured the

---

[1] Cf. M. Buber, Königtum Gottes, Berlin, Schocken Verlag, 1932, pp. 47-60 who himself, had on this subject, stated, "daß alle semitischen Völker sich ihre Götter als Könige vorstellen", p. 47.

[2] S. Mowinckel, The Psalms in Israel's Worship, Vol I, New York, Nashville, Abingdon, Oxford, Blackwell, 1962, p. 114.

[3] See J. B. Pritchard, Ancient Near Eastern Texts Relating to the Old Testament, Third Edition, Princeton, 1969, p. 114.

[4] On Yoruba creation myth, see Frobenius, The Voice of Africa, Vol I, pp. 283-284.

wellbeing of his people, the Oriental king proved himself king to his people by sustaining them in their land.

The basic structure of the Oriental myth of creation has much in common with the myths of origin in Africa and the kingship traditions sustaining them. In Ganda royal myth, for example, the sacred origin of Kintu, the first *Kabaka* is no less dissimilar with that of *Nyikang*, the proto *Reth* of the Shilluk or with that of the *Nkosi* of the Zulu. All these sacred kings had their beginnings described in mythical narratives. In the Ancient Near East, such myths were widely diffused. What appears to change in the narratives is usually the name of the god-king. In nearly all the accounts, the royal founders were believed to have descended from a god, married, begotten children, conquered chaos and non-being, established a dynasty and above all assumed as their responsibility the functions of the protection and custody of their kingdoms on behalf of their peoples' collective survival through time.[5] In Babylonia, it was non other than *Marduk*; in Assyria it was *Asshur*; in Ammon it was *Milhom*; in Tyre, it was *Melkart* and in Africa his various appelations indicate his Sovereignty.[6] In Israel, the Yahwists, the Psalmists and even the Chronicler portray a God who is far greater and a univeral Father and King than the henotheistic deities of the surrounding nations.

7.2.1   KINGSHIP IN THE OLD TESTAMENT

In the OT scriptures, kingship is an integral component of the Kingdom of God in history. As D. M. Howard contends "an impressive theology of kingship" is portrayed in the OT narratives.[7] Progress in contemporary OT research indicates that from the beginning of Israelite history, God had made provisions for the rise of kings from Abraham's tribe. On this issue, Howard quite auspiciously states:

---

[5] Here, I draw on similarity of ideas from B. Ray, The Kabaka as Symbolic Center of Buganda, p. 7.

[6] See J. S. Mbiti, Concepts of God in Africa, London, S.P.C.K., 1970.

[7] D. M. Howard "The Case for kingship in the Old Testament Narrative Books and the Psalms" *TrinJ 9NS* (1988)19-35, p. 19.

140

The texts prior to the deuteronomistic history present the earliest history of God's dealings, and they show kingship in Israel to be one of his intended blessings on his people and the nations, at least, from patriarchal times.[8]

Inspite however of the apparent literary tension in the narratives of the Historical Books, Howard rightly opines that "the prevailing pictures of the idea of monarchy in the OT are consistently positive ones ..."[9] According to him, G. E. Gerbrandt's recent study shows that the view in the Deuteronomistic History (DtrH) of the institution of kingship in Israel is essentially a favourable one, not negative as is commonly supposed"[10] This positive approval of kingship has further been noted by S. L. McKenzie who argues that:

In the Prophetic Record kingship is the gift of Yahweh and not, as according to 1 Sam 8; 10,17-25; 12, the result of popular demand or the rejection of Yahweh.[11]

However, at the centre of the controversy represented in those traditions was the question: what kind of rule would the monarch exercise? In the sense of the Oriental god-king myth (à la Mowinckel), the king was expected to be a godly king who trusted in Yahweh. In his surrogate position, the king was to lead his people and among other things, administer the covenantal obligations. In such a situation, he trusts Yahweh to deliver his people from their enemies. As Howard remarks, Gerbrandt avers: "At the heart of this covenant was Israel's obligation to be totally loyal to Yahweh".[12] Such kings who kept the ordinances of the Law and trusted in Yahweh were the righteous kings of Juda: David, Hezekiah and Josiah. We can then, from this brief exploration on the propriety of kingship in Israel argue that the idea

---

[8] *Ibid.*, p. 20.

[9] *Ibid.*

[10] *Ibid.*, pp. 19-20, esp. n. 1 where G. E. Gerbrandt, Kingship According to the Deuteronomistic History, SBLDS 87, Atlanta, Scholars Press, 1986 is cited. See also, J. K. Wiles, "Wisdom and Kingship in Israel", *AJT 1(1987)*55-61.

[11] S. L. McKenzie, The Trouble with Kings. The Composition of the Book of Kings in the Deuteronomistic History, Leiden, E. J. Brill, 1991, p. 12.

[12] Gerbrandt, Kingship, p. 102 cited in Howard, *art. cit.*, p. 20, n. 3.

of kingship in ancient Israel was concretized in the period of the monarchy. Or to put it in another form, the institution of kingship though an old idea, came into full expression during the monarchical period. Kingship was therefore an office held on behalf of God, the Supreme King. The chosen king ruled over Israel and sat on the throne of the Lord. It is in this sense, according to G. W. Buchanan, that the close nexus between sonship of God and kingship should be understood.[13] Exploring thus further with Howard, I wish to take note of the importance of Dt 17 which had been acknowledged by OT scholars as the Charter for Kingship. The injunctions it hands down suppose that the institution was thought of as good for the people. Even H.-W. Jüngling has, in a recent study on a portion of the Book of Judges, noted that kingship in Israel was favoured by the Israelite public.[14]

A few passages in both Genesis and the Book of Numbers, two dependable portions of the Pentateuch composed centuries before the real serious demand for the monarchy in Israel arose, help put us on the right track. Among the divine benedictions given to the Patriarchs, the promise of kings was never excluded. Echoes of these are found on God's blessings upon Abraham and his family indicated in Gen 17,6,16 and Gen 35,11.[15] The tribe of Juda received a royal promise as suggested in the prophetic symbol of the sceptre as recorded in the *Testament of Jacob*.[16] According to Howard, most commentators and translators understand this passage as a messianic prophecy. For them, he observes, sceptre, and the ruler's staff and vv. 10b, 11-12 furnish evidence of royal imageries indicative of an earlier notion of the God-king in Israel.[17] Thus Juda provided this royal leadership in the

---

[13] G. W. Buchanan, The Consequences of the Covenant, NovT Suppl. 20, Leiden, Brill, 1970, pp. 56-57.

[14] See H.-W. Jüngling, Richter 19 - Ein Plädoyer für das Königtum. Stilistische Analyse der Tendenzerzählung Ri 19,1-30a; 21,25. AnBib 84, Rome, Biblical Institute, 1981, who, though pre-occupied with the stilistic structures of the pericope, makes an effort to demonstrate that in Judg 19 there is "eine pragmatische Rechtfertigung des Königtums", p. vii and also pp. 292f.

[15] See Howard, *art. cit.*, p. 21.

[16] Gen 49,10. Recall that in Yoruba tradition an *Oba* (king) acceeds to the throne on ground of his acquisition of the *are*, the sceptre derived from the divinity he is viceroy of.

[17] See Howard, "The Case for Kingship", pp. 22-23 for fuller details.

person of David from whose tribe the evangelists, Matthew and Luke see in Jesus the ultimate fulfillment.[18]

In the Book of Numbers, the Balaam Oracles (Num 24,7), once again, draw our attention to the promise of the rise of the supremacy of the king of Israel and the might of his kingdom over his enemies. Num 24,17 is yet another prophetic text which makes use of the regal imageries of star and sceptre to announce the divine promise. When one compares the texts of Genesis and Numbers, one sees that the promises often couched in prophetic oracles suppose that Israel would have her own kingdom whose king's rule, might and success would indicate God's choice and blessings. Thus, the king who holds the office is God's vice-regent. In Exodus, the lived experience of the people had made them to express the omnipotence of the one who caused wonders to happen within their history as Saviour (Ex 14,13). Later on, and in light of the divine prodigies wrought in their sight, Israel began to recognize God not only as Creator but also as King over all that exists (Zach 9,9; Ps 74,12). The existence of God meant for them that he acts and reigns. According to Isa 60,1//Ps 47,6-7, God holds a throne in heaven and the world is his footstool. So in a number of texts of the Hebrew Bible, God is spoken of as King. There are two formulas used by the authors of the Hebrew scriptures: (a) Yahweh as king of the gods, though rare, is found in Ps 95,3: "For Yahweh is a great god, a great king over all the gods"; and (b) Yahweh as king of Israel. The idea that Yahweh is king of Israel is attested in Judg 8,23; 1 Sam 8,7. In Isa 41,21; 45,6 Yahweh's kingship over Israel is given full expression. Pss 47,3; 93,1 and 97,1 depict God as king over creation. His kingship is expressed in his other attributes: He is a warrior-king; a conqueror of all forces of chaos (Ps 46; Isa 40,21-26) and the Saviour of those afflicted (Ps 22; 90; 126; Isa 9) and in the oracles of prophets Zephaniah and Amos, God is the Almighty Judge (Zeph 1,14-18; Amos 5-6). In Ps 22,28 kingship (*melukhah*) belongs to Yahweh who alone possesses the divine *malkhut*. In Ps 29,10, we read:

> Yahweh is enthroned since the flood. Yea, Yahweh assumed the throne as king for eternity. Yahweh will give his people strength. Yahweh will bless his people with wellbeing.

---

[18] See Matt 1,1-6: "The Book of the genealogy of Jesus Christ the son of David, the son of Abraham. ... and Jesse the father of David the king".

According to J. Gray, this is one of the enthronement Psalms in which the reign of God is explicitly depicted. The song sung at the autumn festival of Yahweh (Judg 21,19; Hos 9,5) fetes the kingship of Yahweh during the covenant renewal feast. The installed Yahweh is pictured settled on the throne since after the catastrophe of the Flood. He rules for eternity and provides his people, *le àmmo*, (the sacral community) with the gift of *shalom*, material wellbeing and the gift of strength. His installation marks the renewal of nature's bounty.[19] Thus, God' s Almighty power is variously sung in the Enthronement Psalms. Ps 89,6-19 affirms the kingship of God and lauds his victory over the unruly waters.[20] In vv. 10-13, creation is shown as the sign of the order and government of the Divine King. This notion re-stated in Ps 93,1, is represented as a function of the Reign of God. The Psalms of kingship are usually hymns of praises. In them, the psalmists praise, among other things, "Yahweh's mighty acts of vindication, his epiphany as an effective king and the establishment of his government, *mispat*",[21] often conceived in terms of judgement among his people.

7.2.2   JUDAISM

In the literature of early Judaism, the concept 'kingdom of God' or 'reign of God' rarely appears except in a few insignificant texts.[22] In these instances, J. Jeremias maintains that the concept is conceived as a not-yet event, and never thought of in spatial or static ideas but as a dynamic reality open towards a future realization.[23] And in pre-christian Jewish

---

[19] J. Gray, The Biblical Doctrine of the Reign of God, Edinburgh, T. & T. Clark, 1979, pp. 39-46.

[20] See *ibid.*, p.49.

[21] *Ibid.*, p. 71.

[22] See 2 Chron 13,8; Ps. 103 (cxii),19; Ps cxlv,11 and Obad 21.

[23] J. Jeremias, The Eucharistic Words of Jesus, London, New York, 1960, Second Rev. Edition p. 184; *idem.*, New Testament Theology, Part I, The Proclamation of Jesus, London, SCM Press, 1971, p. 98, n. 2. A recent re-statement of the futuristic character of the kingdom of God is made by J. C. O'Neill, "The Kingdom of God", a paper read at the 46th General Meeting of the SNTS, Bethel, Bielefeld, Germany, 29 July-2 August, 1991,

literature, the term was unknown. What is fundamental to early Judaism is the idea of God as king. In Jewish religious literature, the noun, *malkhut*, kingdom, is, as we have seen above, often associated with *melek*, king and it was usually applied to God. In the OT and other Jewish sources, *malkhut* and its cognates bear the meaning, *kingly rule* including the activity of the king himself and the exercise of his sovereign power. Gustaf Dalman had, in fact, confirmed this view since the late nineteenth century. According to him:

> There can no doubt whatever that in the Old Testament and in Jewish literature the word *malkut* when applied to God always means 'kingly rule'and never means 'kingdom', as if to suggest the territory ruled by him.[24]

A critical reader of the OT will discover that it is in the later books and actually late Judaism, that one can find the expression, kingdom of Yahweh and its associated cognates.[25] In the Ps of Solomon 4,21, it is stated:

> And thy goodness is upon Israel in thy kingdom. Blessed is the glory of the Lord, for he is our king.

In the same book in 17,1 it is written:

> O Lord, thou art our king for ever and ever. And the kingdom of our God is for ever over the nations in judgement.

In the Maccabean period, when there prevailed an intense expectation of the end; a further shade of meaning was attached to the concept of the kingdom of God in Judaism. In the Sibyline Oracles 3,47, the revelation states that

---

pp. 1-11. I acknowledge my indebtedness to the author who sent me the reworked manuscript in Frankfurt.

[24] G. Dalman, Die Worte Jesu mit Berücksichtigung des nachkanonischen jüdischen Schrifttums und der aramäischen Sprache, Band 1, Einleitung und wichtige Begriffe, Leipzig, J. C. Hinrichs'sche Buchhandlung, 1898, p. 77 or ET by D. M. Kay, The Words of Jesus Considered in the Light of Post-Biblical Jewish Writings and the Aramaic Language, Vol. 1, Introduction and Fundamental Ideas, Edinburgh, T.& T. Clark, 1902, p. 94.

[25] 2 Chron 13,8; Targ. Micah 4,7; Targ. Onk. Exod 15,18.

... then the mightiest kingdom of the immortal king shall appear over men.

It is Israel that is borne in mind in the oracle. In the War Scroll from Qumran (1 QM VI,6), the kingdom of God represents a period of change and transformation in the world. In this text, the covenanters employ the term, 'thy royal rule' to allude to the general concept and to refer however to the present judicial authority of God.[26] In his study on the Qumran texts, E. Lohse has sufficiently shown that the *berit malkhut*, the covenant of the kingship was invested in the pedigree of David and his descendants who shall ever acceed to it.[27]

In Jewish Liturgical sources in use before AD 70, there is no distinction made between the terms, kingdom and God's kingship. In the *Alenu* text, worshippers chant:

> Let them all accept the yoke of thy kingdom, and mayest thou become king over them speedly, for ever and ever ... for the kingdom is thine, and for ever thou wilt reign in glory.[28]

In the liturgical service for the New Year, *Melok 'al kol-ha 'olam*, God's kingship and kingdom is praised. The text reads:

> ... and whatsoever has breadth in its nostrils may say, The Lord God of Israel is king, and his kingdom rules over all.[29]

Also in the *18th Benedictions*, God is addressed as King.[30] Thus, as it stands, these texts show that in late Judaism, God's kingship was unquestionably acknowledged and proclaimed. It must however be stressed that Judaism made a distinction between two aeons (ages) in its

---

[26] P. Pokorny, The Genesis of Christology. Foundations for a Theology of the New Testament, ET by M. Lefébure, Edinburgh, T. & T. Clark, 1987, p. 17, n. 12.

[27] E. Lohse, Die Texte aus Qumran. Mit masoretischer Punktation, München, Kösel, 1964, pp. 245ff.

[28] S. Singer, *'Alenu.* 19th Ed. 1946, p. 77. For the first portion of the parayer, see Pokorny, The Genesis of Christology, pp. 16-17.

[29] Melok 'al kol-ha 'olam, New's Service, in Singer *op. cit.*, p. 24.

[30] Cf. Buchanan, Consequences, p. 60.

146

conception of the reign of God; namely the present age and the future age.[31] In the Book of
Daniel, for example, this dual view of 'divine kingship' appears quite distinct. Dan 4,34
though put in the mouth of Nebuchadnezzar, makes allusion to the reign of God in the
present age. The text states:

> I praised and honoured him who lives for ever; for his dominion is everlasting
> dominion, and his kingdom endures from generation to generation.

Much earlier, in Dan 2,44 we read:

> And in the days of those kings the God of heaven will set up a kingdom
> which shall never be destroyed, nor shall its sovereignty be left to another
> people. It shall break in pieces all these kingdoms and bring them to an end,
> and it shall stand for ever.

The idea expressed here concurs with Dan 4,3,34 on the fact that the promised kingdom will
endure for ever. The motif is re-utilized in Daniel's vision of what looked "like a son of
man" (Dan 7, 13-14) whose authority would last forever and his kingdom be eternal. On a
rather generic sense, the kingdom shall be set upon "the people of the saints of the Most
High" (Dan 7,27).

7.2.3   CONCLUSIONS

Thus, the available sources show that in Jewish thought, the kingdom of God was conceived
as a coming reign of God. This is tied to the idea of the deliverance of Israel as the people
of God with the eventual re-establishment of the rule of the house of David in Jerusalem.
The psalmists, the liturgical imprecations and the later books, all lay stress on the fact that
Yahweh is the sovereign, the King whose kingly activity is known in history. As N. Perrin
has put it,

---

[31] See F. Nwachukwu & C. U. Manus, "Forgiveness and Non-Forgiveness in Mt 12,31-
32: Exegesis against the Background of Early Jewish and African Thought-Forms"
forthcoming in *ATJ* 21(1992).

Kingship of God is a symbol with deep roots in the Jewish consciousness of themselves as the people of God. Then it functions within the context of the myth of God active in history on behalf of his people.[32]

It is in the light of this Jewish perspective that Jesus' preaching on the concept has its deep background, of course, with its own distinctiveness. To deepen our knowledge of the historical Jesus studied in the previous chapter, I now turn to his idea of the kingdom of God. In the words of Jon Sobrino, "the most certain historical datum about Jesus' life is that the concept which dominated his preaching, the reality which gave meaningfulness to all his activity, was 'the kingdom of God'.[33] This insight further compels us to examine his kingdom preachings.

7.3   THE NT : JESUS' PREACHING AND THE KINGDOM OF GOD
7.3.1   INTRODUCTION

Generally NT scholars and virtually all biblical theologians agree that the central theme in Jesus' proclamation is *he Basileia tou Theou*, the kingdom of God.[34] In the entire NT books, the term with its equivalent, *Basileia twn ouranon*, kingdom of heaven, appears 85 times.[35] Of this number, 63 occur in the Gospels as the very words of Jesus in the following

---

[32] N. Perrin, Jesus and the Language of the Kingdom: Symbol and Metaphor in New Testament Interpretation, London, SCM Press, 1976, p. 32.

[33] J. Sobrino, Christology at the Crossroads. A Latin American Perspective, ET by John Drury, New York, Orbis, 1985 8th Ed., p. 41.

[34] Pokorny, The Genesis of Christology, p. 15.

[35] The form "kingdom of heaven" is much preferred by Matthew where it appears 31 times. It reflects a periphrastic expression employed to substitute the Holy Name. Scholars have argued themselves out as to which form Jesus used in his preachings. Jeremias has argued that prior to Jesus' ministry, the term *Basileia ton ouranon* appears no where in Jewish sources. According to him, it was not until R. Johanan ben Zakkai (c. AD 80) did the term come to be used for the first time in Jewish literature. Thus, Jeremias, concludes that Jesus could not have used an unknown and non existent term. For Jeremias, Jesus had no cause to avoid using the word "God" in teaching. Its preponderant use in Matthew "may be secondary", he opines. For his views, see Jeremias, New Testament Theology, pp. 9-10; 97.

148

order: Mark, 13 times; Q, 9; Matthew, 27; Luke, 12 and John, 2 times. In the Synoptic gospels, the term has been given various shades of meaning by the evangelists. Best rendered "reign" or "rule" of God, it is scarcely employed by non Synoptic authors.[36] It is largely found in sayings attributed to Jesus. Many of Jesus' parables illustrate the nature of the Reign of God such as The Labourers in the Vineyard (Mt 20,1-10.), the entry requirements to and the feasting and eating that happen in the *Basileia tou Theou* (Mt 18,23-25 par). The Last Supper (Mk 14,22-25/Mt 18,11-12//Lk 13,28-29) is the apex of all the drinking and eating in the kingdom of God. Some of the sayings have been given apocalyptic meanings such as those found in Mk 9,42-48//Mt 18,6-9. In Luke-Acts, the term appears only 8 times. It is known once in the Letter to the Hebrews, once in James and twice in the Book of Revelation. In the non canonical literature, *The Gospel of Thomas*, for example, the term appears twice (GS 3,3,5). The near absence of the term in Christian literature of the Early Church may be suspicious. Perhaps, the term's eschatological connotations did not seem to win much of the interest of the Church which was by then getting more missionary conscious than in sedentary theologizing.

In the whole of Pauline epistolary literature, the kingdom language appears 10 times and mostly they are used in the context of his eschatology and paraenesis. In some eight instances, Paul employs the phrase, *Basileia tou Theou* to convey an idea of what God has/is/will do through Christ in human history and on behalf of his people.[37] Some of the texts refer to a future possession of the kingdom, others project the kingdom as a condition the faithful currently experiences. As in his other eschatological discourses, his use of the kingdom language betrays an already and the not-yet aspect of the concept. To my mind, Paul shares a similar perspective on the present and the future dimension of the kingdom with the tradition of Jesus as will be seen presently. In his futuristic view, Paul portrays the kingdom as a realm on earth. In this perspective, he talks of inheriting or being excluded from the kingdom due to ones conduct in the present (Gal 5,21; 1 Cor 6,9-10; 1 Cor 15,50). On another note, when Paul speaks of the kingdom as a reality of the present, he likens it to

---

[36] For a contrary view of this concept, see S. Aalen, "'Reign' and 'House'in the Kingdom of God in the Gospels" *NTS* 8(1961/62)215-246.

[37] It is most to the Thessalonian and the Corinthian churches that Paul handed these lessons. Cf. 1 Thess 2,11-12; 2 Thess 1,5-12; Gal 5,21; 1 Cor 4,20-21; 6,9-10; 15,50; Rom 14,17; Col 4,10-11.

a condition in the life of the Christian and as something one can witness or work for in the present. He however often spiritualizes the issue. Thus, it can be argued that for Paul, the real locus of the reign of God is in the life and character of the Christian on earth and the quality of change his life undergoes. The in-breaking of the messianic kingdom does not seem to challenge Paul so much. 1 Cor 15,24 points to this position and the attitude of Paul.

However, one distictive aspect of Paul's kingdom sayings is his view that the kingdom is a realm to which one can fully become a citizen only through the return of Christ (parousia) and the resurrection of the dead. The kingdom has a limited cosmic significance in Paul. It is an affair reserved to the Parousia and the eventual resurrection of the believers. For Paul, there is therefore need for moral and physical requirements which one must acquire to possessing the kingdom.

Apart however from this brief exposition of Paul's theology of the kingdom, the statistical analysis shows a preponderant occurence of the term in the First Gospel. How may one explain this phenomenon? Is it that Matthew's gospel has a "preferential option" for Jesus' teaching on the kingdom or is it that Matthew's Jesus has, more than his contemporaries, a clearer perspective of the kingdom of God about to dawn on the age? Though these questions be of exegetical interest, scholars agree that Matthew's prolific use of the term arises from his redactional work on the Second gospel (Mark). J. Jeremias, for example, notes that in five cases, Matthew "has inserted the term in the Markan text (Matt 13,19; 18,1; 20,21; 21,43; 24,14)".[38]

7.3.2   JESUS AND THE NEARNESS OF THE KINGDOM

Accepting the priority of the gospel of Mark as a generally acceptable working hypothesis, it is worthwhile to peruse Mark's programmatic proclamation of Jesus on the nearness of the reign of God. According to Mark 1,15:

> *kai legon hoti peplerotai ho kairos kai enggiken he Basileia tou Theou metanoeite kai pisteuete en to evanggelio.*

---

[38] J. Jeremias, New Testament Theology, Vol 1, p. 31.

and saying, "The time is fulfilled, and kingdom of God is at hand; repent, and believe in the gospel".

Even though recent exegesis has established the fact that in this verse, Mark provides us with his own summary of Jesus' entire work;[39] it can be maintained that here is Mark's reproduction of Jesus' manifesto of his mission. The text taken over by Matthew and Luke (Mt 10,7//Lk 9,2) conveys the central theme of Jesus' public teaching, that is, the dawn of the kingly rule of God. This is the imminence or actually the advent of the reign of God proclaimed as the dramatic announcement of good news (Isa 52,7). Matthew and Luke share Mark's logia or source about the proximity of the rule of God.[40] The tradition of the Q-Community represented in the Lord's Prayer plead for the dawn of the reign of God even though some authors see here Jesus'eschatological conception of the kingdom.[41] The community's wish is expressed in the petition: *eltheto he Basileia sou*, Thy Kingdom come (Mt 6,10//Lk 11,2). The in-breaking of the kingdom becomes a visible reality when demons are cast out by "the finger of God" (Lk 11,20).

The narratives on the macarisms of Mt 5,3,10//Lk 6,20b and Jesus' encounter with the *paidia*, the children and his blessing of them (Mk 10,14//Mt 19,14/ Lk 18,16) reflect the status of those who belong to the kingdom of God. In the commissioning sermons of the early Church, the injunction to preach the kingdom of God and to proclaim its eventual

---

[39] R. Bultmann, Die Geschichte der synoptischen Tradition, 8. Aufl. Göttingen, Vandenhoeck u. Ruprecht, 1970, pp. 124, 132; Jeremias, New Testament Theology, p.96; Gray, The Biblical Doctrne of the Reign of God, p. 320; Kasper, Jesus The Christ, p. 72; G. van Oyen, De Summaria in Marcus en de compositie van Mc. 1,14-8,28 SNTA 12, Peeters, Leuven University Press, 1987, pp. 44-52; 129-153; F. J. Matera, "The Prologue as the Interpretative Key to Mark's Gospel" *JSNT* 34(1988)3-20; M.-S. Kim has also commented that the coming of the kingdom of God (Mk 1,15) is as Bultmann has opined "ein Summarium der Predigt des irdischen Jesus". Cf. M.-S. Kim, Die Trägergruppe von Q-Sozialgeschichtliche Forschung zur Q-Überlieferung in den synoptischen Evangelien, Hamburg, Verlag Peter Jensen, 1989, p. 72.

[40] Mk 1,15//Mt 4,17 and Mk 9,1 par.; Mt 10,7 par. Lk 10,11. Here, it is noteworthy to see J. Lambrecht, "John the Baptist and Jesus in Mark 1,1-15. Markan Redaction of Q?, a paper read at the 46th General Meeting of the SNTS, Bethel, Bielefeld, Germany, 29 July-2 August, 1991, pp. 1-22, pp. 5-7; + the Footnotes pp. 24. I remain grateful to the author and my former teacher who later sent the revised manuscript to me in Frankfurt.

[41] See for example, M. Burrows, "Thy Kingdom Come", *JBL* 74(1955)1-8.

nearness remained a major item on the agenda (Mt 10,7//Lk 9,2; 10,9). Even the Reign of God has its own secrets. The right to penetrate this arcane is only given to the disciples (Mk 4,11-12). It is a power only realizeable through the practice of exorcisms (Mt 12,28//Lk 11,20).

7.3.3   THE NATURE OF THE KINGDOM OF GOD

According to the gospel of Mark, the kingdom of God is *musterion*, a mystery (Mk 4,11). In those sayings of Jesus in which "this generation" is addressed, the "kingdom of God" reflects a conglomerate of people among whom are included the recalcitrant "men of this generation".[42] According to the Synoptic evangelists' understanding of the nature of the kingdom of God, it developes from tiny hidden beginnings like a Mustard Seed (Mk 4,30-32 par.); a seed perhaps the size of the African Iroko tree which later grows into a huge tree as the years roll by. If so, the kingdom is self-propagating as in the woman's leaven.[43] Like in the Greco-Roman setting of Mark taken over by the Jewish-Hellenist Christian community of Matthew (Mk 9,19//Mt 12,19); the nature of the kingdom implies a new reality which has broken into human history.[44] Jesus' perspectives on the nature of the dawning reign of God is well illustrated in four types of his sayings; namely those with (a) the subject of verbs of coming, (b) those with the object of the verbs of entering; (c) those insisting on the kingdom as a thing of search and struggle and (d) those showing the kingdom as a locale where a banquet is hosted. What then may one understand from this imprecise portrayal of the nature of the kingdom of God? J. P. Brown proffers an answer. According to him, "in the first group of sayings, the kingdom of God is presented as a quasi-autonomous reality whose arrival is being announced".[45] The second stanza of the Lord's Prayer, "Hallowed be thy name, thy kingdom come" (Lk 11,2//Mt 6,9) and Jesus' mandate to his disciples on mission

---

[42] Lk 7,31-34.

[43] Lk 13,18-21.

[44] J. P. Brown, "Kingdom of God" in Eliade et al. (eds.), The Encyclopedia of Religion, Vol 8, pp. 304-312, p. 307.

[45] *Ibid.*

to heal those who are sick and say to them, "The kingdom of God has come near to you" (Lk 10,9) can be correlated to assert that Jesus assured his audience of the "inhistorization" of the Reign of God. In Lk 17,20-21 Jesus states:

> ... The kingdom of God is not coming with signs to be observed; nor will they say, 'Lo, here it is!' or 'There!' for behold, the kingdom of God is in the midst of you

The numerous accounts of healing miracles by Jesus and his disciples, the victory over the powers of demons, especially the vanquishing of the oppressive, destructive anti-social forces which pontificated as Legion (Mt 5,9) and the condemnation of all vices arising from wealth and its inordinate pursuit described with the Semitic imagery, *Mammon*, riches (Lk 16,13), represent Jesus as the harbinger of God's sovereignty so eagerly awaited by many. Forgiveness is a condition attached to the performance of Jesus' healing miracles. In Mt 9,2; Mk 2,5; Lk 5,20 - all the healed persons are at the same time pardoned of their sins. Thus, forgiveness constituted an integral part of the programme of the new order. It heralded a new aspect of revelation of the nature of the kingdom of God now come in the midst of humanity. The Parable of the Prodigal Son (Lk 15,11-32) is a typical illustration of divine mercy and forgiveness. Concluding his comment on Lk 15,11ff, Gray states: "... this parable is the proclamation par excellence of Divine rehabilitation".

Since the kingdom is come, that is, as a reality broken into history, it must be *peopled*. Jesus' second portion of sayings describe the criteria for the acquisition of its citizenship. One must behave like the poor. This "preferential option" for the poor is expressed negatively in Jesus' statement: "It is easier for a carmel to go through the eye of a needle than for a rich man to enter the kingdom of God".[46] In a few verses before this logion, Jesus makes a positive remark on the criteria for belonging to the kingdom of God. In Mk 10,14-15, he says: "Allow the children to come to me and do not forbid them, for of such is the kingdom of God".[47] The kingdom has thus a lowly beginning. The child in its simplicity is the example of its growth and development.

---

[46] Mk 10,25. Here is in no way a condemnation of wealth as such but the ill pursuit and abuse of it.

[47] See Mt 18,13-14//Jn 3,3-5.

The kingdom of God is a classless society. The tax collectors and harlots acquire citizenship and enter the kingdom even before those who deem themselves righteous.[48] There is room in the kingdom of God for the socially handicapped people (Mk 9,42); the oppressed and the marginalized persons (Mt 5,10) and all those who suffer tribulations of all forms: from structural injustices such as those pepertrated by the leaders of many unjust regimes of our age as in colonial Palestine of Jesus' day. In his Sermon on the Plain, Luke and the community he represents transmit to us Jesus' macarism: "Blessed are you poor for yours is the kingdom of God";[49] and in Mt 5,10:

> Blessed are those who are persecuted for righteousness' sake, for theirs is the kingdom of heaven.

Thus, the Beatitudes which proclaim a reversal of fortunes stress the rehabilitation of the down-trodden faithful; and to stimulate a new ethic, they are begun and ended with a reference to the kingdom of God. As a new order, the Reign of God involves the end of sorrow and suffering (Mt 11,5//Mk 2,19) and so in Isa 61,1f; 65,19. Among other things, death is vanquished in the kingdom of God (Lk 20,36); Isa 25,8. These conquests reflect the victory of the Divine king in traditional Judaism. To ensure the dawn of the Reign of God in his own time, Jesus pursues his healing miracles in earnest. He inaugurates a new programme of rehabilitation and re-creation typical of the king of the old times, indeed a restoration of Israelite community as we are being told by contemporary Jesus scholars. The Beatitudes, otherwise known as the charter of the subjects of the kingdom (Mt 5,3,10), consist of Jesus' rehabilitation programme. In the execution of this new order, he renews the physical, mental and spiritual wellbeing of man. Throughout his ministry, Jesus makes it his major preoccupation to vindicate the poor, the needy and the righteous. He engages himself in the provision of food for the hungry and for those in want in times of shortages. He feeds five thousand peasant poor in the open ground. Luke gives expression to Jesus' immediate solution to such human problems.

---

[48] Mt 21,31.

[49] Lk 6,20.

154

Blessed are you that hunger now, for you shall be satisfied (Lk 6,21a).

Both Markan and Lukan Jesus teaches that possession of the citizenship of the kingdom is a future reward for the poor, the hungry and those who mourn.[50] The injunction to show love to one's enemies is a condition to possessing "nationality" of the kingdom. In these set of sayings, there is clearly implicated the "servant" role of Jesus; a role he enjoins on all who belong to and identify with his movement. To capture the level of appreciation the early church had shown on the criteria for acquisition of citizenship of the kingdom of God, one needs examine the reformulations of such criteria in legal terms. Entry into the kingdom became based, for example, on the keeping of two top commandments; namely the Law of Love of God and Love for one's fellow men and women (Mk 12,38-34); readiness to show persistence (Lk 9,62); to do the will of God (Mt 25,34) to render service to Christ whose face is hidden in the plight of the poor and the weak in society (Mt 25,34); to live above board (Mt 5,20); and in Pauline perspectives, to avoid certain obnoxious evils (1 Cor 6,9-10; Gal 5,21). For Paul, the kingdom of God is not a place for eating and drinking but a place where righteousness, peace and joy in the Holy Spirit prevails.[51] Besides, the kingdom of God is, for Paul, the Christians' true home, "our commonwealth" (Phil 3,20). In 1 Cor 6,9; Eph 5,5; 1 Cor 15,50 the faithful are enjoined to "inherit the kingdom". In Col 4,11, we encounter the expression "fellow workers for the kingdom of God". Exegetes agree that Paul here suggests that the kingdom of God is a reality whose full realization awaits the application of a communal effort.

7.3.4   THE TIME ORIENTATION OF THE KINGDOM

In the kingdom sayings of Jesus, commentators agree that there prevails a certain ambiguity with respect to the timing of the dawn of the kingdom. While the kingdom is said to have come, it is also represented as coming in some future time (à la O'Neill). In Mk 9,1, Jesus advised his disciples that the kingdom would come with power within a generation. The

---

[50] O'Neill, "The Kingdom of God", pp. 5-6.

[51] Rom 14,17//1 Cor 4,20.

Lord's Prayer enjoins the disciples, as we have seen earlier, to pray to God: "hallowed be thy name. Thy kingdom come" (Mt 6,9-13//Lk 11,1-4). In some of his speeches, Jesus gives the impression that the kingdom of God is a present reality. The expression "... the kingdom is in your midst" reflects this ambivalence. Thus the Synoptic reader is moved on a scenario of the *nearness* of the kingdom through its *yet* and its *not-yet* dimensions. How does one reconcile these tensions? Could the discrepancy arise from a mixed conception of the nature of the kingdom on the part of Jesus? Had he no clear-cut idea of the time of the emergence of the kingdom? Scholars have grappled with this difficulty in the texts in their efforts to render account of what Jesus means.

Commenting on the positions of some authors, N. Perrin states that J. Weiss[52] and A. Schweitzer[53] were the earliest scholars to demonstrate that Jesus proclaimed the futuristic aspect of the kingdom.[54] C. H. Dodd's major achievement, Perrin avers, is his argument that the parables teach that the kingdom of God is present in Jesus and realized in his ministry.[55] In a subsequent work, Perrin asserts that for Dodd, the central message of the parables was that the great crisis, the coming of the kingdom "is something present in the ministry of Jesus".[56] Other scholars have by-passed Dodd to re-affirm the future dimension of the kingdom of God in the teaching of Jesus (à la Weiss and Schweitzer). Some others however build on Dodd's findings but go on to assert that "the kingdom of God is both present and future in the teaching of Jesus".[57] According to the views of scholars Perrin had reviewed, Mk 1,15 and 9,1 have a future reference pointing towards the coming kingdom. They even suggest that the Dominical Prayer: Thy kingdom come (Lk 11,2e) and the Lord's

---

[52] J. Weiss, Die Predigt Jesu vom Reich Gottes, Göttingen, Vandenhoeck und Ruprecht, 1892; ET: Jesus' Proclamation of the Kingdom of God, by R. H. Hiers and D. L. Holland, London, 1971.

[53] A. Schweitzer, The Quest of the Historical Jesus, London, Adam and Charles Black, 1954.

[54] Perrin, Jesus and the Language of the Kingdom, p. 37.

[55] C.H. Dodd, The Parables of the Kingdom, London, Nisbet, 1935; 1948 2nd Edition; cited in Perrin, The Kingdom of God in the Teaching of Jesus, London, SCM Press, 1963, pp. 73, 78.

[56] Perrin, Jesus and the Language of the Kingdom, p. 38.

[57] See Perrin, The Kingdom of God, p. 79f on the positions of other scholars.

156

Spper (Mk 14,25) indicate the futurity of the kingdom. For them too, the verbs of "entering" and "receiving" employed by Jesus to describe who shall possess the kingdom point toward its realization as a future event.[58] As Perrin goes on to inform us, both Guy and Fuller demonstrate with some measure of conviction that the "parables of growth" in Mk 4,1-9; 23-29; 30-32//Mt 13,24-30,33 par. imply that the real moment of the kingdom is yet to come.[59] Perrin and his avalanche of scholars dwell so much on the future aspect of the kingdom. Could Perrin's sympathy with the crop of scholars who defend a futuristic dimension explain his interest in claiming that the kingdom of God reflects a *symbol* in Jesus' usages? Perrin and his mentors tend to forget that Dodd was the earliest to assert that the ministry of Jesus heralds into the world of men a new age in which the kingdom of God reflects God's grace and judgment. According to him, in this new age, there is need for a moral ideal, at least, for the "citizens" of the kingdom who must live their lives in the presence of God's grace and judgment now made manifest in Jesus.[60]

Jeremias goes further beyond Dodd's original insight. He syncopates the ideas of Weiss-Schweitzer and Dodd by proposing that the lesson of the parables show that the kingdom has both present and future dimensions culminating into a future crisis.[61] In his German version of *The Parables of Jesus*, he claims that there is a *sich realisierende(n) Eschatologie*, an "eschatology that is in process of realization".[62] For him, the future character of the kingdom are seen in the parables which see in the distant future the fulfillment of what has started to occur in the present in which man's hope is raised. The second group are those parables which allude to a future expectation of an imminent catastrophe on which the present is a moment of serious crisis. The four contrast-parables belong to the first group. All of them portray the unwevering lesson that the divine hour has dawned. Included in this group would be the Parable of the Unjust Judge and the Friend at

---

[58] O'Neill seems to me to represent this school of thought. And so *ibid.*, p. 7.

[59] See Perrin, The Kingdom of God, pp. 80-81 and the useful notes on the studies of these authors.

[60] Dodd, The Parables of the Kingdom, p. 109.

[61] Jeremias, The Parables of Jesus, London, SCM Press, 1954, pp. 81; 89-92; 93-99.

[62] *Idem.*, Die Gleichnisse Jesu, 1960, 5th Ed., p. 194.

Midnight. These two reflect, among other things, the unchanging assurance of the dawn of the future and lay emphasis upon God's mercy towards his people. The near approach of catastrophe is even depicted in the Parable of the Children in the Market-place (Mt 11,16-19//Lk 7,31-35) and other sayings about the Signs of the Times (Lk 12,54-56). In his second volume, *Jesus and the Language of the Kingdom*, Perrin comes to accept that the kingdom of God has both present and future orientation in the teaching of Jesus. He sums up his opinion on the enigma as follows:

> ... in the message of Jesus there is a very real tension between the kingdom as present and the kingdom as future, between the power of God as known in the present and the power of God to be known in the future.[63]

Whether the kingdom of God be conceived as an apocalyptic and imminent reality (Weiss, Schweitzer)[64] or in Dodd's perspective as a realized eschatology or in Bultmann's conception of it as *Zukunft und Zukommendes* (a future and coming) reality in human existence or as Jeremias' eschatology in the process of realization or as a "proleptic eschatology" of R. H. Fuller;[65] what indeed matters is what meaning, not the debate about the nature of the time, does Jesus' preaching on the kingdom bear for African Christians who hear these texts read in their churches, bible classes and homes? What African Christians consider relevant is how to live out in their everyday life the message of Christ about the kingdom already in their midst, the requirements necessary to become a citizen of the kingdom; and its practical consequences in their daily and concrete experiences of suffering in poverty, bad leadership and underdevelopment. For many Africans, traditional kingdoms had offered man a sense of collective survival and cohesion, protection, spiritual and physical

---

[63] Perrin, Jesus and the Language of the Kingdom, p. 40.

[64] Here, see P. Pokorny, The Genesis of Christology, p. 19 who recognizes in the verbs expressing the proximity of the kingdom of God as having their roots in "the apocalyptic imminent expectation" typical of both the Maccabean period and the time of the Jewish War. For Pokorny, Jesus conceived the kingdom as operative in the present even though his preaching is couched "in prophetic-eschatological rather than apaocalyptic terms".

[65] R. H. Fuller, The Mission and Achievement of Jesus, 1954, pp. 26, 32 cited in Perrin, The Kingdom of God in the Teaching of Jesus, pp. 65; 86-87.

wellbeing.[66] Having embraced Christianity and having received the gospel of Christ, the Africans now accept that their traditional value systems are redeemed by the Christ event, and their cultures constitutive of the heritage of the kingdom of God preached by Christ. And given the precarious living conditions and the low life expectancy in Africa, the *present* dimension of the kingdom endears more to the African faithful. What God is doing in the *present* through Christ remains an essential focus of interest by Africans on the goodnews of the kingdom. The present is, for Africans, the time for which *The Lord's Prayer* is intended and most vigorously evoked for it in the present that they bear their crosses of undernourishment and suffering.

I believe that what the scholars passed in review had not taken serious count of is the conception of the kingdom of God in Jesus' own *Sitz im Leben* and tradition at which level the *present* character of the kingdom was taught *vis à vis* the *intentio Evangelii* at which level, after the parousia was not forthcoming as hitherto expected, the futuristic aspect became emphasized. These two levels of the development of NT traditions should not escape us, otherwise propositions about the time of the kingdom will ever remain sterile and mere empty talk. In the next chapter, effort will be made to elucidate how the evangelists had so embellished the Jesus traditions in order to portray his kingship as both a present and future reality. In other words, I will attempt to show that when the proclaimer became proclaimed, his proclamation had become propounded beyond the original proclamation.

7.3.5   THE PARABLES OF THE KINGDOM

As is seen from the foregoing discussion, the kingdom of God constitutes the theme of many of Jesus' parables; that is, those earthly stories with heavenly meanings which he speaks.[67] God's kingdom is illustrated as an object of desire and want for which one should diligently search and struggle. One is enjoined to "seek first God's kingdom" after which all other things shall be added (Lk 12,31). The cost of acquiring citizenship is however high. In

---

[66] Cf. G. H. Muzorewa, The Origins, And Development of African Theology, New York, Maryknoll, Orbis, 1985, pp. 85-86.

[67] C. H. Dood, The Parables of the Kingdom.

Matthew, Jesus tells us that the kingdom is already present in his thought and teaching. This is well expressed in the following parables: The Treasure hidden in a field and The Pearl of great price which only the wise can find (Mt 13,44-46); The Tower-builder and the King going to War (Lk 14,28-32); The Fig Tree (Mk 13,28 par.) and The Light under a Bushel (Mk 4,21 par.).[68]

Following Gray and others before him, the four parables of contrast which Jesus addresses to his hearers can be isolated and categorized: the Mustard Seed (Mk 4,30-32//Mt 13,31-32//Lk 13,18-19), the Leaven (Mt 13,33//Lk 13,20-21); the Seed Growing Secretly (Mk 4,26-29) and the Sower (Mk 4,3-8//Mt 13,3-8//Lk 8,5-8). The first two parables show a contrast between small beginnings seen in the gigantic growth of the mustard shrub and the leaven which, without any human support, the dough swells far larger than the original stuff. The seed growing secretly illustrates a similar kind of development independent of human effort inspite of simple beginnings. In the case of the Sower, the final harvest is rich despite several obstacles at its growth. Jesus uses these parables, mainly the last two on the motif of harvest as parables of promise. As Gray correctly concludes: "They emphasize the irresistible progress of the purpose of the Divine King despite apparently insignificant initial resources and out of proportion to human effort".[69] In sum, these parables provide us insight into the certainty of the realization of God's purpose beyond the limitations of human effort and its associated handicaps and shortcomings.[70] For Pokorny, they are all "parables of growth". Besides the lessons given above, they remind us that the present calls for a time of decision and inner *metanoia*, conversion. To sum up this unit, Pokorny's remark on these parables is worthy of note. According to him, one discovers that the parables urge that:

> Now is the seed being sown, now is the leaven being put into the dough, now are the parables narrated and heard, now can we know what the future brings.[71]

---

[68] N. Perrin, The Kingdom of God in the Teaching of Jesus, p. 74; for a fuller outline see, *idem*; Jesus and the Language of the Kingdom: Symbol and Metaphor in New Testament Interpretation, p. 41.

[69] Gray, The Biblical Doctrine of the Reign of God, p. 331.

[70] Here see also, Perrin, Jesus and the Language of the Kingdom, p. 34.

[71] Pokorny, The Genesis of Christology, p. 19.

7.3.6   THE KINGDOM AS HARVEST

The harvest motif briefly touched upon above needs some further explanations. The motif introduces us into some aspect of the nature of the Reign of God. That God's kingly rule is visualized as harvest can be gleaned from its depiction in Jesus' saying in Mt 9,37//Lk 10,2:

> Then he said to his disciples, "The harvest is plentiful, but the labourers are few".

The extent of *Therismos*,(harvest) urges Jesus on to engage in mission himself and to proclaim the good news of the kingdom. Among the activities of Jesus and those of the required *ergatai* (workers) include the healing of the sick (Mt 9,35). For Luke, it involves the cooperation of all the seventy-two (Lk 10,1). The harvest in these texts as well as in Jn 4,35:

> Do not say, 'There are yet four months, then comes the harvest'? I tell you, lift up your eyes, and see how the fields are already white for harvest.

is quite symbolic of the realization of God's positive purpose in salvation history. To further understand the richness of the harvest motif in the kingdom speeches of Jesus, one needs only reflect how John develops the idea. For the Fourth evangelist, those who reap the harvest in Jesus' time crown the labours of those who have gone before such as the prophets and the others until John the Baptizer.[72]

    Within the scope of the significance of the parables of the kingdom, we must not lose sight of the dynamic grace of God shown in the fact that the kingdom lies beyond men and women's manipulation or determination irrespective of their personal efforts. Jesus gives the Parable of the Vineyard (Mt 20,1-16) to illustrate this situation. Though quite often interpreted in various forms, it is a parable of the kingdom. It reminds us that those who respond to God's challenge to service and cooperation in the harvest even though they

---

[72] And so Gray, p. 332.

engage themselves at the eleventh hour "are" as Gray rightly opines, "no less welcome than those who have long since responded".[73]

7.3.7   THE UNIVERSALIST DIMENSION OF THE KINGDOM

The extent of the kingdom of God is far-flung. In Jesus' thought, it extends beyond "the house of Israel". In what I may term a reprimand on Israel transmitted in Mt 8,11-12//Lk 13,28-30, Gentile converts are promised participation in the end-time banquet with Abraham in the kingdom of God. This open-door character of God's kingdom is the spirit of the Parable of the Feast found in Mt 22,1-14//Lk 14,16-24 and in GS 64. The gospels are redolent with narratives in which Jesus extends this spirit of openness to people of other races. And the huge success of Christian mission in the Third World and the associated conquests of evil forces through miracles and healings being wrought today by several divines in Africa in the name of Jesus support the fact that the Reign of God knows no limits.[74]

7.3.8   THE FATHERHOOD OF GOD

In Jesus' programme, the coming of the kingdom calls for a new way of relating to God as Father. Even though the components of the kingdom of God are so tenaciously taught by Jesus, he does not so often call God King. As is rightly expressed by Pokorny, "Jesus experienced God as Father and so addressed him".[75] Jesus uses the most culturally charged appellation *Abba*, Father as the Yoruba of Nigeria would say *Baba* to an elder as an address of respect to address God (Mk 14,36 par.). In the Lord's Prayer, he employs this local and rich concept to teach his disciples to call upon God (Mt 6,9/Lk 11,2). In trust and faith,

---

[73] *Ibid.*

[74] Cf. C. U. Manus, "Miracle Workers/Healers as Divine Men: Their Role in the Nigerian Church and Society", *AJT* 32(1988)658-669.

[75] Pokorny, The Genesis of Christology, p. 24.

162

Jesus opens his heart to God as his father and teaches his followers to do same. Thus faith becomes a *sine qua non* in possessing membership to the kingdom. On the centrality of faith in the events associated with the dawn of the kingdom, Pokorny advises:

> Faith is bound up with unexpected acts of succour and with miracles, because the person who submits to God in faith experiences his creative power which makes things new. Faith ... anticipates the kingdom of God as the new creation.[76]

7.3.9   THE SOCIAL NATURE OF THE KINGDOM

God alone possesses sovereignty in the kingdom. His kingdom is, no doubt, quite different from the African kingdoms we have already studied. The kingdom of God is not a secular power nor is it a political regime. This may explain why Jesus is silent about describing God as king in it. For Jesus, what is distinctively outstanding is the kingdom's social character. His sayings and deeds speak eloquently of the social aspect of the kingdom of God. In Mt 8,11 par. 22,1-14; Lk 14,16-24; GS 64 the social nature of the table fellowship is depicted. To enhance this aspect of the kingdom, Jesus allows himself to share meals and table conversations with sinners and those persons on the fringe of society (Mk 2,15-16 par; Lk 19,5-7; Mk 14,3-9 par; Lk 7,36-50; Jn 12,1-8). Jesus' socializing policy, in fact, knows no bounds. He freely mixes with tax-collectors and other people society regarded as outcasts. He eats and drinks and speaks well of all of them (Lk 7,34; Mt 11,19).[77] In the kingdom's social context, conversion from and forgiveness of sin occupy important places. In this manner, Jesus lets open the doors of the the kingdom of God to all kinds of men and women to enter and to share in its get-togethers and fellowships. His Last Supper represents a foretaste of the eschatological meal and fellowship in the kingdom of God Isa 25,6; 1 Enoch

---

[76] *Ibid.*, p. 25.

[77] Here, see G. N. Stanton, Jesus of Nazareth in New Testament Preaching, SNTS MS 27, Cambridge, London, 1974, p. 167.

62,14//Mk 14,25//Lk 22,16. In this light Pokorny is right to assert that "with Jesus the kingdom of God comes as gift and as promise".[78]

7.3.10   THE CONSEQUENCES OF THE DAWN OF THE KINGDOM

The mission of Jesus is tantamount to the prospect of the Reign of God in human history. Jesus' life work signals the irruption into history of the effective new order broached by the incarnation of the Son of God, the Messiah-king. His power and authority entail the transformation of situations and the transvaluation of decadent values people hitherto found solace in and the release of new energies as manifest in his prodigious saving acts. This new order (note, since the collapse of Communism in Eastern Europe, politicians now speak of the emergence of a new world order) ushered in the tearing down of all forces which separated men and women from God; those which dominated and subjected humanity in physical and spiritual travail, oppression and alienation (exorcisms). Even though R. Otto argues that Jesus shares with his contemporaries the eschatological and apocalyptic vision typical of the last century B. C. and the first century of the Common Era, he however recognizes the stress and the urgency the dawn of the Reign of God places on man, his hopes and fortunes.[79]

In the person of Jesus, the power of God as King is demonstrated. A new order really commences. Massive healing works became evidence of the arrival of the kingdom of God upon history (Mt 12,28//Lk 11,20). The verbs *engiken* and *ephthasen* in Mk 1,15 and Mt 12,28//Lk 11,20 indeed suggest that the kingdom of God has come (Dodd). It is also important to stress the qualitative sense of the two verbs. *Engiken* (has come near) contrasts with *ephthasen* (has arrived). *Ephthasen* supposes that the Reign of God is already there and that as such it demands immediate and radical response. As Gray correctly opines, "the imperatives in Mk 1,15 are noteworthy, truly reflecting the prophetic challenge of the

---

[78] Pokorny, The Genesis of Christology, p. 29.

[79] Cf. R. Otto, The Kingdom of God and the Son of Man, ET by F. V. Filson and B. L. Woolf, 1938, pp. 48, 54 cited by Gray, The Biblical Doctrine of the Reign of God, p. 319, n. 10.

dynamic Kingship of God".[80] Like in their master's work, the effects of the advent of the kingdom are evidenced in the mission of the disciples and their successes in healing the sick (Lk 9,2; 10,9) and Mt 10,7 where their mission was crowned with the raising of the dead, the cleansing of the lepers and the casting out of demons. Thus, the association of healing, the performance of good works and the provision of wellbeing reminiscent of African kings to their loyal subjects remain important values of kingship but now superseded by and fulfilled *par exellence* in the presence of the Messiah-King. The consequences of the in-breaking of the Reign of God is corroborated in the answer Jesus gave to the disciples of John the Baptizer upon his question: "Are you he who is to come, or shall we look for another?".[81] In sum therefore, among the dynamic consequences of the dawn of the Reign of God are *inter alia* liberation, deliverance, vengeance and judgment.[82]

7.3.11   CONCLUSIONS

My enquiry in this chapter reveals, among other things, that the concept of the kingdom of God belonged to the thought-world of the Ancient Near East and that it persisted in the OT, Judaism and the NT times. The OT understanding of Yahweh as King; especially as was enunciated in Isa 43,15; Pss 5,2; 10,16; 84,3 provides the basis for comprehending Jesus' conception of the kingdom. The belief in the kingship of a God who made history within the experiential circumstances of his people through his salvific interventions in times of crisis deepened the people's faith in God as King who would not allow his people to suffer under the yoke of the *goyim* - the gentile nations and their overlordship. This belief culminated into apocalyptic and messianic hopes as we have earlier on noted. Thus, the survey on the OT indicates that the *raison d'etre* of Jesus' preaching on the Reign of God, his call for conversion and change of heart was to prepare men and women for the dawn of a new order.

Though Jewish mind understood the dawn of the new age in terms of God's display of his omnipotence, Jesus proclaimed the Reign of God which breaks in as divine

---

[80] Gray, p. 321.

[81] Cf. also, Isa 35,5f; 61,1f.

[82] And so Gray, p. 324.

intervention. He stresses the need for a *metanoia* - repentance and change from the old values system. John the Baptizer, Jesus' forerunner, the last of the divine spokesmen, announces the arrival of the Reign of God in Jesus' person and admits that God has become one Being with his creation. The age to come, the acceptable year of the Lord, indeed God's kingdom has already commenced and is noticed in the events happening as preached in the sermon of Jesus to the Jews in Nazareth though completely difficult for them to comprehend. Though what Jesus rehearses is an old prophetic oracle (Isa 61), the manner he discloses what shall happen is quite different from what are expected by the audience (Lk 4,16-21).

The investigation further shows that Jesus proclaims the kingdom of God in a new and in an unprecedented manner even far beevolent that John the Baptist. God's kingdom is a realm of love, pardon, mercy and of the wellbeing of men and women (Lk 6,32; Mt 18,23-35). The nature of the kingdom Jesus proclaims is radically different from Jewish expectations. God's reign as Jesus teaches his hearers is without condemnation and hatred. Its entry and acquisition knows no barriers. Jesus' view of God's reign does not deny the kingdom its right to judge, acquit and to dispense. For Jesus, God's reign can arraign and judge those who do not put God first in their daily lives but only rely on their own capabilities. As Jesus discloses, God's reign brings new perspectives for sinners who refuse to accept the future of God who approaches in grace and for people graphically described by J. Sobrino as those "who refuse to anticipate that future reality in our here-and-now life".[83] This existential dimension or implication of the kingdom of God which Bultmann had earlier pointed out still ought to have impact in contemporary living, otherwise the idea of the kingdom would be merely an abstraction. Thus evidence before us shows that there is discrepancy in the OT, Judaism and Jesus' conception of God's kingdom. The criterion of dissimilarity supposes that Jesus' language about the Reign of God derives from *His-story* and not from the usages of the early church. In this light, it is important to devote special attention in the concluding chapter to the social-political implications of the kingdom of God. The reality of the kingdom of God provides men and women of all ages the vista to judge this world and to renew it through their total commitment to peace, justice, freedom; and as

---

[83] Sobrino, Christology at the Crossroads, p. 53.

an African theologian has put it, to "the covenant for the integrity of creation".[84] It behests all persons who live in the two-thirds world to engage themselves in honest labour and productivity in order to raise the living standards of their teeming population and to reject the installation of irresponsible, wicked and oppressive regimes to power.

It is discovered among other things that Jesus' unique achievement as a preacher of the kingdom of God is his disclosure of a new insight of the Godhead. From his healing acts, he reveals himself as a Son of God, the Messiah-king; a servant-king who is closer to men. In the prayer he teaches his disciples, he reveals God as *Abba*, the Father who, unlike in the ethnic religions of African kings, is the royal progenitor of all men and women (Mk 14,36a; Rom 8,15; Gal 4,6). As mankind's Father, God cares for the wellbeing of his children. The Fatherhood of God demands that we work in community to prosper his reign through sincere commitment on our part to issues relating to our common brotherhood in love, justice and fairplay (Mt 9,12//Lk 7,47). Thus, the conception of God as Father which Jesus stresses is quite revolutionary. According to Aalen:

> Nobody will deny that this implies a break with fundamental conceptions of Judaism, a revolutinary new emphsis of one particular side of the concept which Judaism had of God.[85]

The Reign of God manifests itself in action. As Jesus shows it, it challenges all of us to team up together (international cooperation not, of course, excluded) to renew the potentials of the diminishing resources of the here-and-now. Jesus' good works behest us to work together for better socio-political conditions for men and women of our times. Our personal and social contributions must be geared towards the prosperity and growth of the kingdom of God in the secular city. In the perspectives of contemporary discussions on 'Christology from below' the gospels show that what Jesus proclaims is vindicated in his life-style, a life-style which proves him the One Way for Christians to participate in the realization of God's eternal reign in our midst. To know who the father is, is to know who Jesus is. It is through his life work as Beloved Son of the God-King that the reality of God's kingdom can be achieved in our

---

[84] E. Kandusi, "Justice, Peace and the Integrity of Creation: A Perspective from Third World Theologians", *Scriptura* 39(1991)52-57, p. 56.

[85] S. Aalen, "'Reign' and 'House' in the kingdom of God in the Gospels", p. 218.

world. One thing special about the character of the kingdom of God is the fact that God is bringing about the ideal of the king of righteousness over the years longed for by the people. For the orientals, and for the Africans, kingly rule "in justice and peace" involves protection which traditional kings could offer. The status of Jesus, the Christ in the kingdom which he so ardently proclaims constitutes the task of the next chapter. Let us now turn to what the evangelists tell us about the early church's conception of Jesus' kingship.

CHAPTER EIGHT

THE KINGSHIP OF JESUS : SOME TEXTS AND THEIR EXEGESIS

8.1 INTRODUCTION

In the New Testament, the gospels, unlike in some Jewish literature, rarely speak of God as king. Is it not somewhat astonishing to an observant reader? I am inclined to commit myself to the opinion that the evangelists suppress as much as possible the appellation of God as king because they are out to portray through use of story-telling, legend and OT proof-texts that Jesus, the Son of God is the Messiah-king who had long been expected. There are however a few traditions left untouched. In what belongs to Jesus' *ipsissima vox*, God is described as king. In Mt 5,35, for example, teaching on the impropriety of false oath-taking, Jesus advices that "heaven" is God's throne; "earth his footstool" and "Jerusalem" the "city of the great King". In some parables, Jesus represents God as a king but sometimes one sees that due perhaps, to the redactional hands of the evangelists, the message of the picture-talk can still be assimilated inspite of the royalist character of the narratives.[1] In Jesus' thought and preaching, we have seen that the kingdom of God means kingship or royal power: the reign of God.[2] Certainly, if for Jesus it is God who is king and not himself, this is the reason why an exegetical analysis of the relevant texts constitutes the focus of this chapter. The purpose, among other things, is to discern what paradigms, "scripts" and portraits the evangelists who were confronted with the problem of the inculturation of the Christ event in their communities have bequeathed to us.

In this chapter, therefore, I propose to analyse seven pericopes in which the idea of Jesus as the beloved Son of God in the Davidic dynasty, the *ho erchomenos* (the Coming One) and the Messiah-king are the major motifs (8.2). My exposition of the narratives will

---

[1] See for example, The Parable of the Unmerciful Servant (Mt 18,23-35), The Marriage Feast or The Great Supper (Mt 22,1-14/Lk 14,15-24).

[2] See Aalen, "'Reign' and 'House' in the Kingdom of God", p. 217 who argues for the contrary view.

be presented in order to show how the early church whose faith experience is articulated in those passages conceived Jesus as their king. For want of space, I am limiting myself to the four gospels. However, as an exception to the rule, I will submit to exegetical scrutiny the readings for the *Feast of Christ the King* as found in the Roman Missal (8.3). It is hoped that the analysis will advance our knowledge on the idea and the nature of Jesus' kingship; and to what extent the evangelists have used the OT scriptures to butress their conception, contextualization and inculturational theology of the Christ event. The conclusion will sum up the keynote ideas of the texts studied and their contextual implications.

8.2   THE NEW TESTAMENT TEXTS
8.2.1   THE INFANCY NARRATIVES (Mt 1-2/Lk 1-2)

In their chapters 1-2, the gospels of Matthew and Luke introduce us to the incarnation of the royal Davidic Messiah-king.[3] The earthly Jesus, the man of Nazareth, was for Matthew, the expected royal Messiah from the house of David and the one who fulfilled the OT promises of God to Israel. From the very outset of his gospel, Matthew portrays Jesus in significant Christological titles: Messiah or *Christos*.[4] He is "Son of David" and "King of the Jews" - all emphasizing the fact of Jesus' Messiah-kingship. Matthew consciously employs these titles at the commencement of his gospel to inform members of his church of the divine origin of Jesus, their king and Lord. In Mt 1,1, Jesus is described as "Jesus Christ, the son of David, the son of Abraham" which is somewhat identical to Mark's "Son of God" (Mk 1,1). While Mark traces Jesus' sonship in the Godhead, "Matthew lays more emphasis on Jesus' Davidic

---

[3] The Fourth evangelist is quite vocal on the incarnation motif. In Jn 1,14, we read that "the Word became flesh and dwelt among us", in other words, as Kasper correctly exegetes the text, God "became this man, Jesus of Nazareth"; Kasper, *Jesus the Christ*, p. 198.

[4] See R. E. Brown, The Birth of the Messiah. A Commentary on the Infancy Narratives in Matthew and Luke, Garden City, New York, Image Books, 1979, p. 59. As Brown comments, *Christos* has its most orginal meaning as a translation of the Aramaic *"mesiha"* the messiah or "the anointed one", that is, the anointed king of the House of David".

descent than in his Abrahamic descent..."[5] Thus, Jesus' Christhood (Messiahship) is affirmed in virtue of his Davidic origin. Feeling that the epithet, "Jesus Christ" has become somewhat circumlocutionary, Matthew in 1,16 simplifies it, and with a qualifier formulates it as a throne-name: "Jesus, who is called Christ". And having felt that his addressees have known who is referred to, the evangelist goes on to adopt the non ambiguous title, *Christos*; Messiah (Mt 1,17). In Jn 1,49, Nathaniel, the representative of the true Israelite acknowledges the true king of Israel. Though he combines the two titles, he confesses Jesus as the King of Israel who, in virtue of his anointing, has become "Son of God".[6]

The genealogical table stresses the reality of David's kingship (Mt 1,6). As a means of undergirding sacred positions such as the offices of king and priest as our study of the African traditions show, Jesus' genealogy establishes him as the anointed King, the Messiah who fulfills God's promise to David (2 Sam 7).[7] In Luke, the genealogy starts out from Jesus through Adam and finally to God.[8] Like Matthew, Luke's interest is to show that Jesus has both human and divine origins.[9] The linking with Adam which generically means mankind and with God emphasizes the paradox. As R. H. Gundry opines, "The genealogy has become a large figure of speech for Jesus' messianic kingship".[10] In a similar vein, R. F. Collins concludes that "the purpose of the Lukan genealogy of Jesus is clearly theological - it serves to clarify to some degree the significance of Jesus' messiahship".[11] In Mt 2,2,

---

[5] *Ibid.* See also D. J. Harrington, "Jesus, the Son of David, the Son of Abraham ..."; Christology and Second Temple Judaism", *Irish Theological Quarterly* 57(1991)185-195, p. 185 who opines that with these titles "Matthew 's aim was to show that Jesus, the Son of David and of Abraham, came at the "right" time in Israel's history".

[6] Cf. J. N. Sanders & B. A. Mastin, A Commentary on the Gospel According to St. John, London, Adams and Charles Black, 1968, p. 103.

[7] See, Mt 1,2-17; Lk 3,23-38.

[8] Brown, The Birth of the Messiah, p. 84.

[9] *Ibid.*, p. 91.

[10] R. H. Gundry, Matthew. A Commentary on His Literary and Theological Art, Grand Rapids, Eerdmans, 1982, pp. 14-15.

[11] R. F. Collins, "Luke 3:21-22, Baptism or Anointing", *The Bible Today*, April 1976, pp. 821-831, p. 829.

Jesus is identified as the "King of the Jews" of whom David is a prototype.[12] Thus, for Matthew, it can be argued that Jesus is the Davidic Messiah. According to some exegetes, especially E. L. Abel, in tracing the royal lineage of Jesus, the evangelist draws attention to the kingly qualifications of the Messiah.[13] Mt 1,18-25 has been recognized as an expanded explanation made to demonstrate the fact "of the adoption of the divinely conceived Jesus into Davidic line of Joseph".[14] The divinity of Jesus is told in his birth story. Joseph, son of David (v.20) makes Jesus his son as he accepts Mary as wife prior to Jesus' birth. Mary becomes pregnant after her bethrothal to Joseph before her marriage to and cohabitation with him.[15] As Gundry states, "Mary bore a divine child as a result of generation by the Holy Spirit".[16] Jesus is divine. Joseph names the infant on his birth.

In chapter two of his gospel, Matthew carries forward his determined intorduction of Jesus as the Messiah-king whose birth arouses no small furore in the ruling House of Herod. The Magi, the wise and noble men from the East arrive, seek the locale where the "King of the Jews" is born (Mt 2,2). The enquiry is laid before Herod's household who is not a little upset. Herod immediately summons the religious leaders of the nation to dig into the scriptures and the prophets in order to tell him about the "Christ" (Mt 2,4). He is directed to check up in Bethlehem which old prophets had foretold as a city that shall produce "a ruler who will shepherd my people Israel" (Mt 2,6).[17] The visit and adoration of the Magi underline, according to Verseput, the fact that "the kingly theme is important to the Matthean christology".[18] It appears equally important to stress that the story enhances, as in

---

[12] M. D. Johnson, The Purpose of the Biblical Genealogies, NTS MS 8, London, Cambridge, 1969, pp. 153-279.

[13] E. L. Abel, "The Genealogies of Jesus ho Christos", NTS 20(1973/74)205-206.

[14] D. Verseput, The Rejection of the Humble Messianic King, A Study of the Composition of Matthew 11-12, Frankfurt/Main-Bern-New York, European University Studies 291, 1986, p. 23.

[15] Gundry, Matthew, p. 20.

[16] Ibid.

[17] Cf. F. Martin, "The Image of the Shepherd in the Gospel of St. Matthew", Sc Es 27(1975)272-274 cited by Verseput, The Rejection of the Humble Messanic King, p. 23.

[18] Verseput, ibid., p. 304.

the case of the Centurion of the Passion story, Gentile recognition of Jesus' kingship. Here, as elsewhere, the evangelist shows that Jesus' kingship contrasts fully with Herod's position. Jesus is "King of the Jews" while Herod was not a Jew but a foreign puppet installed into power by the colonial administration who ruled as an instrument of foreign domination.

Throughout his gospel, Matthew minces no words in depicting Jesus as the Messiah-king who is the fulfillment of Jewish messianic hopes. During the reign of the anointed king of the Davidic royal dynasty in Jerusalem, contemporary Judaism regarded the king as the Messiah and hoped on him to deliver Israel from her enemies or from unforeseen disasters. When the reigning king could not achieve such feats, such hopes were dashed and later transferred to his immediate successor. Isaiah's prophecy (Isa 7,14-17; 9,1-6; 11,1-9) reflects one such transfer of hope to yet an unborn royal child, most probably king Hezekiah as the *Immanuel*. As a consequence of the Babylonian Exile (587-539 BC), the Davidic monarchy came to an abrupt end; and there appeared no significant descendant to succeed to the ancient throne, not even from the Hasmonean dynasty. Thus, people looked forward to the emergence of an anointed king of an unspecified age "who would free his people and bring it glory and renown".[19]

This hope gave rise to the expectation of the Messiah, the divinely anointed eschatological ruler of the house of David who would prosecute the deliverance of his people. The Psalms of Solomon, composed about the middle of the first century BC, especially Ps 17 is eloquent on the situation. V. 21 sings:

> O Lord, raise up for them their king, the son of David, at that time in which you, O God, see that he may reign over Israel your servant.[20]

According to the Psalmist (vv. 21-46), this king will subdue foreign dominions, seize Jerusalem from the enemy, purge it of all heathen contamination, judge the tribes of Israel and rule the land in purity and in righteousness so that other nations of this world will come from their far and remote places to see his glory and to look on the glory of the Lord. On his rulership, v. 32 expatiates: He will rule as a righteous king who is taught by God

---

[19] E. Lohse, "huios David" *TDNT* 8(1972)478-488, p. 480.

[20] Text quoted from Brown, The Birth of the Messiah, p. 67, n.9.

himself. In his days, no wrong will be done, for all are holy and their king is the *Christos kyriou*, the Lord's Anointed.[21]

In the first and second century AD, mounting expectations of a son of David with these characteristics was quite current. The historical Jesus was depicted as this royal figure, if not for the Jews, at least for the Jewish Christian church.[22] For Matthew, Jesus' kingship was not in doubt at all. As we have seen above, he is son of David and belongs to the royal Davidic dynasty. As Lohse puts it, he is the second David, the Messiah in whom the Scriptures are fulfilled.[23] According to Matthew, this is the reason why Herod drives him into refuge in Africa (Egypt). This incident is for the evangelist, Jesus' first opposition as a royal contender. But inspite of all, Jesus is portrayed throughout the gospel as a humble king; a theme I will explore later in the study.

8.2.2 JESUS' ELECTION AND ANOINTING
(Mt 3,13-17/Mk 1,9-11/Lk 3,21-22/Jn 1,29-34)

From the discussion above, we note that Jesus appears at a time of intense Jewish eschatological hopes; a last chance as it were; a period whose urgency is suggested by the need for baptism of water unto repentance and the questions about the arrival of the Messiah (Lk 3,15). Among those who come along to submit themselves to the rite at the river Jordan is Jesus of Nazareth (Mk 1,9) as we have already noted. When he emerges from the water, he at once sees the heavens "opened" and the Spirit settles upon him in the form of a dove. Upon this, a voice is heard speaking from heaven

Thou art my beloved Son, with thee I am well pleased (Mk 1,11).

---

[21] Lohse, *ibid*; and my *"Jesu Kristi Oba"*, pp. 318-320.

[22] Recall the probable date of the composition of the Gospel of Matthew as within the time when the idea was already more than current.

[23] *Ibid.*, pp. 485-486.

The Markan narrative appears quite esoteric. Undoubtedly a celestial picture is portrayed. The opening of heaven, the descent of the Spirit and the voice of the Father reflect events of the last times that would herald the momentous choice and election of the king of the end-times.[24] It is in this context that Mark presents Jesus as the only Son of God, one fully chosen and whose Father approves of his programmes and activities.

In their own accounts, Matthew and Luke objectify what Mark has narrated subjectively. While in Mk 1,10 Jesus sees the heavens opened, in Mt 3,16//Lk 3,21 the heavens are opened. While the descent of the Spirit is a visual experience in both Mark and Matthew, Luke objectifies it: "the Holy Spirit descended" (Lk 3,22). Among the Synoptics, it is only Luke who describes the Spirit as "holy" and reports of his descent in physical form - "bodily form" (v. 22//Acts 2,3). In Mark and Luke, the celestial voice speaks in the second person singular "Thou art ...". In Matthew, the same voice is reported in the third person: "This is my beloved Son with whom I am well pleased" (Mt 3,17b). What can one make out of these minor agreements and disagreements? While I agree with most exegetes who recourse to Redaction Criticism for explanations, it is equally important to stress that Matthew sees in the event of Jesus' baptism an occasion for his own *presentation* of the *elected* Son of God, the anointed Messiah-king of Israel. In thus objectifying the event, Matthew informs his readers that God is saying to Jesus: the rite you are submitting yourself to has my fullest support and approval.

Once again, one needs to appreciate the level of contextualization and inculturation the evangelists initiated in the primitive church. While the tradition about Jesus' baptism is transmitted in the three Synoptic gospels, its historicity is not much doubted, not even by the most critical of exegetes.[25] But the demonstartion of the election of Jesus as the Messiah-king required to be "contextualized" through use of the OT proof-texts in order to show that Jesus fulfills the divine plan. Mark (the original composer) in doing exactly this, conflates

---

[24] E. Schweizer, "huios" *TDNT* 8(1972)363-392, p. 368.

[25] The Fourth evangelist does not report of Jesus' baptism, even if John spoke in his gospel of the baptism to come. In Judaism, there is no tradition that the expected Messiah would receive a baptism of water unto repentance.Inspite of these, the Synoptics however give us a historical event in the life of Jesus which each has told in his own manner in order to stress his own Christology. For a detailed treatment of these facts, see Collins, "Luke 3: 21-22", pp. 821-822.

more than one source here. The message from heaven is a combination of Ps 2,7 and Isa 42,1. In Ps 2,7 we read:

... He said to me, "you are my son, today I have begotten you".

And Isa 42,1 reads:

Behold my servant, whom I uphold, my chosen, in whom my soul delights;
I have put my Spirit upon him, he will bring forth justice to the nations

The fact is clear. In the LXX, the Bible of the early Christians in the Greco-Roman world, Mark replaces *pais mou* (my servant/child) of the text of Isaiah with *huios*, son. For Mark, the servant of Isaiah becomes Son of God.[26]

Certainly Mark's composition has, as usual, a Christological tendency. The Markan baptismal narrative portrays a Christological scenario which is similar in its literary form to the enthronement prophetic visions of the OT. Jesus is presented, in Mark here, as a royal figure upon whom the Spirit has come. Jesus is not any king, but the Messiah-king of the end-times. Besides, the baptismal narrative has its own literary function. It serves to prepare the readers, as in Matthew, towards an appreciation of Jesus'programmatic proclamation of the dawn of the Reign of God (Mk 1,14-15). For Mark, Jesus is not only the Messiah-king and Judge of the end-times, but he is the figure to be identified with the Suffering Servant of God. This is why he is son for Mark and his redactors. As stated earlier, though each evangelist has his own Christology to highlight with the baptismal story, one thing basic is that they all agree on the Messiahship of Jesus. For Luke, as Mark has shown, Jesus' bapism anticipates his story of Jesus' preaching in the Synagogue at Nazareth (Lk 4,16-30). Citing Isa 61,1-2 where again the preposition *epi* is found, Luke shows that the baptism of Jesus is his Messianic anointing in the Isaian perspectives.[27] In sum, I agree with Collins that the

---

[26] As for how Isa 42,1 was a customary point of reference in early Christian contextualization, see Mt 12,18 where Matthew cites it in order to show Jesus as fulfilling the Ebed-Yahweh canticles. Also note that Luke changes the preposition *eis* with *epi* (upon) which is used in the LXX Isaian text. Thus, he also contextualizes the Isaian Suffering Servant. The Third evangelist, highlights and presents Jesus as the beloved son.

[27] Collins, "Luke 3,21-22", p. 824.

Lukan genealogy and even the temptation complement the baptismal pericope to stress the significance of Jesus' Messiahship. In conclusion, Jesus' baptism confirms his anointing "as Messiah by his Father through the gift of the Spirit".[28]

8.2.3   THE 'BELOVED SON'

The theme of the "Beloved Son" is fully complementary to the understanding of the significance of the "voice from heaven" in the Synoptic baptism narrative. In Mk 9,7, at the scene of the Transfiguration, once again, Mark re-iterates God's theophanic declaration of special relationship to Jesus before representatives of the ancestral religion. For Mark, Jesus is the Father's "beloved Son" to whom all should listen. In 12,6, he tells us with the aid of a "picture-talk", that an absentee landlord places a productive vineyard in the hands of tenant farmers and travels abroad. The tenants molest the servants who are sent to collect the landlord's profit. Eventually they despatch the master's "beloved Son", the only heir of the estate. In these accounts, the transcendent phenomenon of the "beloved Son", *huios agapetos* looms large. This "beloved Son" is dear to God and so to Mark, the evangelist.[29] As Mark employs the concept to conclude his parable, he literarily connects the figure to the rejected corner-stone mentioned in Ps 118,22. For Mark therefore, the Only Son of the Vineyard story who is rejected and killed represents a *royal figure*. Let us see how this may be understood.

The occasion of the Parable of the Vineyard occurs when Jesus is asked by the Chief Priests, Scribes and Elders to explain his credentials for the astonishing things that are done by him (Mk 11,27-33). Jesus corners their question by raising the issue of the origin of John's baptism: "from heaven or from men" (11,30). No answer comes from them and Jesus in turn gives no response to their query. The Parable with its stress on the rejection of the corner-stone is, to my mind, Mark's portrayal of Jesus' response to the religious leaders. The Parable, unlike the preceding ones told in Mk 3,23-27; 4,1-34 and even in 13,28-29, is

---

[28] *Ibid.*, p. 831.

[29] See Mk 1,1,11; 3,11; 9,7; 13,32; 15,39.

rather an allegory directed to the religious authorities.[30] They quickly catch the taunt and show their resentment by attempting to arrest him. As an allegory, the Parable draws our attention to the wickedness of the tenants who represent the religious leaders; the servants as the prophets and the only son as Jesus.[31] The question now is: how then is the "only son" king in Mark's understanding?

The text of Mark is emphatic that Jesus is God's son. According to Schweizer, the expression, *en soi eudokesa*, "in him I am well pleased" alludes to 2 Sam 22,20.[32] In that text, we read:

> He brought me forth into a broad place, he delivered me, because *he delighted in me*.

Here, David raises a praise-song to God for delivering him from the cluthes of his enemies, especially Saul. Commentators have shown that the verb, *eudokeo* is usually a term employed in referring to divine election and the choice of humans.[33] The context in which it is used is within the prayer tradition of king David himself. As the royal Son, Jesus is the prototype and inheritor of the Davidic promises.[34] Thus, the use of Ps 2, Isa 42 and 2 Sam 22 hark back to the Davidic royal theology. All the texts are employed to demonstrate Jesus' kingship. In this light, I agree with Matera that "if Mark has drawn a relationship between the only son of the parable and the only son of the baptism and transfiguration, then he

---

[30] Here, see M. Hubaut, La parabole des vignerons homicides, Paris, Gabalda, 1976.

[31] Jewish NT exegetes and scholarship, in recent times, are contesting this reading of the passage. Cf. J. Neusner, Messiah in Context: Israel's History and Destiny in Formative Judaism, Philadelphia, Fortress, 1984; A. Milavec, "The Identity of "the Son" and "the Others": Mark's Parable of the Wicked Husbandmen Reconsidered", *BTB* 20(1990)30-37, p. 32.

[32] Schweizer, *"huios"*, p. 368.

[33] See for one, G. Münderlein, "Die Erwählung durch das Pleroma", *NTS* 8(1961762)264-276, p. 266.

[34] Cf. F. J. Matera, The Kingship of Jesus: Composition and Theology in Mark 15, SBL DS 66, Chico, Scholars Press, 1982, p. 78.

understood this son as a royal figure".[35] Besides, most exegetes agree that the only son of the parable is the very son whose divinization had been declared at the baptism and the Transfiguration episodes and the one whose royal Sonship is proclaimed in these passages. What the nations did to God's anointed (David) as is related in Ps 2, the tenants did in a harsher manner to the Son in order to disinherit him. My presentation on the transfiguration will provide more insights.

8.2.4 THE TRANSFIGURATION
(Mt 17,1-9/Mk 9,2-10/Lk 9,28-36)

The account of Jesus' transfiguration is graphically told in the Synoptic gospels as we have briefly remarked in the last section. As usual, Luke introduces his own additions to the Markan text. The reference of the transfiguration in 2 Pet 1,16-18 intimates us that the church of the New Testament had considered Jesus' transfiguration a significant event worthy to be preached about for faith development of the members. Scholars would not doubt the theological importance of the narrative of the Transfiguration of Jesus. Its documentation in the Triple Tradition has however made E. Debrowski who wrote in the early thirties to argue in favour of its historicity;[36] a position no longer taken by mainline Roman Catholic exegetes today. The story is well known to us. It is not my intention to reproduce it here. The references are given above. For me, what counts are the theological highlights of the incident. Can we, from the narrative, gain insight into early Christian messianic understanding of Jesus? The discussion that follows attempts to clarify this question.

W. H. Kelber believes that the incident happened at Mount Tabor; according to him, the only high mountain scene in Mark.[37] This opinion hails from the gospels which narrate that before and after the incident Jesus was yet in the area of Galilee. The appearance of Moses and Elijah has no small consequences to the faith of the three apostles who were in

---

[35] *Ibid.*

[36] See E. Debrowski, La Transfiguration de Jésus, Scripta Pontificii Instituti Biblici 85, Rome, 1933.

[37] Cf. W. H. Kelber, Mark's Story of Jesus, Philadelphia, Fortress, 1979, p. 53.

the company of Jesus at the occasion. The Transfiguration marks the dawn of a new revelation. The presence of the hero figures of the ancestral religion, according to A. Plummer, gives encouragement to "the three witnesses who had been perplexed and depressed by the announcement that the Messiah must suffer and die".[38] The incident makes the apostles to come to the realization that even though Jesus is the Messiah-king, his kingdom is not of this world; an issue obliquely hinted at in Jesus' elusive response to Pilate in the trial scene. The occasion reveals the glory of the Messiah, though not yet made public, it is however in itself an encouragement to Jesus.

In Jewish religious sources, Elijah was expected to return before the close of the present age in order to announce the advent of God's kingdom and to prepare the people for it. The appearance of Moses was not a popular Jewish article of faith. According to the evangelists, the ancient figures participate in the theophany as representatives of both the Law and the Prophets. Moses' appearance in the vision of the apostles signifies that the great Law-giver confirms and approves the choice and election of Jesus as the one in whom all the promises are fulfilled and who now possesses all the rights of Moses to speak for God (here recall the status of the Reth-elect in his relation to Nyikang in Shilluk theology). Elijah's appearance with Jesus in the vision means that he too endorses Jesus as the Messiah-king, the proclaimer of the kingdom of God. According to J. L. Mishkin, Elijah appears in the story to assure Mark's church that "... God's Son will return in glory".[39] Thus, the presence of the culture-heroes re-assures the apostles that the Messiah-king has not come to reverse the Law and the Prophets but to herald the arrival of a new era of salvation. Peter pleads for a postponement of Jesus' passion, at least, to an indefinite time.

The cloud which overshadowed the witnesses is described as a luminous cloud. It represents the Divine presence, the *Shechinah* in whose presence no one who beholds the characteristic awe and the feel of the presence of the Ultimate Reality would not tremble. There occured a divine voice:

---

[38] A. Plummer, The Gospel According to St. Mark, Thornapple Commentaries, Grand Rapids, Michigan, Baker, 1982, (Repr. of 1914), p. 213.

[39] J. L. Mishkin, Elijah Transfigured: A Study of the Narrative of the Transfiguration in the Gospel of Mark, Ann Arbor, University Microfilms International Disseration, N.D., p. vi.

This is my beloved Son; listen to him. (Mk 9,7c)

This is my beloved Son, with whom I am well pleased; listen to him. (Mt 17,5d)

This is my Son, my Chosen; listen to him. (Lk 9,35b).

As I have already shown earlier on, the divine voice is similar to that which is heard at the Baptism of Jesus (Mk 1,11). Notice the variation in Luke. The "beloved Son" of both Mark and Matthew is decribed as the Chosen Son by Luke, a concept very similar to the progenitors' chosen prince in the African sacred kingship traditions. As the "beloved Son", Jesus is superior to all those who had been called sons of God in the OT: Israel, the kings and in later Jewish literatures.[40] This time around, the apostles are addressed. They are called to recognize that in Christ, the Messiah, the Law and the prophets are complemented; and thus all his followers are to listen to him. As Plummer lovely puts it "This Voice assured the apostles that, although the Jews might reject Him and the Romans put him to death (viii. 31), yet He was accepted and beloved by God".[41]

Thus, we can agree with Hurtado that the Transfiguration of Jesus is "a powerful disclosure of his true significance as the Son of God".[42] The motif of glory is a distinctive quality of the Messiah, the celestial Christ; an essential figure of the Parousia. The motif of the cloud also indicates the coming of the Messiah, a feature typical of the events of the eschaton. The presence of OT sacred figures and such motifs as these attest that Jesus is the Messiah who fulfills the hopes for the dawn of God's Reign. Besides, all three evangelists concur on the shiny aspect of Jesus' clothes. Exegetes accept that the "glistening, intensely white" clothes of Jesus refer to a theophanic vision like that of Dan 7,9.[43] Matthew and Luke commenting on Mark and other possible Q material, portray the mystical experience of Jesus and the apostles in the light of Dan 7,9-14.[44] For Luke, the Christ who is here

---

[40] L. W. Hurtado, Mark, NIBC, Peabody, Massachussetts, Hendrickson, 1989, p. 146.

[41] Plummer, The Gospel According to St. Mark, p. 215.

[42] Hurtado, Mark, p. 145.

[43] Cf. *ibid*.

[44] See also Isa 6,1-13; Ezek 1,4-28; 8,1-4.

transfigured is the one who receives the Spirit at baptism and the one who ascends to heaven (Acts 1,11); and he is the one who comes soon. For the three evangelists, Jesus' Transfiguration in this theophanic environment establishes him not only as the Messiah, but as a divinely chosen king who is to rule in God's name. By his choice and election, he is himself fully clothed in divine glory; an unparalleled glory and divine favour.[45]

8.2.5   JESUS' ENTRY INTO JERUSALEM
(Mt 21,1-9/Mk 11.1-10/Lk 19,28-40/Jn 12,12-19)

The New Testament portrayal of Jesus as a royal figure is noticeable in more than the instances so far shown. In the context of my discussion, an analysis of Jesus' Triumphal descent into Jerusalem according to the gospels becomes quite apposite. In the exegesis that follows, the questions I will address myself to are: in what manner was the Messiaship of Jesus explained to the earliest Christian communities and apologetically defended before Jewish unbelievers? Are the categories used in the passages far-fetched and far-removed from acceptable and prevailing traditions? Does the story in anyway refer Jesus' experience to his ancestral stock as has already been noted in the previous passages?

The account of Jesus' Triumphal Entry into Jerusalem is transmitted in the four gospels, a fact which suggests the historicity of the event in the life and ministry of Jesus. Vincent Taylor cautiously observes that in the Markan pericope, there are combinations of literary elements of both messianic and non-messianic character which make its analysis somewhat difficult.[46] The theme of the descent of a royal figure into the Holy City and his inspection of the Temple which is alluded to in the OT books is freely utilized in this narrative.[47] Jesus' main destination is the Temple.[48] He does not commune with ancestral

---

[45] Hurtado, Mark, p. 146.

[46] V. Taylor, The Gospel According to Mark: The Greek Text with Introduction, Notes and Indexes, 2nd Edition, New York, St Martins Press, 1966, p. 452.

[47] Cf. Zech 9,9; Gen 49,10-11; 1 Kgs 1,38-40; 2 Kgs 9,13.

[48] J. Beutler, Das Markusevangelium (Kap 8,27-13,37). Vorlesungen Phil.-Theol. Hochschule Sankt Georgen, Frankfurt am Main, 1991/92, p. 87.

spirits like the African princes and kings-elect but he only examines the Temple locale and moves swiftly to Bethany (Mk 11,11). In Mt 21,10, the evangelist introduces into the Markan text literary elements from Zech 9,9 to vivify his own description of Jesus' arrival at the Temple Mount.[49] According to Matthew, the city is thrown into uproar at Jesus' arrival.[50] Luke, as usual, portrays a much more vivid picture. Jesus descends from the Mount of Olives. The disciples hail him as "... the king who comes in the name of the Lord" (Lk 19,38). A good theme-to-theme or step-by-step comparison between the evangelists reveals some striking agreements and disagreements in the narrative. On what I may refer to as the fifth-level agreement, Mark, as well as Luke offer a macarism on the kingdom of "our" forefather, David. For Mark, the ancient promises that the kingdom would come find their fulfilment in the approach of Jesus and his procession into the city of Jerusalem. He lauds the event with a *Hosanna*, a praise-song. Here, except Matthew, Luke and John do not adopt the *Hosanna* chant as Mark does. Perhaps, the literary difference can be understood in the context of Mark's Messianic secret; a specific feature of Mark's gospel which the other evangelists do not share with him. At this juncture, I consider Beutler's comment on Mark quite pertinent.[51] The literary differences however indicate how Matthew and Luke using Mark (other sources not excluded), detail out a crisp story of the Messianic entry of Jesus into Jerusalem despite how each stresses his own theological point of view. Luke, for instance, omits a Holy Week chronology and the waving of branches.[52] The sum total of this discussion is that while Mark sees in the event the coming kingdom of their Father David (vv. 11,10), Luke describes Jesus on the occasion as "the king who comes in the name of the Lord" (19,38) and Matthew sings his arrival in: "Hosanna to the son of

---

[49] Cf. E. D. Freed, Old Testament Quotations in the Gospel of John, NovT. Suppl., Leiden, Brill, 1965, pp. 8-10.

[50] Note the forensic use of the verb *eseisthe* in v. 10.

[51] Beutler, Das Markusevangelium, p. 87:

> Die "Herrschaft unseres Vaters David" in V 10 ist whol beeinflußt von Jes 55,1-5;2 Sam 7,8-16; Ps 89,28-38. Diese Herrschaft wurde zur Zeit Jesu als kommend erwartet. Es handelt sich hier also um eine messianische Begrüßung Jesu. Doch wird der Königstitel vermieden (anders als bei Mt, Lk und Joh: s.u., e).

[52] Cf. O. C. Edwards, Luke's Story of Jesus, Philadelphia, Fortress, 1981, p. 80.

David! Blessed is he who comes in the name of the Lord" (21,9b). John whose literary affinity to Luke is defended by many critics, especially the Leuven school, appends to the Synoptic chorus the cliché: "even the King of Israel" (12,13). Thus, the Fourth evangelist, like Matthew and Luke do in their Infancy narratives, claims kingship for Jesus.

Let us now briefly examine some OT accounts of Royal enthronement narratives in order to understand the possible background of the story. In 1 Kgs 1,38-40, the enthronement of king Solomon is narrated; and in 2 Kgs 9,13, we are informed of king Jehu's accession to the throne. In the case of Solomon, he is made to ride on king David's mule to Gihon by the king-makers. The priest Zadok anoints him. He receives the sceptre and they blow the trumpet. The people shout: "Long live the King". Much merriment and jubilation follow thereafter. In 2 Kgs 9,13, a crowd of commanders strip themselves, decorate the steps with their garments, blow the trumpet and shout: "Jehu is king". In 2 Sam 15,10, the rebellious Absolam was proclaimed king by his faction with the shout "Absolam is king at Hebron". In all three the traditional structure of hailing and welcoming newly proclaimed kings pervade through. These stories, well known in those days, especially in the circles of Christian teachers and evangelists would naturally have influenced the church's contextualisation praxis and thus the composition of the texts concerning a figure whose mission and life-work suggested the happenings associated with the expected Messiah.[53] Beutler opines that the *Gattung* of the narrative is that of story-telling-*Geschichtserzählung* and legend - *Legende*.[54] Truely the narrative is expanded to include the legend and the custom of the time by which the king would usually send his courtiers ahead of him to prepare for his entry into a city.[55] By sending his disciples to fetch the colt ahead of him and the message they are to bring to the owner (Mk 11,3), Jesus is being portrayed as exercising a royal authority of "conscription".[56] Jesus enters the Temple royally and cleanses

---

[53] Here, I refer to J. Osei-Bonsu, "The Contextualization of Christianity: Some New Testament Antecedents", *IBS* 12(1990)129-148 who however neglects to illustrate this interesting subject of research from the use made of the OT scriptures by the evangelists.

[54] Beutler, Das Markusevangelium, pp. 84, 87.

[55] See 2 Sam 15,18.

[56] J.-Duncan M. Derret, "Law in the New Testament: The Palm Sunday Colt", *NovT* 13(1971)241-258; p. 246 who has recognized the phenomenon as *angaria*.

it of all impurities and wantonness introduced by the activities of the businessmen and money changers who made "a house of prayer" into a mercantile premises.[57] In using the customary motif, the evangelists emphasize Jesus' prophetic insight. But as he shows this foresight, he is also presented as the royal figure acting with a characteristic air of authority in the land which he rules. For Matthew, the Triumphal entry into Jerusalem and the Temple, and the Cleansing of the Temple, the healing of the blind and the lame and the Hosanna-shout of the children constitute a single unit of information (Mt 21,1-17). N. Lohfink recognizes the scene as the approach of the Messiah-king with his poor followers to Zion.[58] For me, Jesus, by his action is challenging the status quo. His cleansing of the Temple is a Messianic act typical of the coming Messiah-King who would proclaim a Jubilee in the spirit of the Law of Leviticus 25. In other words, the proclamation of the *Goodnews* of the Kingdom must be matched with action. The Kingdom comes true as the hungry are fed, the sick healed and justice given to the poor and the needy. Jesus offers a different vision, and calls for a totally variant attitude to action instead of the non-engaging ideology offered to the people by the Pharisees, Sadducees and the belligerent Zealots.

At this juncture, let us consider Zech 9,9 and Gen 49,10-11 to see what light they shed on the foregoing discussion. In Zech 9,9 we read:

Rejoice greatly, O daughter of Zion! Shout aloud, O daughter of Jerusalem!

Lo, your king comes to you; triumphant and victorious is he, humble and riding on an ass, on a colt the foal of an ass.

Due to the literary resemblance of Mk 11,2-5 to Zech 9,9, a number of exegetes in recent years agree that the OT oracle of Zech 9,9 had influenced, if not Mark's major motifs, at

---

[57] And so Edwards, Lukes's Story of Jesus, p. 81.

[58] N. Lohfink, "Der Messiaskönig und seine Armen kommen zum Zion" in: L. Schenke, (Hrsg.), Studien zum Matthäusevangelium, Fs. W. Pesch, SBS, Stuttgart, 1988, pp. 181-200.

least, the tradition received by him.[59] According to some authors, the case of Gen 49,10-11 is rather fascinating.[60] The text reads:

(10) The sceptre shall not depart from Judah, nor the ruler's staff from between his feet, until it comes to whom it belongs; and to him shall be the obedience of the peoples.

(11) Binding his foal to the vine and his ass's colt to the choice vine, he washes his garments in wine and his vesture in the blood of grapes; ...

In this oracle, Jacob swears that the sceptre will not depart from Judah until *Shiloh* (MT) comes to bind his foal to the vine. Both the MT and the LXX texts point towards a figure described as the *Coming One*. Seen in the light of Ps 118,22 which is frequently applied to Jesus as the "Corner-stone", it does appear that it is Jesus who comes in the guise of Shiloh to claim what is reserved for him. Shiloh is quite an enigmatic figure. It however reflects a person of gentle and humble character in prophetic literature. Isa 8,5 employs the figure to allude to a rejected source of life and deliverance. It is probably in this light that it is ascribed to Jesus like the motif of the rejected *Corner-stone*.

In the Qumran and the Targumin, Gen 49,10 is understood quite messianically. 4 Q Pat. Blessing reads:

The explanation of this is that (1) a monarch will not be wanting to the tribe of Judah when Israel rules, (2) and a descendant seated on the throne will not be wanting to David. For the (commander's) staff is the covenant of kingship,

---

[59] Cf. A. Ambrozic, The Hidden Kingdom: A Redaction-Critical Study of the References to the Kingdom in Mark's Gospel. The CBQ Monograph Series 2, CBAA, Washington, 1972, p. 37; F. F. Bruce, "The Book of Zechariah and the Passion Narrative" *BJRL* 43(1961)336-353; L.Gaston, No Stone on Another: Studies in the Significance of the Fall of Jerusalem in the Synoptic Gospels, NovT Suppl. 23. Leiden, Brill, 1970; W. H. Kelber, The Kingdom in Mark: A New Place and a New Time, Philadelphia, Fortress, 1974; D. Juel, Messiah and Temple: The Trial of Jesus in the Gospel of Mark, SBL DS 31, Missoula, Montana, Scholars Press, 1977.

[60] Cf. J. Blankinsopp, "The Oracle of Judah and the Messianic Entry", *JBL* 80(1961)55-64; H.-W. Kuhn, "Das Reittier Jesu in der Einzuggeschichte des Markusevangeliums", *ZNW* 50(1959)80-91, who have put the weight of their argumentation on the phrase, *polon dedemenon*.

(3) [and] the feet are [the Thou] sands of Israel. Until the Messiah of Righteousness comes, the Branch (4) of David; for to him and to his seed has been given the Covenant of the Kingship of his people for everlasting generations, because (5) he has kept [...] the Law with the members of the Community. For (6) [...] is the synagogue of the men [of mockery ...][61]

The Targum Onkelos interpretes Gen 49,10 as follows:

The transmission of dominion shall not cease from the house of Judah, nor the scribe from his children's children, forever, until the Messiah comes, to whom the kingdom belongs, and whom nations shall obey.

On the passage, the Targum Jonathan is much more particular. It states:

Kings and rulers shall not cease from the house of Judah, nor scribes who teach the Torah from his seed, until the time when the king Messiah shall come, the youngest of his sons, and because of him shall nations melt away.[62]

These strands of tradition suppose that there prevailed hopes, as we have earlier seen, in the coming Messiah whose triumphal entry into the Holy City is perceived in the perspective of Gen 49,10. Without doubt, this contemporary thought permeated the Markan church, and hence the other evangelists following him conceive Jesus' descent to the Holy City as a fulfillment by the Messianic king.[63] Therefore, for the evangelists, the story of Jesus' entry into Jerusalem has a royal significance. Jesus is the royal figure who comes on the *polon dedemenon* (a colt tied ...) and the one who fulfills the promise made to David. He is the one who comes as *Shiloh* and to whom the sceptre (*ade*) belongs. He comes to take charge

---

[61] Text taken from Dupont-Sommer, The Essene Writings from Qumran, ET by G. Vermes, Gloucester, Massachussetts, Smith, 1973, pp. 314-315.

[62] Text taken from S. H. Levey, The Messiah: An Aramaic Interpretation. The Messianic Exegesis of the Targum, MHUC 2, Cincinnati, Hebrew Union College-Jewish Institute of Religion, 1974, pp. 7, 9.

[63] J. Dupont, "L'Arrière-fond Biblique du Récit des tentations de Jésus", *NTS* 3(1956/57)299; B. Gerhardsson, The Testing of God's son: An Analysis of an Early Christian Midrash, Lund, Gleerup, 1966; M. D. Goulder, Midrash and Lection in Matthew, London, SPCK, 1974, p. 245.

of it, not as a victorious and a triumphant conqueror but as a humble king. As I would prefer to state it, J. K. Elliott vividly sums it up well:

> The triumphal entry thus becomes a coronation procession reminiscent of the procession in 2 Kgs 9,13 after Jehu's anointing, when the crowd placed their garments under the newly elected king (cf. Mk 11,8).[64]

8.2.6 THE ANOINTING IN BETHANY
(Mt 26,6-13/Mk 14,3-9/Lk 7,36-50/Jn 12,1-8)

In these passages, an unknown lady (except Jn 12,3 where she is named Mary, the sister of Lazarus) comes forward to Jesus in a party. She offers him a precious gift of her love as a sign of his Kingship of the world. It is in the context of the recognition she gives him that Jesus speaks well of her:

> And truly I say to you, where the gospel is preached in the whole world, what she has done will be told in memory of her (Mk 14,9).

The action of the woman described as "a sinner" (Lk 7,37,48) in this pericope is shrouded in symbolism suggestive of honours done to a Messiah-king. While the religious authorities of his nation seek opportunity to do away with him, the woman does what is good. She is an exemplary lady to whom much appreciation is owed by mainline feminist theologians today.[65] The woman lavishes a full pack alabaster flask of oil, her tears, her sweat and time. The unction is her faith and preparedness to celebrate God's salvific work made manifest in Jesus, the King-Saviour who is to die in the coming Passover. In other words, the story is a Markan insertion into the Passion Narrative as Elliott contends.[66] In the light of his Christology in the Passion narrative, Mark first tells the story of the anointing woman "as a

---

[64] J. K. Elliott, "The Anointing of Jesus", *ExpT* 85(1973-74)103-107, p. 107.

[65] See for one, Elizabeth S. Fiorenza, In Memory of Her.

[66] Elliott, "The Anointing of Jesus", p. 106.

Christ-figure".[67] Thus, it can be argued, as Barton obliquely draws our attention to, that there is a messianic orientation in the passage. Even the author of Hebrews in 1,9 makes reference to Ps 45,7 which, in its ancient usuage, refers to the anointing of the king in preparation for a wedding feast. Reworking this *Vorlage* for his community's christological inculturation, the Son who has "loved righteousness and hated lawlessness" now becomes anointed "with the oil of gladness" (LXX Isa 61,3) as the Messianic king.

Some scholars have interpreted the passage literarily; other some symbolically. Suffice it just to name two. J. Delobel, my former teacher at Leuven and now dean of the ancient Faculty, has a detailed essay, some of the results of his doctoral research, in which he critically analyzes the compositional technique of Luke, the evangelist. He argues, among other things, that Luke has redacted the story on the basis of the hellenistic *symposion*.[68] On the signification of the story then, Delobel opines that Luke demonstrates in the action of the woman "un temoignage admirable de la foi en Jésus, salut des pécheurs".[69] J. K. Elliott gives a brief but succint exposée of the gospels' accounts of the story.[70] After a balanced overview of the differences and similarities of the account in the four gospels, Elliott observes that even though Luke's is quite remarkably detailed, all four evangelists intend to tell us that "Jesus was at one point in his ministry anointed".[71] What then is the importance the evangelists attach to this story? In Matthew and Mark, the anointing is made on Jesus' head as "the definite and symbolic act of acknwoledging a king's consecration"[72] Apart however from this Messianic significance of the woman's action, three of the evangelists tell us that the use of the oil and the anointment foreshadow Jesus' burial anointing (Mt 26,12/Mk 14,8/Jn 12,7). There is indeed an underlying connection between the anointing of the living Jesus and the anointment of the dead Jesus. For me, apart from conventional burial

---

[67] Cf. S. C. Barton, "Mark as Narrative. The Story of the Anointing Woman", *ExpT* 102(1991)230-234, p. 232.

[68] J. Delobel, "L'Onction par la Pécheresse. La Composition litteraire de Lc, VII,36-50", *ETL* 42(1966)415-475.

[69] *Ibid.*, p. 475.

[70] Elliot, "The Anointing of Jesus".

[71] *Ibid.*, p. 105.

[72] *Ibid.*

rites then current in the Eastern Mediterreanean, the relationship resides in the fact that the full acquisition of Jesus' Messiah-Kingship is achieved through his death on the cross, burial and the resurrection; his eventual glorification and enthronement. In a final submission, Elliott categorically states: "Jesus is here clearly being anointed as king".[73] H. Schlier sees the act or the unction performed by the woman as pointing to Jesus' exalted status as that Son who has loved righteousness in the Godhead. It is by this singular act, according to him, that Jesus has become the *Christos*, the Christ.[74]

Elliott further underscores our position. He remarks that Jesus' baptism is his anointment with the Spirit as the Son of God and the Messiah. The accounts of Mark and Matthew in which the head of Jesus is anointed by the woman reminds us once more of its OT antecedents. We have seen that in 2 Kgs 9,1-13, Elisha's servant anoints Jehu and the commanders proclaim him king over Israel.[75] In Elliott's words, and I quite agree with him, "the original core of the story of Jesus'anointing therefore tells of his consecration as king ..."[76]. Besides, in view of the ancient belief that "kingship descends from heaven",[77] and given the role of oil and its smearing on the body (vide the coronation of the Zulu *Nkosi*), I am of the opinion that the action of the anonymous woman reflects, on the one hand, evidence of divine choice and election mediated through the devotion of a representative figure, this time around, a woman, and on the other hand, the fact that Jesus' forgiveness of the anointer's sin sheds light on the role of the Messiah-king as God's regent whose task, among other things, is to heal and to repair human brokenness and disorder. Here, I hope to have fairly bridged the gap between the literarist (Delobel) and the symbolist (Elliott). Moreover, the story of the anointing is to be read together with the preceding Synoptic Triumphal Entry into Jerusalem where the same Messiah-king is hailed and honoured. But the placement of the story in John immediately before the Triumphal Entry suggests that

---

[73] *Ibid.*

[74] H. Schlier, "elaion", *TDNT* 2(1964)470-473, p. 472.

[75] There are other passages in the OT which show that anointing with oil is a visible sign of royalty. See 1 Sam 10,1,1 Kgs 1,38-40, Ps 133,2.

[76] Elliott, "The Anointing of Jesus", p. 106.

[77] Cf. H. Frankfort, Kingship and the Gods, Chicago, The University of Chicago Press, 1965, p. 237.

John sees the anointing as a royal coronation rite performed in Bethany before Jesus' last entry into the Holy City. In conclusion, I concur with Elliott that "having been anointed at Bethany, Jesus straightaway enters Jerusalem triumphantly as the newly acclaimed Messiah-King (Jn 12,13)"[78]

The notion that Jesus is king is equally a Lukan theme. Twice in Luke-Acts, he tells us that Jesus is king. In Luke 23,2, among the triple charges brought against Jesus is that he claims "that he himself is Christ a king". In Acts 17,7, the uproar in Thessalonica was raised on the accusation by the Jews against Paul, among others, that he and his co-workers said "that there is another king, Jesus". As I have tried to demonstrate elsewhere, Luke so skillfully tells these stories in such a way that historical evidence and literary artistry blend together to produce a theological vision specifically Lukan.[79] In sum, the picture which emerges is that Jesus is, at least, for the evangelists (apart from Mark yet) the Messiah-king.

8.2.7   MARK 15 AND THE KINGSHIP OF JESUS

In all the passages so far analysed, Mark no where calls Jesus "king" like Luke and John, even though his redactional hand had worked with material derived from ancient royalist sources and traditions. Why then did Mark restrain calling Jesus "king" if the other evangelists readily recognized him so? Some authors hold the view that Mark has purposefully "reserved" the title until he comes to his chapter 15, the scene of Jesus' trial before Pilate who, in the course of his interrogation, makes the character of Jesus' kingship public.[80] The literary-critical solution offered by W. Wrede in his *Das Messiasgeheimnis ...*, (1901), *The Messianic Secret,* can help us explain the absence of the title so far in Mark. In

---

[78] Elliott, "The Anointing of Jesus", p. 107.

[79] For further insight, see my "Luke's Account of Paul in Thessalonica (Acts 17,1-9)" in R. F. Collins (ed.), The Thessalonian Correspondence, BETL 87, Leuven University Press, 1990, pp. 27-38, pp. 33-35.

[80] Matera, The Kingship of Jesus: Composition and Theology in Mark 15; H. Conzelmann, "History and Theology in the Passion Narrative of the Synoptic Gospels" *Interpr.* 24(1970)178-197, p. 183; J. Gnilka, Das Evangelium nach Markus, 2. Teilband Mk 8,17-16,20, EKKNT 2, Zürich, Benziger Verlag, 1979, p. 120.

the rubric of Wrede's theory, the correlative titles "Christ" and "Son of Man" appear to have been employed by Mark to insist on silence about Jesus' Messiah-Kingship. Thus as a dogmatic proposition created by Mark and received from the tradition on which he drew, Wrede stated, may explain the delay of the title, "King" for Jesus in this penultimate chapter.[81]

It appears that for Mark, the consultation of the priests' council over the Jesus problem; their accusations before Pilate; the mockeries railed against him by the guards and the passers-by; the inscription over his head on the cross - all described in chapter 15 speak much more eloquent in determining Jesus' kingship than the boisterous entry into Jerusalem. In the words often spoken by others in the process of Jesus' trial and execution, Jesus is shown as Son of God and Messiah.[82] For Mark and his church, kingship does not consist in the power to rescue oneself and others from imminent danger nor in flamboyant street shows and processions and such other ostentatious feats as are suggested by Satan in the temptations (Mk 1,12-13 par.). The real King is a *crucified Messiah*.

While Mark has not yet used the title, "king", his gospel already alludes to Jesus' kingship in a number of passages apart from those we have studied. In 1,3, Isaiah's prophecy points to the *kyrios* of 11,3 who has need of the colt. Is it not the same muted Messiah-king whom David should call Lord (12,37)? Is *ho erchomenos* of Mk 11,9b not the figure spoken of by John the Bapitizer in 1,7-8 as one mightier than himself? Is he not the one with all the characteristics of the Messiah-king of the end-times who will baptize with the Holy Spirit? In 13,26, the Messiah-king will erupt onto the clouds with power and majesty and in 14,62 with the affirmative formula, *ego eimi*: "I am", Jesus admits before the High Priest's Council that he is the Messiah-king who will be "seated at the right hand of power, and coming with the clouds of heaven". In the end, I wish to commit myself to the belief that the concepts *kyrios* and *ho erchomenos* are chosen Markan synonyms for *King* which anticipate full revelation in the Markan Passion Story of chapter 15. Really the content of Mk 15 is emphatic on the kingship of Jesus. As Matera elegantly sums it up:

---

[81] Cf. Kasper, Jesus the Christ, p. 105.

[82] Manus, "The Centurion's Confession of Faith (Mk 15,39)".

Jesus is tried as king of the Jews (vv. 1-15)
Jesus is mocked as king of the Jews (vv. 16-20a)
Jesus is crucified as king of the Jews (vv. 20b-26)
Jesus is mocked as Messiah-king of Israel (vv. 27-32)
Jesus cries out as Messiah-king (vv. 33-34)
Jesus is mocked as Messiah-king (vv. 35-36).[83]

Thus for Mark, kingship of Jesus is achieved through the cross. This is one great difference between his gospel and the "oralture" of African kingship institutions.

8.3 THE FEAST OF CHRIST THE KING. EXEGESIS OF THE LESSONS
8.3.1 INTRODUCTION

In this section, I wish to examine the texts chosen as readings on the Feast of Christ the King in the Sunday Circle B as contained in the Roman Missal.[84] Apart from hundreds of Christian establishments such as schools, hospitals, clinics and charitable organisations dedicated to *Christ the King* in Africa today, let us remind ourselves of the origin and history of the Feast in the Roman Catholic Calendar. Christ the King is a feast whose origin dates from Pope Pius XI's Encyclical, *Quas Primas* of December 11, 1925.[85] Though an "honorific" and "idea feast", the feast was set up by the Pope in order to counteract the growing laicism, secularism and atheism which engulfed the world of his time.[86] According to O'Shea, the feast celebrates "the triumph of the King of kings, the ascended Lord and the heavenly High-Priest".[87] Since its inception, the solemn feast had been celebrated on the last

---

[83] Matera, The Kingship of Jesus.

[84] H. Winstone (ed.), The Sunday Missal. Texts Approved for use in England and Wales, Scotland and Ireland, and Africa, London, Collins, 1985, 12th Ed. pp. 550-552: "Last Sunday of the Year: Christ the King" <B.

[85] Cf. my *"Jesu Kristi Oba"*, pp. 318-319.

[86] See, W. J. O'Shea, "Feast of Christ the King" in New Catholic Encyclopedia, Vol 3, pp. 627-628.

[87] *Ibid*, p. 628.

Sunday of October every year. But in the Revised Liturgical Calendar of Pope Paul VI, it has been moved up to the Last Sunday of the Ordinary Time of the Liturgical Year in November where it currently stands. While there may exist some echoes of triumphalism noticeable in the language and theology of the *Litterae Encyclicae* establishing the feast,[88] I am here only interested in showing by way of the exegesis of the scriptures chosen as the Readings on the occasion of the Feast how the Universal Church magnifies herself in the Kingly status of Jesus, the Christ and the esteem this ideology must continue to enjoy in the African Christian Churches. Thus what is proposed here is a sort of a *sensus accomodatio* for the Church in Africa. In light of the exegetical findings, I do recognize that in their contexts, some of the texts, especially the OT passages do not speak of Christ not to talk of Christ as king. However, their polemicization against the other gods do qualify them to enter the Church's sacred liturgy which celebrates Christ's Kingship over misguided wielding of might by the powers that be.

The texts are chosen from Dan 7,13-14 whose theme is on the eternal sovereignty of "one like a son of man". Ps 92 (MT 93) which provides the Responsorial hymn has the Lordship of the King who is robed in majesty as its theme. The Apocalypse 1,5-8, whose focus is on Jesus Christ as the Ruler of the kings of the earth and John 18,33-37, where the nature of Jesus' Kingship is given expression constitute the third and the fourth readings respectively. I will examine the texts according to the sequence in which they occur in the Missal.[89]

---

[88] See, "Acta PII PP XI, Litterae Encyclicae".

[89] I am aware of the existence of another set of readings for the Feast of Christ the King in Circle C. Cf. Winstone, The Sunday Missal, pp. 720-723. These texts put stress on Christ as our anointed King who, through his passion, has delivered us into his kingdom of light. The Scriptures chosen for the Circle are equally christologically dense. Space and time do not permit full exegetical analysis of those texts. Suffice it however to note that like the other royal texts, the motifs of (a) the king as shepherd of his people (2 Sam 5,1-3); (b) thrones of judgment set in the royal House of David (Ps 121); (c) the kingdom of the Son in whom all powers and principalities were created (Col 1,11-20) and (d) the *Christos* (Messiah), whose kingdom is paradise (Lk 23,35-43) constitute the central themes of the lessons of the occasion in this Circle.For an African exegete's treatment on the concepts of Powers and Principalities, see B. Obijole, "St. Paul's Concept of Principalities and Powers in African Context" *ATJ* 17(1988)118-129, p. 125; also *idem.*, "Principalities and Powers in St. Paul's Gospel of Reconciliation" *AJBS* 1(1986)113-125.

194

8.3.2 Dan 7,13-14

The central focus of this text is on the Son of Man. Much has been written on the nature and identity of the Danielic Son of Man.[90] In the fifties, scholars have continued to maintain that the messianic ideas about the Son of Man in Dan 7,13-14 had had quite an early development as is shown by its representation in 1 Enoch xlvi,2ff, xlviii,2; 4 Ezra and the NT.[91] Many a recent interpreter offer a "collective view" of the concept of the Son of Man and others a symbolic view. As Hartman-Di Lella would want us believe, the Son of Man is nothing more or less than a symbol of "the holy ones of the Most High".[92] Scholars employing the History of Religions approach have drawn attention to the Ancient Near East; especially the Baylonian Tiamat mythology as possible origin of Dan 7.[93] Unfortunately the findings of the *Religionsgeschichtler* have not received much approbation among scholars. Towards the end of the sixties and the decade after, many authors shunned the symbolic and preferred a Christological interpretation of Dan 7,13-14. J. Massingberde Ford is one of those who commit themselves to the view that the concept Son of Man is interchangeable with the Son of God in John and should thus be regarded as a "euphemistic appellation for Son of God".[94]

Even though in its context the text in which the title is used does not speak of Christ; but from the manner it is used in the words of Jesus himself in the gospels, I am of the view

---

[90] For one, see J. M. Ross, "The Son of Man" *IBS* 13(1991)186-198. I however do not subscribe to Ross' position as indicated on pp. 193-196.

[91] Cf. H. H. Rowley, Darius the Mede and the Four World Empires in the Book of Daniel, Cardiff, University of Wales Press, 1959, p. 62, n. 2; also T. W. Manson, "The Son of Man in Daniel, Enoch and the Gospels" BJRL 32(1950)171-193.

[92] Cf. L. F. Hartman and A. A. Di Lella, The Book of Daniel, AB 23, Garden City, New York, Doubleday, 1978, pp. 85, 97.

[93] See H. Junker, Untersuchungen über literarische und exegetische Probleme des Buches Daniel, Bonn, Haustein, 1932, p. 58; E. G. H. Kraeling, "Some Babylonian and Iranian Mythology in the Seventh Chapter of Daniel" in J. D. C. Pavry (ed.), Oriental Studies, London, Oxford University Press, 1933, pp. 228-231.

[94] J. M. Ford, "'The Son of Man': A Euphemism?" *JBL* 87(1968)257-266; *idem.*, Revelation. Introduction, Translation and Commentary, The AB, New York, Doubleday, 1975, p. 16.

that it stands for Jesus as a specific self-designation that points up his Messiahship as one who does not count anything personal to himself nor demand any personal tribute to himself but as one who proclaims himself a servant to fellow human beings and an obedient tool in God's hand. It would seem to me that Isa 53 contributed much to Jesus' self understanding of his role as the Servant Messiah. This is, for me, the quintessence of the messainic irony, the irony of Jesus' Kingship, a servant-King. Thus, Jesus' personal use of this epithet supposes that Dan 7,13-14 is recognized in Jewish religious circles as a messianic text. The content of the text prefigures Christ's incarnation in human history, the bestowal of royalty, glory and kingship on him by God and the followership and service accorded him by believing gentiles. Some other authors are compelled to hold the expression, "coming on the clouds of heaven", as an indication of Christ's second coming. And perhaps, this may be one reason why the Church has chosen the text for a feast that marks the commencement of the *Advent* in the Christian Calendar. But is this idea vindicated by results of sound exegesis? The crux of the matter is: who is the Danielic figure? Has the choice of the text been determined by a clear understanding of and the parallelism between this figure and the Christ? These are questions whose answers the science of exegesis can provide in a book-size of its own. Meanwhile, I wish to limit myself to the explanation of the close association between the Son of Man and the Messiah.

Given the fact that the term, *Messiah* is generally understood in biblical contexts as the Anointed descendant of the House of David whose monarchy is depicted as perfect and righteous and the one who will reign over Israel, I would say that the Messiah and the Danielic figure share many ideas in common. Besides, the text of Daniel offers the following features of the Son of Man: (a) he acquires dominion, glory and the kingdom; (b) all peoples, nations and languages will do him service and (c) he has an everlasting and indestructible kingdom. All these themes reverberate in the passages we have already seen in Section 1 of this chapter. In vv. 13-14, the motif of royal investiture is palpably noticeable. It can therefore be argued that theological affinities exist between the Danielic Son of Man and the Messiah. In sum then, I would conclude that following Jesus' tradition, the early church and the evangelists had no hesitations whatsoever to ascribe the concept to Jesus as the Messiah-king. Thus, the Church who has chosen the text for this solemn and august feast is certainly re-affirming the deposit of faith bequeathed to her by her earliest forebears; a tradition quite familiar in African traditional patriarchal systems.

8.3.3   Ps 92, 1,2,5

Ps 92 (93) is one of the enthronement hymns such as Pss 47, 96-99 generally sung at the New Year Festival. In each of these, one outstanding feature is the chant: "Yahweh is King" or "Yahweh has become King" over the earth and all its peoples. Likewise, Ps 92 praises and acknowledges the kingship of Yahweh as the Supreme God to whose Will all peoples owe obedience.[95] In a Commentary claimed to have been prepared "in consonance with the insights and understanding transmitted through over three millenia of Torah tradition"; and said to be "faithful to the insights of the Talmud ..." a group of Jewish commentators recognize Ps 92 (93 MT and the RSV) as containing "pronouncements that will be made in the Messianic era".[96] According to Rashi, the Psalm celebrates God's supremacy when all men will again recognize God's majesty. For the Jews, the Psalm emphasizes the reality of the future kingdom. This is due to its *Sitz im Leben* in the post-exilic cult and at the liturgical service of the renewal of God's kingdom.[97]

> V. 1:   Right from its first verse, the tone of the Psalm is decidedly polemical. The Psalmist acknowledges God's sovereignty over all creation. God alone is the only One robed in grandeur. This is a taunt against Gentile kings such as the Pharoah of Egypt, Nebuchadnezzar of Babylon and Senanacherib of Assyria who held themselves as king-gods and defied the Almighty-King of Israel. According to the Psalmist, earthly power comes from above. Israel's judges and kings, even though they had been clothed in majesty, they had received their rulership from God. Even though "they sat upon a throne, yet they were

---

[95] G. A. Buttrick et al (eds.), The IDB, Vol IV, New York, Abingdon Press, 1955, p. 502.

[96] Rabbis N. Scherman & M. Zlotowitz (eds.), Psalms 73-150 (Tehillim). A Traditional Commentary on the Books of the Bible, Art Scroll Tanach Series, Mesorah, 1985, p. 1158. According to the commentators, the Psalm in Midrash Shocher Tov teaches, among other things, that the throne of God and the King-Messiah antedated even creation; *ibid.*, p. 1159.

[97] IDB, IV, pp. 502-504.

there not in their own right but as representatives of the King of kings".[98] The Psalm, therefore, emphasizes God's eternal exercise of kingly power.[99]

V. 2: Here, the text's orientation is futuristic. It affirms that when the world shall have rightfully been established in the messianic era, then shall all people realize that God's permanent control of the universe was set right from the very moment of creation; and thus that God's kingdom is not a new event. God's sovereignty has never changed since time. His rule and the moral order it institutes are ever indestructible. It will ever endure till end of days for God is eternity.

V. 5: This verse sings the Lord's victory. According to the Psalmist, the New Year Festival is celebrated precisely because of God's triumph over chaos. All the laws, promises, decrees and utterances of God must be trusted since he is the Lord of the universe. The worship of the only and Almighty God is extolled and will ever endure, for there is no other God that should claim the allegiance of humans. Thus, the Psalmist acknowledges God's dominion, power and eternal glory.

Seen in the light of its deeply religious creeds and faith in God's sovereignty, power and glory, one can agree that the features of Ps 93 complement those of the Son of Man text of Dan 7,13-14. Hence their use as Lessons in a Feast established in the Western Church to laud the Kingship of Christ in the Church and society over the arrogance of human kings and princes is quite appropriate.

---

[98] *Ibid.*, p. 503.

[99] J. W. Rogerson & J. W. McKay, Psalms 51-100, The CBC, London, C.U.P, 1977, p. 210.

198

8.3.4   Apocalypse 1,5-8

Apoc 1,5-8, in its context is generally considered part of a "preliminary section" which belongs to chapters 1-3 with a high Christology. This block of material has been described by J. M. Ford as "much more advanced than that in the rest of Revelation".[100] Chapter 1,5-8 appears to be a prelude to 1,12-16 which concentrates attention on the portrait of one like a Son of man. Most exegetes fear a strong influence of Daniel and Ezekiel in this unit.[101] The chosen passage for the Feast possesses Christological features such as "Jesus Christ", a rare title in the Book of Revelation.[102] In the opinion of Ford, the text reflects a later Christian addition made to underscore the concept of witness in a community suffering under persecution.[103]

V. 5:   In this verse, Jesus Christ is designated a "faithful witness". The notion that Jesus is a "faithful witness" is shown to be the model of a martyr's death in so far as Jesus, as an ideal martyr, is the firstborn from the dead and ruler of the kings of the earth.[104] Jesus' universal kingship with its eternal glory and power; his eruption from the clouds and the eventual elevation of the believers to the status of kingship and priesthood constitute the central themes of the

---

[100] Ford, Revelation, pp. 40-41, p. 41.

[101] See ibid., p. 40.

[102] Cf. R. H. Mounce, The Book of Revelation, Michigan, Eerdmans, 1977, p. 64.

[103] Ibid., p. 12.

[104] Here, the idea reminds us of a major theme in Ps 89,27 which says of David:

I will make him the firstborn,
the highest of the kings of the earth.

This is a royal theology which refers to David and his descendant, the Messiah. Ps 89 is a post-exilic prayer for the restoration of the Davidic kingship which later crystalized into messianic hope. As a prayer which invokes God to establish his rule among men, "Christians have seen its answer in the life and continuing influence of Jesus Christ". Cf. Rogerson-McKay, Psalms 51-100, p. 189.

passage.[105] For the author of Revelation, the Risen Christ exercises sovereign control, so that the faithful share in his reign (20,4-6).

The influence of Ps 89,27 on the author of Revelation is not in doubt. As I have tried to explain in the note below, the meaning that Jesus is "ruler of the kings of the earth" is a direct *reportage* from Ps 89,27. In Rev 17,14; 19,16, the author refers to the open manifestation of Jesus as King of kings, an epithet we have seen ascribed to God in Ps 92. What Jesus denies to accept from Satan - "all the kingdoms of the world and the glory of them" (Mt 4,8-10), he has received through his faithful obedience unto death. The resurrection is his vindication. By his elevated status he is acknowledged as the supreme ruler.[106]

V. 6: Through, his death, his great sign of obedience to the Father, Jesus constitutes his followers into a kingdom. In the OT, the Jewish people, through obedience to the yoke of God's Law were established as "a kingdom of priests and a holy nation".[107] The early church ascribed this royal and sacral heritage to herself in the light of the exaltation of Christ as sovereign of all earthly kings. They also believed that their priesthood rested on the merits of Christ's sacrificial death on the cross.[108]

V. 7: Dan 7,13 where the figure like a son of Man comes with the clouds of heaven and Zech 12,10 where the Jerusalemites shall "look on him whom they have pierced" and "mourn for him" are taken over by the author, re-adapted and employed "to describe the impending advent of the victorious Christ and the

---

[105] See Ford, Revelation, p. 40.

[106] And so Phil 2,10-11. This is a Christology I have recently discovered in Matthew's Commissioning pericope. Cf. C. U. Manus, "'King-Christology': The Result of a critical study of Matt 28:16-20 as an example of contextual exegesis in Africa".

[107] Ex 19,5-6/Isa 61,6.

[108] Cf. Mounce, Revelation, p. 72.

response of a hostile world to the revelation of his universal sovereignty".[109] Jesus comes with the clouds, that is, within divine presence, a *theophaneia*. At his arrival, all the tribes without any barrier will mourn for the divine judgement which he shall execute (Rev 16,9,11,21).

V. 8: The Reading is concluded with a divine voice. God declares that he is *Alpha* and *Omega* which literally means the first and the last letters of the Greek Alphabet. As an inclusive concept, Alpha and Omega supposes that "God is sovereign Lord of all that takes place in the entire course of human history".[110] He is the beginning and the end. As sovereign Lord, he is the Almighty. As Mounce correctly opines, the title points "to God's supremacy over all things".[111]

To bring the discussion on Apocalypse to a close, I would state that in light of this brief analysis, the reasons for its choice into the liturgical rite of the Feast of Christ the King equally appears obvious: its high Messiah-King Christology; its relationship with and the continuation of the themes of the Danielic Son of Man prove beyond reasonable doubt that the early Christians, especially those whose suffering faces are reflected in the Book of Revelation employed the titles as legitimate proof-texts for their inculturation of Christ's Kingship in the context of the persecuted churches in Asia Minor.

8.3.5   Jn 18,33-37

This reading is taken from John's Passion Narrative. It describes the first interrogation scene before Pilate, probably in the Praetorium (vv. 33-38) and it includes in its context Jn 19,9b-

---

[109] *Ibid*.

[110] *Ibid*, p. 73.

[111] *Ibid*.

10a,15a.[112] A. M. Hunter supposes that the court of Pilate was at the Fortress Antonia.[113] Whereever it might have been, what matters is that John tells us that Pilate cross-examines Jesus. His first question is: "Are you the 'King of the Jews'" (v. 33b)? The use of the title, *rex Iudeaorum* by the Governor was by no means accidental. Why? The environment had been obsessed with the hope of the emergence of a national liberator popularly styled 'the King of the Jews'.[114] It seems that Pilate's question reflects both doubt and uncertainty. Jesus' answer which in the Synoptics is "You say so" has, in John, become returned as a question: "Do you ask this of your own accord or have others spoken it to you?" (v. 34). M. Sabbe defends the view that here is "a redactional elaboration of the Synoptics by the Johannine author"[115] According to Sanders-Mastin, Jesus' question seeks "to know the background to the question", whether it is "the basis of the charge against him" or simply to satisfy the questioner's own curiosity.[116] Pilate's answer, "Am I a Jew" (v. 35a) may well reflect both a slight arrogance and a ridicule against the Jewish authorities who laid such charges against Jesus.[117] I agree with Brown that Pilate's question suggests that he had no prior knowledge of Jesus except the information passed on to him by those who charged him to his court.[118]

---

[112] J. N. Sanders & B. A. Mastin, A Commentary on the Gospel According to St John, p. 396.

[113] A. M. Hunter, The Gospel According to John, The CBC, Cambridge, C.U.P., 1963, p. 171.

[114] Cf. Brown, The Gospel According to John (XIII-XXI), AB, New York, Doubleday, 1970, p. 851; R. Kysar, John, ACNT, Minneapolis, Augsburg Publishing House, 1986, p. 277.

[115] Cf. M. Sabbe, "The Trial of Jesus Before Pilate in John and its Relation to the Synoptic Gospels", in *idem.*, Studia Neotestamentica: Collected Essays, BETL 98, Peeters, Leuven University Press, 1991, p. 471.

[116] Sanders-Mastin, A Commentary, p. 396.

[117] See Hendricksen, New Testament Commentary, p. 407.

[118] Brown, John, p. 852.

A crowd gathered. One may wish to agree with Sabbe that in the trial scene, the Jews renounce their expected Messiah and prefer the Roman emperor.[119] The presence of the crowd described in John as "your own nation and the Chief priests" reflects Jewish nationals to whom Jesus belongs and their religious authorities. The complicity of the Chief Priests and the Sanhedrin which they represent appears a conscious exoneration of the Romans and the inculpation of the Jews.[120] Pilate's question, "... what have you done?" (v. 35c), by which the Governor seeks to know what crime he has committed is subtly cornered by Jesus. Exegetes consider it a much more fundamental question. A judge cannot pass fair judgement without hearing the defendant's version of the case preferred against him. Instead, Jesus answers: "My kingship is not of this world ...". The response appears partly an answer to the very first interrogation in v. 33: "Are you the King of the Jews?".[121] In other words, Jesus denies the charge and explains the true nature of his kingship, that is, what it is not; namely that it is in this world yet it is not of this world. What a paradox! Perhaps, it is better for our African readership to be familiarized with an interpretation of this verse offered by our "great ancestor" in faith, St. Augustine of Hippo. According to the ancient exegete, "His kingdom is here till the end of time but ... it does not belong here because it is in the world only as a pilgrim".[122] Our brother, Augustine had employed concepts derived from the Greco-Roman thought-world in which he drank deep. What is the meaning of "end of time" and "pilgrim" for the majority of Africans whose worldview have no such concepts of time and ideas? Can Augustine's explanation still help us in our search? While we may jubilate over the fact that the idea of the *Pilgrim Church* is a theological construct an African had bequeathed to the Church Universal, we must not loose sight of the fact that

---

[119] Sabbe, "The Trial of Jesus", p. 473. According to Sabbe, the action of Jews who refuse to enter the Praetorium for fear of defilement is ironical and "... those who present themselves as faithful to their own laws (18,28c,31b; 19,7) are ready to reject their Messianic king and to submit to Caesar", *ibid*, p. 496.

[120] See my "The Universalism of Luke and the Motif of Reconciliation in Luke 23:6-12", *ATJ* 16(1987)121-135; also Kysar, John, p. 277.

[121] Brown, *ibid.*, who notes that Jesus lays stress rather on the Kingdom instead of addressing himself to the issue of the controversial kingly title; also see Hendriksen, New Testament Commentary, p. 408.

[122] Augustine, In Jo. cxv 2; PL 35: 1939 cited by Brown, John, p. 852.

early African Church Fathers highly treasured Julius Caesar's proverbial pronouncement: *ex Africa semper aliquid novi* (out of Africa, there is always something new). Still holding Caesar's dictum with pride, we should do well to realize that the motif of withdrawal from the *kosmos* (world) is Johannine.[123] For John as for Africans, the world is a hostile environment infested with forces that inhibit the developement of the fullness of man and his wellbeing.

Jesus' "men" or "subjects" (v. 36b) is a *crux interpretum*. Once again, this is due to the paradoxical nature of Jesus' kingdom. Brown's exegesis of the concept is impressive. But if I may remind ourselves of part of the data furnished by my *religionsgeschichtlich* approach in the study of African kingships namely, that a kingdom is unimaginable without a people, I am inclined to conclude that even if Jesus' kingdom be celestial, its sovereignty is deeply anchored in human history. Its inhabitants and prospective members are men and women of flesh and blood. There is no other way Africans would perceive it. It is senseless mystifying the concept. Africans think concretely and not in abstract terms.

In Pilate's question: "so you are a king", one can see that the interrogator now avoids adding "of the Jews". Probably Jesus' anti-Jewish polemic has rightly penetrated his ear. In what follows thereafter, Jesus admits that Pilate has rightfully said what he is, "a King". Let us settle therefore with the fact that what Jesus gives is an evasive reply.[124] According to one author, Jesus' "answer is neither a denial nor an affirmation".[125] He does not deny that he is king.[126] As E. C. Hoskyns rightly points out "Jesus ... states quite clearly that a kingdom and sovereign authority and power are His by right, but that the source of his authority is not of this world". Commenting further, he says "He does not say that this world is not the sphere of his authority, but that his authority is not of human origin".[127] Much as it appears true as Brown states, that "king is not a title that Jesus would spontaneously

---

[123] See Jn 14,2-3; 17,24 etc.

[124] Cf. Sabbe, "The Trial of Jesus", p. 497.

[125] Kysar, John, p. 278.

[126] Sanders-Mastin, John, p. 104.

[127] E. C. Hoskyns, The Fourth Gospel, London, Faber, 1947, p. 520.

choose to describe his role";[128] there is scriptural evidence that Jesus conceived his kingship in messianic terms. Did Jesus rebuke the two brothers, James and John who had applied for posts of esteem in the kingdom he was going to set up (Mt 20,20-23)? Besides, Jesus promised the Twelve special governing roles: each one ruling over one of the twelve tribes of Israel once the Son of Man was enthroned (Mt 19,28). Buchanan has correctly shown that the faith of the NT church as attested in the gospels supposes that Jesus is the Messiah-king. Jesus, he asserts, promised the Twelve "many material rewards when his administration was installed"[129]. In his opinion, the Twelve had invested heavily in Jesus' campaign ... and when the kingdom came, they would receive many times more things than they had given up (Mt 19,29; Mk 10,29; Lk 22,29-30).[130] And to cap it up, Buchanan states:

> ... there was a man, nearly two thousand years ago, named Jesus, a Jew, who lived in Palestine. He was called a "Messiah" which meant "anointed king"; "Son of God" which is a title for king; "Son of Man", which is a mythical title for king; and he was given the title "king" itself.[131]

This will remain to be true unless there is sufficient evidence to doubt the authenticity of Jesus' response: "Yes, I am a King", despite the Johannine expansion of it (I was born for this, I came into the world for this: ... v. 37) as an *ipsissima vox Jesu*. However, let no one misunderstand us. What is meant is a non-political kingship. When we use contemporary political language, we are using conventional expressions to create meaning of the texts written in thought-forms our age does not so easily understand than to spiritualise the whole affair about Jesus and his life work. Jesus' kingship is one of *koinonia*, (communal living and sharing) and with an integrative sense of *diakonia* (service). Thus, we are reckoning with a sublime Christology: Jesus is the Messiah-King who wins his glorious crown through suffering and humility.

---

[128] Brown, John, p. 854.

[129] Buchanan, Jesus. The King and his Kingdom, p. 38.

[130] *Ibid.*

[131] Buchanan, Jesus, p. 12.

V. 37c: And all who are on the side of truth listen to my
            voice.

Jesus is the harbinger of truth. Brown appositely remarks: "... Jesus' birth was the coming into the world of divine truth".[132] For John, Jesus' singular role in testifying to the truth is quite clear. It is seen in the very fact that he belongs to the above (Jn 8,23,28,38; 12,49; 14,10). Already, John has made us know that Jesus descends from heaven (3,13; 8,42). He knows the Father and the Son has himself listened to the Father (8,26). He is the truth in itself (14,6). By his numerous healing acts and exorcisms, he demonstrates the dawn of the true kingdom and salvation unto God's glory (14,6).[133] The Johannine verb, *akouein*, to listen, has attracted much interest of exegetes. In good translation it means, "to hear" (10,3). Usually it is the sheep bred in the Palestinian environment that when called "hears" the voice of the shepherd (10,3). Recently a number of exegetes of the SNTS have addressed themselves to the shepherd motif and its background in the Fourth Gospel.[134] Most believe that the Ancient Near Eastern mythology where the shepherd is the figure of the king provides the thought-form. The "sheep" are those who are faithful and believe in the truth Jesus has come to deliver. They are called into being by the Father and constitute the citizens of the kingdom. Here, again, John offers us a Christology of the Messiah-king who brings revelation and the soteriological aspect of truth.[135] Akin to John 10 is Mt 25,31-46 where in an eschatological scenario of the end-time, the Messiah-King will dispense judgement as the shepherd.[136] In light of the above exposition on the verse, it becomes obvious that

---

[132] Brown, John, p. 854.

[133] Cf. D. Zeller, "Jesu Ankündigung des Reiches Gottes - ein uneingelöster Scheck auf Zukunft?" in H. Wißmann (Hrsg.), Zur Erschließung von Zukunft in den Religionen: Zukunftserwartung und Gegenwartsbewältigung in der Religionsgeschichte, Würzburg, Königshausen & Neumann, 1991, pp. 89-102, p. 91f.

[134] J. Beutler, R. T. Fortna, The Shepherd Discourse of John 10 in its Context, SNTS 67, Cambridge, CUP, 1991.

[135] Cf. Sabbe, "The Trial of Jesus", p. 502.

[136] See my "'King-Christology': Reflections on the Figure of the Matthean Endzeit Discourse Material (Mt 25,31-46) in the African Context", Acta Theologica 11(1991)19-41.

Jesus' declaration reflects the reality of his kingship; a kingship established in truth and faith and to be lived in the hearts and lives of those who "hear" and "follow" him.

8.3.6 THE REJECTION OF THE MESSIAH-KING
(Mt 11,16-19/Lk 7,31-35)

The theme of the rejection of Jesus as the Messiah-King must have been an essential ingredient in the proclamation of the New Testament church to the extent that it is well documented as early as Lk 2,22-40. The theme runs through John's Passion Narrative as we have seen above. That the Jewish religious authorities prefer the Roman emperor to Jesus "the King of the Jews" is a Johannine nuance of the Rejection-motif in the teaching of the early church. Matthew, Luke and the Q-community preserve a tradition of repudiation by "this generation" or by "men of this generation". In these pericopae, the 'hardness of heart' of the Jewish people is the centre and focus of the picture the evangelists portray. In contrast to the saving opportunity provided to the people, the generation of Jesus still repudiate the mediation and wellbeing promised through him as the Messiah-king. D. Verseput has, in a recent work, *The Rejection of the Humble Messianic King*, detected a hidden parable cast "in a typically rabbinic manner" in the Matthean pericope.[137] According to Verseput, Matthew shows "deep frustration with the problem of a Messiah rejected by his own people" which "has led him to characterize Israel as closed front of opposition against the messengers of God".[138] The generation in question is non else but "Jesus' Jewish contemporaries who encountered his ministry".[139] These are the people whose attitude to Jesus (and John the Baptizer) are compared to the behaviour of the recalcitrant children who refuse to participate in the games proposed by their play-mates.

The main objectives of the evangelists in using the motif is to draw attention to the fate of a Messiah-king disowned by his own people. They use the title "Son of Man" to describe the coming of Jesus and his mannerisms. He is an eschatological figure, and as I

---

[137] Verseput, The Rejection of the Humble Messianic King, pp. 104-105.

[138] *Ibid.*, p. 106.

[139] *Ibid.*, p. 107.

have much earler shown, the harbinger of salvation. Inspite of the disbelief of his contemporaries, he proclaims the Reign of God. In the taunt: "... Behold, a glutton and a drunkard, a friend of tax collectors and sinners" (Mt 11,19b/Lk 7,34b), the evangelists sum up the accusations of the opponents of Jesus. As Verseput puts it: "They neither prepared themselves for the kingdom, nor participated in the joys brought by the appearance of their Messiah".[140] In sum, Matthew, Luke, John (and Mark before them) use the motif of rejection to delineate man's abject lack of appreciation in "God's wise design or purpose for man".[141]

This motif, and many such others in the NT have partially been responsible for the traditional Christian teaching that God sent his Son, Jesus to be the Jewish Messiah-king but that the Jews rejected him and became guilty of compassing his death (deicide). It is important here to underline the fact that the position of the churches on this "teaching of contempt" has now changed.[142] Contemporary ecumenists, exegetes and most biblical theologians agree that the charge of deicide is false. A distorted view of Judaism, especially of the Second Temple period and the contemporary Pharisaism as well as a bizarre secularization of NT texts have partially been the cause of this form of thinking. Jesus died for the sins of all mankind and for the wellbeing of the whole world.[143] It is through the surrender of his life for all that he has become a Servant-king, the real irony of his kingship. All Christians, the African Christendom, of course not excluded, should pay heed to the warning in the Vatican Document, *Guidelines* against distorting the scriptures "especially when it is a question of passages which seem to show the Jewish people as such in an unfavourable light" as objective science of exegesis reveals, *inter alia*, that such texts "have their historical contexts in conflicts ... long after the time of Jesus".[144]

---

[140] *Ibid.*, pp. 111, 117.

[141] *Ibid.*, p. 115.

[142] Cf. M. Braybroke, Time to Meet, London, SCM Press, 1990, Part One.

[143] Cf. C. U. Manus, "Jesus and the Jewish Authorities in the Fourth Gospel" in W. Amewowo et al. (eds.), Johannine Communities, Actes du Quatrième Congrès des Biblistes Africains, p. 149.

[144] *Ibid.*, pp. 151-152 notes 28, 29.

8.3.7   THE RESURRECTION OF JESUS
(Mt 28,1-8/Mk 16,1-8/Lk 24,1-12/Jn 20,1-13)

The Resurrection of Jesus is an essential article of faith in the early church; and in contemporary Christian religion, it is central to the Christian faith. It represents the fullest divine act of installation of Jesus as the Messiah-king as it marks the realization of God' saving activity for the world and for man (1 Cor 15,14-17). A glance at K. Aland's *Synopsis* (p. 325), shows that the Resurrection is a four-gospel account though told in each with some minor variations. The women disciples who came to anoint Jesus' body testify to the fact of the empty tomb. The *"angel of the Lord"* (Mt 28,2), Mark's *neaniskos*, youngman (Mk 16,5-6) and the *"two men"* (Lk 24,3) are encountered by the women. They encourage the frightened ladies (Mt 28,5/Mk 16,6/Lk 24,5-7) and *re-assure* them that what happened is a supernatural intervention in favour of Jesus.[145] They are directed to report what they saw to Peter, the head and spokesman of the eleven. And in his appearance to them, Jesus himself re-assures them that he lives (Mt 28,10/Jn 20,17; Lk 24,36-43). All these figures, some human, some mythical, and some merely symbolic representative figures re-assure the disciples through the women members of the exaltation of Jesus, the Messiah-king. The angel who announces the conception of the Messiah-king at the onset of the gospels (Mt & Lk) is here referenced to. Thus in an *inclusio* style of narrative, the angel's testimony confirms the re-assurance of faith in the event.

    The Markan *neaniskos*, is, as D. E. Nineham maintains "undoubtedly an angelic being...".[146] This is corroborated in Luke 24,4 where the clothes of the two men are described as 'dazzling'. The basis for this claim appears to depend on intra-gospel comparisons. The term *neaniskos* is quite commonly used in the New Testament and more often than not it refers to human persons (Mt 19,20,22; Lk 7,14; Acts 5,10, 1 Jn 2,13-14 and so on). In Mark, 14,51-52, the account of a young man who dared to follow the squad that arrested Jesus but fled naked when pursued readily calls to mind. I am however aware of the different interpretations of scholars on the Markan *neaniskos*. Personally I doubt much

---

[145] A. K. Jenkins, "Young Man or Angel?" ExpT 94(1983)237-239, p. 239.

[146] D. E. Nineham, The Gospel of Mark (1963) cited by Jenkins, *ibid.*

if the *neaniskos* of Mark is indeed an angel. I really have my reservations and would seem to agree with Jenkins that:

> ... the fact that angelic beings are mentioned in the other gospels does not therefore necessarily mean that Mark meant the young man to be taken for an angel. Indeed it may be asked whether, if we did not know the other gospels, there would be any question of assuming the young man to be an angel.[147]

Matthew and Luke following Mark agree that the women are recognized as seeking Jesus of Nazareth who was crucified but has risen (Mt 28,5/Mk 16,6/Lk 24,5). "To seek", (*zeteo*) in its Greek meaning is simply used for looking for lost or misplaced objects of value. It was also used to express the search about philosophical and religious truths. In the LXX, the Greek Bible, the verb is employed in a rather technical sense to express the search for Divine Wisdom as the Sapiential books make clear. The very equivalent of the verb in Hebrew is *darash* which in Jewish literature is usually found as *darash ha Torah*, meaning the studious search and interpretation of Scriptures. Given these manners in which the verb is used, it appears that Mark is saying that the women disciples are in quest not only of the person of Jesus but of the revelation which he imparts because by his Messiahship, Jesus has become the embodiment of Divine Wisdom, hence the object of search.[148] The "two men" of Luke hark back to the adoration of the "three wise men" of the infancy narratives. Matthew underlines the fact that the resurrection is Christ's glorification and exaltation (Mt 28,17).[149] In his commissioning narrative (Mt 28,16-20), he gives expression to the divinized status of the resurrected Christ to whom all *proskynesis* is given.[150] Mt 28,18 confirms that the installation to kingship of the risen Jesus has become an accomplished reality.[151] For Matthew, the risen Lord "who directs, commissions and is worshipped by the

---

[147] Jenkins, p. 238.

[148] Cf. R. F. Collins, "The Search for Jesus: Reflections on the Fourth Gospel" *Laval théologique et philosophique* 34(1978)27-48, esp. pp. 35-36.

[149] See Mackey, Jesus, p. 119.

[150] H. Greeven, "Proskyneo", *TWNT*, 1959, pp. 750-767.

[151] Manus, "'King-Christology': The Result of a Critical Study of Matthew 28,16-20", p. 37.

210

eleven is the enthroned and exalted Lord, who has been justified by the Father and granted authority to reign in his stead ..."[152].

In his earthly ministry, Jesus claims that with his person the Reign of God and the realization of God's Kingship for the world has broken in. Now his resurrected status implies that, in raising him, God confirms his presence, his love and power in the person of Jesus. As in the case of the African kings, enthronement is the peak of royalty. But Christ's installation as King is far more sublime. His resurrection is the greatest event of his enthronement. The resurrection marks the occasion when he is placed at God's right hand and made Lord and Messiah (Acts 2,32-36). The evangelist Matthew makes it plain that Jesus, as Son of Man shall "be seated at the right hand of Power" (Mt 26,64).[153] But Jesus' Lordship and Kingship is service. For Jesus, true kingship consists in being a servant (Mk 10,42-44).

8.3.8   CONCLUSIONS

The investigation undertaken for this chapter has sought to study how the early Christians conceived the nature and kingship of Jesus and the theological rationale for the Church's choice of the Lessons for the *Feast of Christ the King*. Since some African Christologists are under the impression that to cast Jesus as an African King is a disservice to African Christian theology, the findings of this chapter on how the early Christians and their evangelists understood Christ's kingship and contextualized it in the light of OT scriptures help us disabuse our erroneous minds. The texts so far analysed and the others too numerous to treat in this volume indicate that Jesus was confessed as the Son of David, the expected and the anointed king. As in the Judean royal ritual, the king was declared "son of God" on his

---

[152] *Ibid.*, p. 42; and also see, Kysar, John, p. 139.

[153] The declaration reflects the oracles of the Davidic coronation psalm (Ps 110,1). "'The Lord said to my Lord (the king), sit at my right hand, till I put thy enemies under thy feet'" (Acts 2,34-35; Heb 1,13; 10,13).The context is the installation of the king by God. Luke-Acts adopts this coronation motif to describe the resurrection of Jesus (Acts 13,32-35). Once again, these are good examples of the adoption of the OT to contextualize the Christ event in the NT Church period.

enthronement, so is Jesus anointed "Son of God", the Messiah-King, the King of kings and Lord of lords in these events. Besides, Jesus' saying in Mt 11,27//Lk 10,22:

> All things have been delivered to me by my Father and no one knows the Son except the Father, and no one knows the Father except the Son and any one to whom the Son chooses to reveal him

resonates the unique authority he claims as the Messiah-King. This authority is rooted in prophetic literature. In the royal accession oracle, paralleling African royal enthronement rites, prophet Isaiah says of the Davidic king:

> The Spirit of Yahweh shall rest upon him,
> A Spirit of wisdom and understanding,
> A Spirit of Counsel and power,
> A Spirit of knowledge and fear of Yahweh (Isa 11,2).

In his activities, especially in his healing acts, Jesus recognizes himself as fulfilling the royal ideal. He recognizes that his kingship rests on how well he brings about the Reign of God as the anointed Son of God. In Lk 4,16-20, patterned on Isa 61,1-2, Jesus informs the Galilean audience that he is "the anointed deputy of the Divine King".[154]

The title "Son of David", implies that Jesus is remembered in his earthly life, in his activities and mission. By using this epithet, the evangelists make it clear that Jesus relates to God in an analogical manner as that relationship between David, the old king and God. This is the point of Ps 2.7. His choice is perceived as similar to that of his ancestor, David.[155] In his person, the eternal dominion promised to the son of David who comes forth from his body has in the Easter events fully been realized. The Easter events mark his exaltation into the realm of the Spirit, a status which his baptism already indicates. The Resurrection is his establishment as the promised Son of God who is now vested with authority and power.[156] He exercises his kingship over the Christian community; a

---

[154] Gray, The Biblical Doctrine of the Reign of God, p. 336.

[155] Cf. J. D. Kingsbury, The Christology of Mark's Gospel, Philadelphia, Fortress Press, 1983, p. 47.

[156] Manus, "'King Christology': The Result of a Critical Study of Matt 28:16-20", p. 37.

community whose members are marked by *agape, diakonia* and *koinonia*. It is also discovered that the kingship of Jesus is non-political though its universal significance bears much on the relevancy of Christian leadership in contemporary society; especially in the developing nations of Africa and rest of the Third World.

In the Triumphal entry into Jerusalem, it is noted, among other things, that Jesus humbly rides into the Temple precincts and conducts himself as a teaching messianic king and not like the Zealots whose cleansing programme is characterized by violence and militancy. The teaching which Jesus gives is prophetic and kingly. It is universal. His rulership brings all nations under his sovereignty. His Messiahship has its central manifesto as *CHANGE*; a U-turn towards the dawn of a new order, a reality which his parable of the patch of new unshrunk cloth on an old garment and the new wine in old wineskins (Mk 2,21-22) and the Matthean end-time judgement scene (Mt 25,31-46) allude to.[157] This order is to be tabernacled in a new temple built on faith, love and justice in which relationships between members are far more effective than those founded on cultic rites and sacrifices. For his revolutionary teaching, it is noted that his opponents reject him and plan to kill him. In the trials that ensured upon his arrest, the nature of his kingship is actually revealed. He is a low-profile Messiah-king, a servant king, one who shepherds those who hear and follow the truth his rulership offers mankind.

It is noted that his birth is rooted in sacred history, his election, choice and anointment with the Spirit of power are the consequences of his Baptism. The Transfiguration episode confirms his divine Sonship; the Triumphal entry is the sign of his royal coronation procession and the Bethany anointing foreshadows his passion and suffering through which he rides to the pinacle of his kingship (Mk 14,3-9/Mk 15,1/Lk 24,1). Pss 2,7; 110,1; 118,22; Isa 42,1; Zech 9,9 and the other OT texts serve to prove that in Jesus, the ancient promises are fulfilled, the divine plan realized and the Reign of God inaugurated.

My analyses of the Readings of the Feast of "Christ the King" show the wisdom of the Church in the choice of those dense Christological texts. The OT texts of the Readings (Dan 7,13-14 and Ps 92) with their topical messianic motifs re-confirm the Church's tradition already began by the evangelists; namely that the scriptures are "good news"

---

[157] C. U. Manus, "'King Christology': Reflections on the Figure of the Matthean Endzeit Discourse Material (Mt 25,31-46)", pp. 38-39.

because they speak not only of the Kingship of God in the OT history but the Messiah-Kingship of Jesus. They attest that in Jesus the old promises made to David and his lineage have come true. In choosing the OT texts, the Church shows herself in solidarity with the Jewish people and faith in acknowledging God's universal sovereignty but goes ahead of them in confessing Jesus as the Messaih-King and God's Regent on earth. The passages of the Apocalypse and John complement the OT to establish Jesus as the Messiah-king who has come. Jesus is king not of the profane world but of the People of God who listens to the truth which he has come into the world to bring. Nevertheless, the People of God are flesh and blood men and women who are inhabitants of the city of man. Thus, *King-Christology* is the face of Christ that ultimately emerges. As the Sovereign Lord, Christ is indeed the ruler of all persons, families, the human society, the state and the whole universe.[158] He is the King who has obtained his regency through obedience to the Father and his submission to death on the cross. He is nothing if not the Saviour-King, the Servant-King, the only Son of God who reveals the truth of the Reign of God and the One who goes between all humans and the Father.

---

[158] Cf. J. Lambrecht, "Christus muß König sein", *Communio, Internationale katholische Zeitschrift* 13(1984)18-26.

CHAPTER NINE

KINGSHIP : AFRICAN AND NEW TESTAMENT IDEAS

9.1   INTRODUCTION

This chapter presents the summation of the study. Firstly, it presents, in a discursive manner, a summary of the main ideas from the anthropological and ethnographical data on African kingship systems in the pre-contact period. It provides a review of the processes which established African kings-elect in office, the court theology which grounded the kingships they occupied and the consequences of kingly rulership in African traditional communities. In the second step, the phenomenon of kingship is interpreted in its cross-cultural contexts. What constitutes the essential components of kingship be it African or scriptural is highlighted. A crisp but brief review of the NT central thought on the kingdom of God and Jesus' kingship is presented in the third step. Since the NT is a much familiar and well-known material than the exposée on African kingships, the discussion concentrates on highlighting the topical themes in the later. Fourthly, there follows comparisons of African ideas with those of the NT. A tabular presentation of the major commonalities opens the comparative section.

It is however neither claimed that there are exact parallels in the African "graphies" with the NT "scripts" nor are there identical theological evidence approximating one another in terms of dates, origins, derivatives and even genealogy. Neither do both originate in the same culture zones nor do I draw the conclusion that there exist any literary relationships. What is relative to my proposal in this study is the analogy with the humanity of Christ; that is, the manner in which African categories of kingship apply by similitude to the NT ideas about the Messiah-King. The striking similarities and contrasts help us recognize the full implications of the kingship of Jesus in the African contexts. The principle objective of the chapter is therefore to outline the motifs that are similar (if any) and those which are dissimilar. It is the similarities and dissimilarities of ideas, themes and thoughts that clarify in what manner Jesus is or is not the African King. This chapter may not therefore be fully understood without a thorough reading of the preceding sections. The conclusion is a reflection on the immediate implications of King-Christology which arise from the insights gained through this comparative approach.

The comparative method has a value. I believe that the introjection of African kingship concepts and ideas into the Christian theology of Christ the King helps identify autochthonous African categories with a traditional Christian doctrine. Moreover, it allows the categories permeate theological reflections of a revealed truth. This is in itself, I believe, apropos to the task of re-contextualizing in the African context the contextualized NT thought on the Christ event. The paragraphs in this section may be short as each is designed to stress a particular point. Aware of the dangers of parallelomania characteristic of European and American biblical scholarship in recent years,[1] I prefer to invest my interest on the analogical thematic features derived from longitudinal rather than from punctiliar parallels.

9.2   DISCUSSION

The making of the African kings involves elaborate and complex procedures. It comprises the consultation of the gods (Ifá in Yoruba tradition); the trials, fights, seizure and capture of the kings-elect (Yoruba, Shilluk); the public proclamation of the kings-elect (Yoruba, Shilluk); the summoning of the communities' nobility (Yoruba, Ganda, Zulu); the enstoolment, ensoulment and anointment of the candidate (Yoruba, Ganda, Shilluk and the Zulu); the swearing of the oath of office (Zulu, Shilluk, Ganda); the paying of homage to the newly coronated king (Yoruba, Ganda, Shilluk and Zulu) and the concluding speeches and banquets (Yoruba, Shilluk, Ganda). These processes ensure the rightful establishment of the kings as natural substitutes of their progenitors. The enthronement rites have been seen to portend in themselves some aura of mystery. The kings are believed to be "captured" or "seized" by the kingship prior to the enstoolment; and thereafter are enthroned on sacred stools or are stood on the tribal sacred coil like the *inkatha* of the Zulu Nkosi the symbol and the embodiment of the royal ancestors. It is discovered that such is the moment of their transformation and re-possession by the spirit of the progenitors and the culture-heroes of the race. Royal drums beat consistently. Praise singers address the enstooled kings. They are

---

[1] Cf. S. Sandmel, "Parallelomania" *JBL* 81(1962)1-13, p. 1.

honoured as the re-incarnations of the founding fathers of the tribal kingship. Public presentation of the kings mark the completion of the installation ceremonies. It is found out that the announcement of the throne-names taken by the kings; the addresses made by chiefs and the responses the kings return are social rhetorics which function to cement the installation rituals to the customs and laws of the land.

The eventual withdrawal into the chambers, the observance of taboo prescriptions; personal seclusion and ritual obligations of kingship enhance the royalty and sacredness of the incumbents. Their *status remotus* is therefore founded on the ritual maxim that whatever is sacred is hidden from sight and elevated in height.[2] The African examples of kingship indicate that for most African traditional communities, Kingship has been the apex of the social-political organisation and through it the *Pax et Securitas* of the state had been achieved and maintained. As a communal institution, the offices derive their efficacy in the context of the responsibility of the incumbents towards the politico-jural community which establishes them.[3] Without people, no king reigns. Prudent evidence uncovered in the investigations indicate that Africans conceive their kings in numinous and mystical terms; a conspectus which supports belief in the divine origin of the kings.[4] Kingship is thus seen as transcendent and the throne held as ever enduring as all the items of the royal paraphernalia indicate. Subjects revere the kings as the centres of their social and natural order.

On the other hand, kings are humans entrusted with the onus of implementing the rules of kingship. As royal office-bearers, they possess immense privileges and prerogatives. They have access to material wealth and are entitled to services ordinary peasants cannot receive. In the societies studied, there is no doubt that kingship confers on the holders power over the destiny of the people. They rule their people as supreme judges and lords. The kings' political and judicial authority confer on them absolute right over the care of their subjects, land and cattle. They operate the distribution of all kinds of bonanzas, slaves, war booty, cattle, tribute goods and perform as the chief tax collectors (through agents) and the

---

[2] Ray, The Kabaka as Symbolic Center of Buganda, p. 12.

[3] For some of these ideas, I am indebted to Fortes. Cf. his "Of Installation Ceremonies", p. 8.

[4] For similar and general ideas on kingship, cf. I. Engnell, Studies in Divine Kingship in the Ancient Near East, Uppsala, Almqvist, 1945, p. 4.

giver of all state appointments. Like any occupation, kingship has its own hazards, but these are reduced to a minimum through the vigilance of many powerful individuals and chiefs who are usually conferred with royal favours and in turn, offer defense to the realm.

Quite typical of the African installation ceremonies are the presentation of relics in such forms as the spear and the shield for the kings of the hunting and pastorlist societies and the beaded crowns and the sceptre for those of the forest regions. All these "material insignia of office symbolize more obviously the powers and capacities that pertain to the office".[5] The materials derive from the store-house of the founding patriarchs. Their presence at the ceremonies lend an aura of sacrality to the ceremonies "since they go back to the beginnings of the coronation rites and symbolize also the majesty of the monarchy".[6] The insignia represent the means of the continuity of office from ancestral times; and as Fortes correctly states, "they symbolize the powers and prerogatives, secular as well as mystical and spiritual, vested in it".[7] Apart however from mere symbolic values, the attainment of the kingly office is consummated when the bearers take possession of these relics. In possessing them, kingship takes possession of them. The Yoruba *Oba* gains possession of the *Obaship* when he dons the *ade*: the *Kabaka*, when he takes the *Lumansi* jaw-bone and the umbilical cord; the *Reth* when he takes possession of *Nyakwer* after the exasperating mock battles and the *Nkosi* gains possession of his office when he receives the *isiJula*, the hurling spear said to stand for ever as well as a new *Nkartha*. In the light of such investiture rites , it is arguable that kingship is a sacred legacy of the ancestors who are devoted to the guardianship of the customs and laws they had bequeated to posterity.

Kingship is however temporary in the hands of the bearers. They bear it for and on behalf of the society. Parts of the installation rituals take place in the royal palace as in the Yoruba and the Shilluk traditions or at the national sanctuary like those of the Ganda and the Zulu. In each instance, worship is conducted by the head-priests. Prayers, sacrifices and libations of wine are poured and the kings are presented to the Patriarchs whose blessings are solicited. In some tribal traditions (Yoruba, Ganda), the kings-elect are moved into the quarters of a chief who is the principal custodian of the court treasures. Periods of over forty

---

[5] Fortes, "Of Installation Ceremonies", p. 16.

[6] *Ibid.*

[7] *Ibid.*

days are spent in such seclusions. Here, it is found that the kings are instructed in the arts and obligations of kingship, informed of the treasures and wealth of the realm, the people and its major ethnic groupings . They are coached in the ritual duties which now devolve on them. This period of apprenticeship is noted to be crucial in the steps leading to the kings' accession and their ascent to the hereditary residence at the palace.

Finally, it is pertinent to discuss the notion of "eating" during the rituals installing some of the kings in Africa. The Yoruba Oba "eats" his predecessor's heart and "drinks" a portion from his skull.[8] The Kabaka eats and drinks various herbal concoctions the totality of which is recognized as "eating Buganda". The Nkosi drinks herbal mixtures in order to be fortified against all kinds of evil. The rites of "eating and drinking" at the installation ceremonies signify the incumbents effective occupation of their offices, the virtual identification between them, the progenitors and the kingship they have "eaten". These acts of ingestion are not only ritualistic, but also symbolic. As Fortes opines, they reflect something sacramental in sofar as the rites happen in the context of community sacrifice.[9] The newly elected kings recognize through the eating and drinking as Fortes further avers, the authority and power of the ancestors and other supernatural agencies, place themselves under them and pledge themselves to fulfil all the obligations of their offices.[10] Besides, the comingling with the ancestral spirits has a powerful symbolic dimension. It separates the kings from the subjects and endows them with mystical forces and the charisms which grant them the vital force to bear the responsibilities of their office. It is precisely this gift of mystical powers which sets the kings apart from the 'impure' world; makes them the only persons authorized to transcend the others and to instill awe and fear in their subjects.[11] Such powers are meant to ensure that kings adhere strictly to taboos and the rules of the game of kingship. Besides, it is found that kingly powers guarantee supernatural sanction to

---

[8] See P. Morton-Williams, "The Yoruba kingdom of Oyo" in D. Forde, P. Kaberry (eds.), West African kingdoms in the nineteenth century, London, OUP, 1967, pp. 53-54; also Fortes, *ibid.*, p. 17.

[9] *Ibid.*, p. 19.

[10] *Ibid.*

[11] Cf. J.-Claude Muller, "'Divine Kingship' in Chiefdoms and States. A Single Ideological Model" in Cleassen and Skalnik, *op. cit.*, pp. 239-230, pp. 241-242.

the political and juridical authority which the bearers wield.[12] Given these facts, I agree with Max Weber's theory that the validity of the claims to legitimacy such incumbents make, as the case of the African kings make clear, is founded on traditional basis where authority rests on a community's established belief in the sanctity of time immemorial mores and customs as well as the obligations such imposes on the agents exercising authority to uphold the claims.[13]

9.3 THE NEW TESTAMENT: A BRIEF OVERVIEW

My expositions of the Synoptic gospels, John and the random forays into the Deutero-Pauline epistles provide the scriptural basis for the discovery of the importance early Christians attached to Jesus' teaching on the kingdom of God. My analyses shows that God, the "Great King" acts in and through Jesus whom he confirms his "Beloved Son", the Messiah-King in his stead. It is found that in the Synoptic gospels, Jesus' activity is portrayed as focusing largely on what he does to bring about the Kingdom of God. And that he lives to proclaim the kingdom and dies to reign over it. My exegesis shows that the Reign of God and its eventual in-breaking in human history bridges the gap between the past and the future in order to emphasize the *present* as the hour of the reign of God in everyday life. Mk 1,15: "The time is fulfilled and the kingdom of God is at hand ...", is discovered to be generally agreed to reflect Mark's programmatic summary of Jesus' messianic mission towards the realization of the reign of God in our midst.

In Jesus' teaching and especially in the parables he tells, it is noted that his religious vision has nothing so much to do about himself and his personal identity but the nearness of the Reign of God.[14] He comes to reveal not so much himself but the Father and the Father's kingdom. In this manner, his life is a God-the-Father-centred life. In the healing acts he

---

[12] *Ibid.*

[13] See M. Weber, Economy and Society. An Outline of Interpretative Sociology, G. Roth & C. Wittich (eds.), New York, Bedminster Press, 1968 (1921), p. 215; also, see, B. Schnepel, "Max Weber's Theory of Charisma and its Applicability to Anthropological Research" *J. Anthrop. Soc. Oxford* 17(1987)26-48.

[14] Sobrino, Christology at the Crossroads, p. xviii.

performs, he testifies to his audience the power of God who works through him. For the early Christians, Jesus must be the *Christ*. My discovery of the contextualizing programmes of the evangelists in this regard, therefore, attests to the effort of the early Christian teachers and evangelists to grapple with the problem of the inculturation of the Christ event as the Messiah-King and as the *ho erchomenos* (the Coming One) who fulfills the divine plans. Certainly this notion of a kingdom must be different from those of the Africans yet there exist relative analogues which help us perceive, however dim it may be, the mystery of the kingdom of God and Jesus' kingship in it.

9.4 INTERPRETATIONS

My discussion on the cross-cultural patterns on the African kingships assist us uncover a number of features which, *inter alia*, confirm that traditional kingships are indeed associated with some transcendent qualities. Let me outline here such components of kingship as are gleaned from the systems examined. Parallel data from the four African kingship systems and the biblical view are not unsupportive of the characteristics of kingships in general. The discussion helps us achieve a break-down of the procedures of kingship installation and rites in traditional Africa. Now it becomes possible to perceive, at least, four inter-related components which are inherent in the structure of kingship itself; namely

    (a)   sacrality,
    (b)   rulership and authority
    (c)   protection and,
    (d)   benevolence.

When the incumbent kings satisfy these qualities of kingship, their regimes are said to be God-given and legitimized before their subjects. Let us briefly discuss the components.

9.4.1 THE SACRAL STUTUS OF RULERSHIP

According to mainline theorists in contemporary anthropological research, "the basic characteristic of the sovereign is his sacral status".[15] While the kings are not deities on earth as Frazer (1905) had thought, they are held as descendants of the "gods". Their pedigree in divinity makes them stand in better relationships with the gods of their lands than all other members of their communities.[16] According to Abéles, they, in fact, incarnate a legitimacy which transcends their powers.[17] This consists in their sacral status which establishes them as active intermediaries between their people and the gods whose viceroys they are. In this light, I readily agree with Abéles that the kings belong to the whole society but on the other hand find themselves projected above the same society because they are living incarnations of the totality of society, but yet transcend all its groups and members.[18]

9.4.2 THE COMPONENT OF RULERSHIP/AUTHORITY

As rulers of kingdoms, the kings reign over their lands and subjects. In secular contexts, this is a governmental component, part of which is realized through consultations with advisers, committees and councillors; and through the audience they grant to numerous people and representatives of other rulers. In carrying out this function, Claessen observes that the kings meet with their subjects and listen to their wishes and petitions.[19] In most of the communities I have studied, the kings judge their people and settle cases and disputes, even if their faces are never beheld by ordinary mortals. The authority of kings extends to the right of appointing ministers, essential services functionaries, chiefs and the royal guards.

---

[15] H. J. M. Claessen, The Early State, The Hague, Mouton, 1978, p. 577.

[16] Claessen, "Kingship in the Early State", p. 125; cf. also *idem.*, "Specific Features of the African Early State" in Claessen & Skalník (eds.), The Study of the State, pp. 59-86.

[17] Abéles, "Sacred Kingship", p. 2.

[18] *Ibid.*, p. 3.

[19] Claessen, "Kingship in the Early State", p. 119.

222

They lay down laws and in themselves embody law and order.[20] Laws and regulations are promulgated in their names. In the four representative African kingdoms studied here, the incumbent kings represent the supreme judges and the sole administrators of justice except in a few cases where the Prime Minister acts on the king's authority as the Ganda and Zulu traditions attest. Death sentences remain the prerogatives of the kings.

9.4.3   THE COMPONENT OF PROTECTION

The kings fulfil the important function of providing protection to their people and the strangers in the land.[21] They appoint military leaders and the commanders of their armies. This is true of the *Bashorun* in the Old Oyo Empire in Yorubaland who leads the national army in wars instead of the kings. Kings are known to "protect their people from all kinds of natural and supernatural dangers".[22] They are the protectors of orphans and widows, especially those of the dynastic lines (Ganda, Yoruba). They assure their own wellbeing through the agencies of courtiers who perform various duties aimed at protecting the kings and the inmates of the palaces or royal enclosures.

9.4.4   THE COMPONENT OF BENEVOLENCE

All African kings are respected by their subjects as kind and generous donors; the benevolent lords of the people. Kings achieve and maintain their legitimacy by ensuring the subjects of ample food supply and traditional health care. Various systems of trade and transfer of goods and services are evolved. Goods and funds accruing from market tolls and sometimes war booty are distributed to many wards, cultic groups, various ranks of chiefs and to powerful age-grades and social clubs. This early idea of re-distribution of wealth flourished as part of the economic system of African states in the pre-contact period. The kings establish their

---

[20] *Ibid.*, p. 120.

[21] See *ibid.*, p. 121.

[22] *Ibid.*

own markets, oftentimes, sited opposite the royal palaces. The states survive from funds and revenues derived from trade and commerce carried on in the kings' markets (Yoruba) and from inter-state trade. There are central food storage facilities built in many quarters of the kingdoms to provide food in times of shortages or famine. There is self-sufficiency as subjects work hard under a prosperous king and his leadership. As benevolent and open-handed rulers, African kings are known to grant royal gifts, titles, chieftaincies and rewards to valiant and successful subjects and also to distinguished princes, nobles and chiefs, especially to those who regularly send the tributes of their wards to the courts. In Baganda, for example, every act of the king, is reckoned as benefits and every deed done to his subjects as a gift.[23] Thus one can see that reward is granted for loyalty to the kings and that on the part of the subjects, such is seen as royal generosity. Royal gifts and honours therefore help to ensure loyalty and followership.

9.5   COMPARISONS

In this section, five distinct stages in the structures in which the communities legitimize the kingship of African traditional kings and those through which the God, the Father approves Jesus' divine kingship are outlined in a tabular form. Recall that I have advised that there are no exact parallels. However, the differences enhance the quality of Jesus' Royalty. Here, we go:

African kings have their pedigrees in mythical origins. They are acclaimed descendants of the gods. Their long lists of genealogies point to this. The Oba from *Oduduwa*, the Kabaka from *Kintu*, the Reth from *Nyikang* and the Nkosi from *Dingiswayo* - all culture-heroes begotten by the gods, and the progenitors of the race.	Jesus' ancestry is traced to its origin (through David to God [Mt 1,1-17]), and Son of God (Mk 1,1). As John puts it, he is the only Son "who is in the bosom of the Father (Jn 1,18b), and according to Paul, he "... was in the form of God, did not count equality with God ..." (Phil 2,6)

---

[23] CF. J. H. Speke, Journal of the Discovery of the Source of the Nile, Edinburgh, Blackwood, 1863, p. 255.

The choice and election of the Kings are dependent on the will and the confirmation of the deities/culture-heroes.	The choice and election of Jesus of Nazareth is the will of the Father: "Thou art my beloved Son, with thee I am well plaesed" (Mk 1,11); "This is my beloved Son; listen to him" (Mk 9,7b par).
The installation, coronation, the ensoulment and the enthronement of the kings are communal events. The rites are witnessed and feted in the open spaces or palaces by the members of the local communities.	The installation of Jesus to Messiahship happens in community contexts. The Transfiguration on the Mountain is witnessed by the Jewish socio-religious heroes and the three apostles as representatives of the *Qahal Yahweh*, the ecclesial community. The Royal procession into Jerusalem is witnessed and hailed by the crowd. The Anointing at Bethany happens at a Party. The Trial takes place in a Court-Room before a crowd. The glorification of the Risen Lord is attested to by disciples of the Christian community. His Ascension is his enthronization at the right hand of the Father (Mk 16,19/Lk 24,51).
By the concoctions they drink; the oil and the ash smearing rites and the putting on of the royal regalia; reception of throne-names; and by their insignia of office, African kings become "anointed" as their communities' *reges et sacerdotes* (kings and priests) to perform as ritual heads, to enact and defend the laws of the land; to heal and to protect the health of the community (wholeness of life).	By his anointment with the Spirit of God at his Baptism (Mk 1,9-11 par), Jesus in Galilee, shows himself designated as the Messiah to usher in the Reign of God, to re-enact the Laws, to offer liberation and to provide fulness of life in abundance.
The enstoolment/the crowning rituals of African kings, their possession of and their re-incarnation of the soul of the founding heroes ensure the transmission of mystical quality of rulership and continuity of kingship through time.	At his baptism, the Spirit takes possession of Jesus in "bodily form" (Lk 3,22). The voice from heaven and the presence of ancestral socio-religious leaders: the Lawgiver (Moses) and the Prophet (Elijah) confirm the transference of mystical quality of Kingship and its roots in distant past to him.

9.6   ANALYSIS

Though these five parallel items roughly reflect a summary, we should recall such other parallel features as divine descent; and election usually expressed as "capture" and "seizure"; baptism or lustration, that is, ritual cleansing as is known in Zulu coronation ceremonies. The anointing and investiture with new regalia (in the case of Jesus, the shiny white garments at the Transfiguration scene), enthronement (in the case of Jesus the resurrection), throne-names (in the case of Jesus, Mt 1,16: Jesus who is called Christ), presentation to the ancestors and divinities (Yoruba: king visits the *Bara*; Ganda: the shrines are the homes of the royal ancestors; Zulu: king enters the temple to pay respects to the *amaKosi*). In Shilluk, the Reth passes through stringent trials symbolized in the water ordeal; and above all, his right to the throne is validated by his emerging the victor over *Nyikang* in the gruesome mock fights. In Jesus' case, he communicates with the principal representatives of the ancestral religion at his Transfiguartion. He enters the Temple as a royal figure. The event parallels the triumphant return of Gondongwana to the Zulu capital to take the reins of power upon the demise of his father; but more than this African king's triumphal return, Jesus conducts himself in a prophetic manner, another aspect of his kingship. Inspite, however, of some of these commonalities, there is certainly an intrinsic discontinuity between the NT texts and the "texts" of African royal creeds.

9.7   INSIGHTS FROM ANTHROPOLOGY

The similar and dissimilar elements can further be expatiated in the perspectives of mainstream anthropological categories typical of kingship studies in general.[24] While among Africans recogition and certification of the legitimacy of the kings-elect to the throne are required by the Royal Council, such as by the *Oyo Mesi* in the Old Oyo kingdom of the Yoruba, for example, Jesus is born king (Mt 1-2//Lk 1-2). According to Johannine christology, he came into the world precisely for that (Jn 18,37). He has no contender even

---

[24] Such as the perspectives developed by A. M. Hocart, Kingship, London, Watts Press, 1941.

226

if the Jewish crowd would prefer Caesar to him. Thus, his legitimacy is not in doubt by men of goodwill. In traditional African kingship systems no heir-apparent seizes, by legal, moral or religious right, power to proclaim himself king over the people. The NT shows that, inspite of the contention of "the men of this generation" who try to incite the Romans against Jesus as a messianic pretender, and unlike the Zealots, he makes no force, either by moral, legal or political means to acquire his kingship. Kingship is thrust upon him as the Son of David, the expected Messiah. While in the African traditonal systems, kingly authority is transferred to the prince-candidates by functionaries (like Semanobe at the Buddo Hill in Ganda tradition; the *Olori Marun* of the Yoruba royal culture) who themselves claim no aspirations and rights to the office of kingship, Jesus' kingship is his birth-right as indicated in all the episodes in his life where God approves of his royal right.

In the coronation rituals of African kings, the transferring agent, like Semanobe or Mainja (Ganda), or the Queen Mother (Yoruba), is usually a representative or one who acts on behalf of the community in light of the requirements of its moral and religious traditions. He or she performs the rite in consonance with traditions acquired from belief in the intervention of supernatural agencies. Such beliefs are sustained by cosmological beliefs embodied in myths and the worldviews of the people. In Jesus' case, there is no such ritual agent or agents. Though Moses and Elijah may fulfil such roles, God himself gives him his royalty from above. In his life work, Jesus ushers in the Reign of God and acquires its throne of glory through his suffering and death. African subjects recognize that by the public rite of investiture, such as in the case of Shilluk's Reth involving competitive mock combats, the royal office and kingship are symbolically acquired by the victorious candidate. For the early Christian communities represented in the gospels of Mark, Matthew, Luke and John, God's approval that Jesus is his beloved Son to whom all should listen and the context in which the election is proclaimed, is far more sublime in so far as God himself declares Jesus as his royal Son. In God's kingdom, competition is out of the way. As G. O'Collins states, Jesus' unique relationship with God is certainly far more superior. Jesus' Sonship alludes "to an intimate link that communicated divine salvation to human beings".[25]

There is no tradition that any of the four African kings studied or their predecessors resurrected from the dead as one would find in the Osiris myth of Egyptian religion. The

---

[25] G. O'Collins, "Jesus", p. 19.

resurrection of Jesus is a unique and superlative event. It expresses God's omnipotence which affirms Jesus as the Lord. His glorification as the Risen One, as has already been noted, is his installation and coronation *par excellence*.

9.8   MISCELLANOUS FEATURES

The triple components of kingship examined above can further be broken down into several small units of motifs which help facilitate our comprehension of the commonalities between the African and NT kingshp idealogies.

9.8.1   KINGSHIP AND COMMUNITY ACCLAIM

Even though as in the Yoruba case, some of the preliminary rites of the coronation ceremonies of an Oba-elect are performed in private, the community participates as a congregation and witness to the solemn event through its corps of delegated chiefs. In the NT, the women disciples, the unknown youngman of Mark and the "two men" of Luke who are witnesses to Jesus' resurrection and glorification are representative figures who speak on behalf of the believing early Christian communities. Witness is therefore an important aspect of confirmation of installation to kingship. Thereafter, the crowned kings are acclaimed by the communities as they mount the throne in the capital. Jesus' royal procession into Jerusalem is hailed by the crowd with songs and decorations with Olive branches. African kings-elect are received by the Royal Councils and ritual authorities who are the custodians of the kingship. In the African kingship ceremonies of installation, I have shown that the highlights of the ceremonies consist in the handing over of the royal insignia, material relics and other reverent instruments of office to the new kings. These constitute the paraphernalia of kingship and the symbols of royalty; the signs of the continuity of the office and the transference of regal charismata from distant past. In Jesus' case, he is not handed over any material object by any officiating prelate. But right from his cradle, material insignia suggestive of his kingship are donated to him by the Magi in the forms of gold, frankincense and myrrh. The three relics combine to indicate the fulness of his kingship in its inclusion of the offices of priesthood and prophethood.[26]

9.8.2   KINGSHIP AND PURITY

While the installation processes divest the African kings-elect from their lay, secular, profane and social states in life to purify them of all earthly dirty qualities (the Zulu Nkosi) and to create them into a personality proper and ritually "fortified" to bear the office of kingship "whose transcendence and perpetuity is pictured in dogmas about its sanctity and ideal inviolability",[27] Jesus, the Christ is born holy and pure as he "was conceived ... of the Holy Spirit" (Mt 1,20b) and in a lineage entrusted with the divine right of kings.

9.8.3   KINGSHIP AND THE CULT

Most African kings are known for their ritual leadership. Some of the kings pontificate in the major worship ceremonies of their kingdoms, and other some in the daily cult and at the great national festivals. They officiate as priest-kings even when they are not the Chief-priests of the states. By the sacrifices they make to propitiate ancestral spirits, it is noted that wellbeing and cosmic harmony thrive. In the Letter to the Hebrews, we encounter one of the NT's loudest preaching on the eternal high priesthood of Jesus, the Son of God whose place in the "highest heaven" is the assurance of divine bounty and grace.[28] The kings of Africa made expiatory sacrifices to atone for the evils of their communities and used scape-goats to send off known and unknown evils in order to ensure fullness of life for themselves and for

---

[26] For further interpretations on the legend of the Magi's gifts and their place in Christian art, see D. Rudloff, "Die Drei Könige im Geschichte und Kunst", *Die Christen-Gemeinschaft* 51(1979)15-22.

[27] Fortes, "Of Installation Ceremonies", p. 19; also see, M. Palau-Marti, Roi-Dieu au Benin, Sud-Togo, Dahomey, Nigéria Occidentale, Paris, Collection Mondes d'Outre Mer, 1974, p. 133.

[28] Heb 4,14-16.

the states because they live, according to the author of Hebrews, in the limitations of weakness.[29] Christ's high priesthood transcends the priestly functions undertaken by the African kings. As God's Son, approved and called to the ranks and as "a priest of the order of Melchizedek, and for ever",[30] Jesus lives for ever and as such his priesthood is perpetual and has a far more wholistic soteriological value as the intercessor "for all who come to God through him".[31] While the African priest-kings perform their ritual services annually to fulfill the requirements of routine state cultic rites and to placate the spirits and the divinities when disasters and catastrophic events strike or when the climate is unclement, Christ appears in the real presence of God on behalf of all humanity and offers himself only once. African royal rituals are annual, but Christ' sacrifice, according to Hebrews, is never repeatable. He is himself the victim of his sacrifice. He offers himself as ransome for many.[32] The author of Hebrews recognizes the enthroned status of Christ "at the right hand of God" from where he reigns.[33] The singular value of Christ's once-and-for-all sacrifice is re-emphasized. Its soteriological consequences are far-reaching and tops all of Africas' royal rituals. Even though the author places much emphasis on sin and the value of "sin offering", themes not unfamiliar in the African concept of sacrifice, the major contrast is that Christ's sacrifice "has achieved the eternal perfection of all whom he is sanctifying".[34]

9.8.4 KINGSHIP AND RULERSHIP

African kings ruled with authority and led their subjects as their owners and as the administrators of justice. Theirs was a society where the kings were seen as gods incarnate; as 'Igba keji Orìsà, the next in rank to the divinities, as in Yoruba tradition. Many praise-

---

[29] Heb 5,1-6.

[30] Heb 5,6.

[31] Heb 7,23-28.

[32] Heb 9,24-28.

[33] Heb 10,11-14,18.

[34] Heb 10,18.

names we have already seen are used to laud their divine statuses and majesty. In all the traditions, installation confers on the invested kings full entitlements to their offices and the responsibility to cater for the wellbeing of their people. Jesus' elevated status and enthronement as the King establishes him as One with all authority "in heaven and on earth" (Mt 28,18b). In the performance of the signs and wonders granted him by God, his authority as King is the central focus of the evangelists' portrait of his mission. Here, I freely quote myself from an earlier study:

> The sum total of the work of Jesus and his Christship constitute his authority
> in heaven and on earth. Thus, for Matthew (see Matt 11:27a/Lk 10:22) and
> the Q-Community, Jesus is the recipient of divine prerogatives, charisms only
> bestowed at the occasion of his enthronememnt and installation.[35]

Jesus executes a God-given authority more than the authority kings exercise in Africa over their states and people. Jesus' authority is quite often considered awesome and even frightening by those who encounter him. He however does not dominate; he rather leads people to understand by words and action.[36] His authority extends to his teaching and healing activities. He struggles against oppression and lives out the standards of his own ethical proclamations. Jesus is not only the embodiment of law and order in the kingdom of God, he interprets with confidence God's will on legal issues, establishes the importance of some over others and abrogates certain written laws. He even condemns oral traditions and disallows some irrelevant religious and pious practices. He applies the law in personalistic circumstances and interprets many of the hash statutes in favour of people and as an expression of love of neighbour. Indeed he is the one whom God firmly establishes in authority as King over all peoples. The Parable of the Vineyard illustrates how the Son is designated over the slave to inherit authority over the vineyard. I have shown elsewhere that according to Mt 25,31-46, at the end of time, Jesus will appear in glory at the right hand of God to judge with authority the peoples of the earth.[37] Thus the Risen Jesus possesses

---

[35] Manus, "'King-Christology': The result of a critical study of Matt 28,16-20", p. 37.

[36] Rhoads-Michie, Mark As Story, p. 104.

[37] Manus, "'King-Christology': Reflections on the Figure of the Matthean *Endzeit* Discourse Material (Mt 25,31-46) in the African Context", pp. 36-37.

"universal authority which empowers him to discharge his duty as the Christ, the King, to the community".[38] Besides, Jesus is the Good Shepherd. He promises shelter to the homeless, not transient shelter but eternal and everlasting home for all who prosper the dawn of the Reign of God.

9.8.5   KINGSHIP AND ROYAL FUNCTIONS

One specific royal function executed by African kings is the purification of cultic places and sacred spots. Some of them are Temple-builders; supporters and preservers of national deities. Many appoint and consecrate curators and priests (Yoruba, Ganda and Zulu). In Jerusalem Jesus cleanses the Temple. The gospels tell us in graphic terms how he overturned the tables of those who carried on business in the Temple. For Jesus, the Temple is a place of prayer. Besides, he foretells the destruction of the same Temple when it outlives it usefulness (Mt 24,1-2 par.). He promises to destroy the visible Temple and to rebuild it in three days. Is Jesus here not a Temple builder; namely his Church? Does Jesus not appoint the Twelve, ordain and send them out to go and spread the goodnews? Jesus, in fact, fulfils these kingly roles in a much far-reaching fulfilling manner pleasing to God, the eternal King.

9.8.6   KINGSHIP AND ANOINTING

Bethany as the spatial setting of the Anointing of Jesus by the unknown woman in the Synoptic gospels and the symbolism her action evokes is not unconnected with the social significance consequent upon the Messiahship of Jesus. Like in the installation of African kings, the value of cleansing and anointing is noteworthy. The Nkosi is anointed in the state's palace-hall by an officiant of the national priesthood. Unlike the African king, Jesus is not anointed in the Jewish national Temple. The national priesthood unlike in the case of African tradition is in opposition. It is rather a simple woman who anoints Jesus in a private house, the home of a leper, and at a Party. Thus, for Mark and the other evangelists, in the

---

[38] *Idem*, "'King-Christology': The result of a critical study of Matt 28,16-20", p. 37.

Reign of God sacred space is no longer Jerusalem and the Temple. The house of the leper, the unclean, impure and unholy spot has become alternative space as the locale for the sealing of Jesus' kingship. Herein lies one of the greatest significance of Jesus' Messiah-kingship: his kingdom knows no spatial limitations, no racial, tribal or social distinctions and boundaries. Jesus' Messiah-kingship supercedes the African traditional kingship rites in so far as the kings and their courtiers attach importance to cultic rights performed in particular sacred spots and for particular ethnic peoples. Luke points out that Jesus' positive approval of the woman's action portrays him as the King who liberates and saves persons who find themselves subjected to all forms of man-made degradations and barriers or as in many places in contemporary Africa, all tyrannical systems which are not in consonance with the promotion of the fullness of man (Lk 7,48-49).[39]

9.8.7   KINGSHIP AND SERVICE

African kings are never regarded nor regard themselves as servants to their subjects. The protective or defensive functions fulfilled by them are not seen in terms of service or servanthood. Rather they keep a retinue of court servants and slaves who, like in the Ganda tradition, bear the king on their shoulders during public ceremonies and outings. But servanthood is the hallmark of Jesus' kingship. He sees his role as a suffering servant in the perspectives of Isaiah (Isa 52,13-53). Jesus lives not to be served but to serve (Mk 10,45; Lk 22,27). Jesus' destiny as a servant can further be explained in light of Jewish sociology. In the Jewish patriarchal system, every minor son is *de facto* a servant (*pais*). In religious services, the quality of being "son" and "slave" *doulos* are closely related. In Exod 4,22-23; Jer 3,9, God claims Israel as his "first born son" and in turn, the people are his "servants" (Ezek 28,25; 37,25) or even "servants" (Isa 54,17; 56,6). Aware of this biblical background, Mark shows Jesus proclaimed by heavenly voices as the "beloved Son" (Mk 1,11;9,7). At the same time, Jesus, on his own part, looks upon himself as a "slave" (Mk 10,43-45; 9,35). It is in this context that Jesus' kingship implies both sonship and servanthood.

---

[39] Cf. E. E. Uzukwu, "Evangelization in Context: Human Promotion and Liberation", *AJT* 5(1991)274-285.

9.8.8   KINGSHIP AND MEDIATION

The ritual sacrifices African kings make on behalf of their people portray them as intermediaries between the gods and the people. Their sacred statuses has been shown to portend this function. There is however no myth or legend about the kings I have studied here dying a vicarious death on behalf of their people. But some of them like the Shilluk Reth in the mock combats and the Zulu Nkosi who, in the event of an outbreak of national wars, stay in the battle-fronts, lead his troops and never runs back from the enemy demonstrate acts of valour which may explain a latent vicarious sacrifice on behalf of their nations and peoples when it is possible.[40] In the OT, a king is a leader of his people. As D. T. Williams reckons, the king "was engaged in warfare both for, and with his people and sought to benefit them by his victory".[41]

For African Christians, Jesus is the only and one mediator and intermediary between man and God. He has conquered on the side of humanity all opposing forces and has given himself up as ransome for his people. He is therefore a *Rex Victor* - the victorious King (Mbiti 1972:52) in whose victory we share. He is our King because of his conviction of "being absolutely reliable in mediating the divine will and grace to others"[42]

9.8.9   NATURE OF JESUS' KINGSHIP

The kingship of Jesus is never exactly like any of the earthly African kingships. This fact lies at the heart of the comparisons made in this chapter. Jesus' kingship is of a higher realm. He has come to bear witness to the truth from above (John). His kingship does not originate from the world of humans. It is not confered by any earthly authority, not even by the satan (Mt 4,8). Its nature and character is totally different. He has no armed officers and retinues

---

[40] According to S. O. Abogurin, "the idea of an intermediary and sacrifice are areas which bring Christianity and traditionalists together ..." , cf. Abogurin, "The Cosmic Significance of Jesus Christ in the African Context. An Exegesis of Philippians 2:5-11", *Orita, Ibadan Journal of Religious Studies* 20(1988)3-14, p. 14.

[41] D. T. Williams, "The Four-fold Office of Christ", *ExpT* 100(1989)134-136, p. 135.

[42] O'Collins, "Jesus", p. 18.

nor councillors such as the *Lukkiko* (Ganda) or the *indunas* (Zulu). He has no police force as the Oba's *efa* or as those of the Nkosi who could have fought under his command to defend him from arrest in Gethsemane. He choses the low-profile manner and the way of suffering to realize and consolidate his kingship. The Church is today his visible kingdom.

9.8.10   JESUS' KINSHIP AND HIS HUMILITY

The outstanding quality of Jesus' kingship worth stressing is its meekness and humility. In the rejection narrative (Mt 11-12), the evangelist highlights the lowliness of Jesus' Messiahship. In the Triumphant entry into Jerusalem, Jesus rides on the back of the colt, the mark of the advent of a humble and powerless king. In his humiliation and rejection in the trial scenes, Jesus conducts himself as a gentle and quiet king. He accepts suffering as a means to receiving his crown. He ushers in the the Reign of God and assumes the challenging tasks of healing the sick, pardoning evils and the sinful persons; raising the dead and expelling the demons. In his crucifixion and execution, he humbly surrenders to death. Here is, as I have stated earlier on, the paradox of his kingship.

The evangelists depict a king who is at the same time a Servant of God. This is the distinctive aspect of *King-Christology*. Here is a category not found in the African kingship, not even in those cultures that practised ritual and symbolic regicide. Christ, the King is a meek, humble, quiet and simple King who ministers to the poor; delivers the afflicted and goes about as the messenger of salvation. His humiliation does not detract from his messianic roles. Here, I find myself at one with B. Combrink and B. Müller, two white South Africans who, in their comment on one of my recent articles on *King-Christology* published in their country, had this to say:

> ... there can be no doubt that honour and status is not to be sought in symbols of power and prestige, but in situations of lack of power, low rank and social insignificance, even dishonour (Malina & Neyrey 1990:116). The fact that Jesus' kingship is rejected, does not imply that his kingship is not real and true. The important thing is that in this way Jesus embodies the pattern of a

king who is rejected by his own people, a ruler who is truly a servant, the first who becomes the last.[43]

Jesus' enthronement and status as the *Rex Victor* behests us to join the earliest believers to continue to chant *Mara-natha*: Lord come, come soon.

9.8.11   KINGSHIP AND REJECTION

The theme of rejection is found in both the African and the NT traditions. African kings can be deposed, forced to kill themselves or even be slain, deserted and boycotted when they abuse their positions. Thus Kings who violate the rules of kingship to the detriment of the commonweal trade their positions with rejection and violent death. Some of the kings can even be subjected to the disciplinary control of their concillors, elders and the dignitaries who elected, invested and installed them. Inspite of their apprenticeship in the arts of kingship, they may still not possess the whole truth and wisdom about their kingdoms. Here lies the limitations of the earthly kings. In a somewhat similar way, the most explicit references to Jesus' kingship are located in the context of conflicts and oppositions. Jesus is rejected by the Jews on a flimsy excuse of provoking the Romans against the people (Jn 11,47b-50). But through his rejection and death, unlike the African kings whose rejection put an end to their regimes, Christ's kingship is permanently established. In the kingdom of God, there are no king-makers except the Father. And Jesus is the Chosen One, the Beloved Son to whom all should listen to. He is born to bring the truth about the kingdom and those who "hear" the truth he imparts are the *sheep*, that is, the faithful. The supremacy of Christ's kingship is nondescript.

---

[43] B. Combrink & B. Müller, "The Gospel of Matthew in An African Context - in dialogue with Chris Manus", *Scriptura* 39(1991)43-51, p. 47.

9.8.12   KINGSHIP AND DEATH

While kings die, kingships live for ever. This is a dictum predicated upon the mortality of our human kings. The occupants of royal offices in Africa and elsewhere are transitory bearers. Their majesty and powers are fleeting and short-lived. Inspite of their sacral statuses, they pass away and create vacancies on the throne which, many a time, are hotly contested by rival princes. Jesus' kingship is eternal. He died once but now he lives in perpetuity. His kingship has no end. There are no rivals and no successors. Once and for all God has crowned him the Everlasting King. God, who is Alpha and Omega as the author of Revelation maintains, transfers his kingly powers to him. The Christian Church acknowledges this since time immemorial. The ancient faith is expressed in the Apostles' Creed:

> ... and (he) is seated at the right hand of the Father. he will come again in glory to judge the living and the dead, and his kingdom will have no end.

9.8.13   THE CROSS AS PARADOX IN JESUS' KINGSHP

The cross, with the infamous inscription *INRI*, is, *par excellence*, Jesus' insignia of kingship. As the African kings are captured and "tied" to their kingships, Jesus is arrested, judged, executed and "nailed" to his kingship on the cross. What is the purpose of the inscription? Yes, at face value it appears derisive. But God who knows the human mind does not err. The authors of the inscription have said the obvious: Jesus is King. Did they not put a crown, though made of thorns, on his head? Did passers-by not jeer at him and hail him as King? Was Jesus not clothed in purple reminiscent of the flowing large regalia of the Yoruba Oba and the Shilluk Reth? Did the torturers not do him obeisance? The mockery and derision of his captors and executioners reveal the opposite. As a matter of fact, the evangelists describe the scenes with irony the purpose which is to reveal Jesus' kingship in its truest light. By his death, Jesus became God's reigning King. That is the paradoxical character of his kingship. It is its specific distinction and the major factor which explains why he is King of kings and the King of all Africa and the world. The fact that Jesus acquires his kingship through his death on the cross remains the perplexion of many a ruler. The climax is seen when he entrusts his spirit to the Father who receives it : "Father unto your hand I commend my spirit" (Lk 23,46).

9.9 CONCLUSIONS

The discussions, interpretations, reflections and comparisons, similarities and dissimilarities now equip us with new perspectives towards a broader understanding of the ideas of kingship in both pre-contact Africa and the New Testament. The visions and the conceptions of the African kingship cultures can now be seen to enrich New Testament ideas, at least, for the African readership and mind. The commonalities and parallel features that exist in both traditions prove beyond doubt that African ideas of kingdom, kingship and king are not valueless but possess positive ideas and notions useful for pragmatic inculturation of the mystery of Christ's Kingship in the African Christendom.

The components of kingship found common to the traditions but in which Jesus contrasts superiorly to those of the African kings indicate that *King-Christology* transcends African traditional religious cultures. Like the evangelists noted, the kingship of Christ is a traditional article of faith. Its complementarity with African kingship cultural thought-forms can be pressed and thereafter be harnessed to profit the most audacious of inculturational programme of the Church in Africa today. When inculturation is understood as the effort by a local Church to incarnate the Christian message in its cultures; namely to demonstrate how Christian faith must be lived in the local situations, then the *nativization* of the gospel to the African kingship ideas in theology, ecclesiology and liturgy shall be seen to belong intrinsically to the process of making the goodnews of Christ's kingship more meaningful and intelligible to the African peoples. Inculturating Christ's kingship presupposes, of course, that certain unwholesome elements in traditional African kingship systems be judged by the gospel and be rejected, modified or adapted.

What my King-Christology aims at, therefore, is the disengagement of the supra-cultural aspects of the gospel on the subject of Christ's kingship from its Western cultural trappings in order to profit the African situations. This is perhaps one of the ways its eventual contextualization within the African familiar concepts, thought-forms and expressions an be realized. The envisaged change must be allowed to pemeate Africa's social institutions in order to achieve the transformations of some of the traditional religious practices still associated with the installations of kings and chiefs being currently revived in contemporary Africa. This is important in so far as the manner or forms in which man, especially the African personlity responds to God is closely tied to his culture and thus relative. Acceptance of Jesus of Nazareth as African King implies making him at home in Africa's rich spiritual universe as one who fulfills Africans spiritual hopes and aspirations. A King-Christology which springs from the African context and from the African joy and experience of the Christian faith cannot be in anyway inferior as against any other form of conceiving who Jesus is to Africans and their descendants everywhere. What matters is how well such a Christological perception faithfully reflects biblical witness and traditional Christian faith.

My exegesis of the relevant texts confirms, among other things, that Jesus is the Son of David, the Son of God, the Servant King and Saviour. He is such a King precisely because of the authoritative acts he performs to herald the dawn of the Reign of God. In view of the fact that rulership in traditional African kingdoms involved a certain perception of the kings' benevolent and protective roles and the consequences these have upon the cosmic and material wellbeing of human existence, King-Christology with its insight into the redemptive role of Christ remains a bounteous substitute in the African religiosity. This is made possible by the fact that the New Testament stories contain a way of life, that is, how to live as a loyal citizen of the Kingdom of God. This way of life no doubt, finds its congruence in the Africans' experience of kingships and kingdoms and our strong sense of community. Besides, the multifarious political problems of the African peoples, even in times when kingship has become (in the states where it still survives), an institution of little political importance, clamour for the popularization of a virile Christology in which Christ should be emulated as a Servant-Leader. In other words, who Jesus is in the African heritage of spirituality cannot be removed from the significance of a Christ who in his sacrality, rulership and authority is himself African and addresses himself to modern African crises as manifest in ecclesiology, liturgy and above all in her endemic leadership problems. Thus, the experience of bad and inhuman political systems in many regions of contemporary Africa and our readiness to *change* make sense when we believe that Jesus ushers in the Reign of God daily and reigns over Africa precisely because he is the exalted and glorified Servant-King.

CHAPTER TEN

GENERAL CONCLUSIONS

KING-CHRISTOLOGY. IMPLICATIONS

10.1   INTRODUCTION

My study has shown that Christology is indeed a biography but a bigraphy with a difference. Jesus of Nazareth is such a versatile figure whose transcendence has, from the NT times, been expressed in various portraits. He is versatile precisely because of the responses each faith community in the early church gave to the meaning his person evoked in their concrete life experiences. Many African theologians have, as my review of literature reveals, begun to see from different angles in which the Christ is African. My King-Christology catches up on the idea but zeroes in from another perspective. From the insights of the African traditional kingship cultures and the NT history, I offer a horizon in which Jesus of Nazareth relates to Africans as the Christ and Lord of history. This understanding of the biblical Christ in the light of a specific African cultural paradigm has far-reaching implications in the church and society. It points up the historical and the cosmic relevance of the kingship of Christ for the life and praxis of Christians in today's Africa. I judge this factor quite significant in view of the fact that the personality of Jesus continues to make and shape history in the present world order which, no doubt, influences the future orientations of a large portion of humankind. Indeed Jesus' past illumines the present and opens us towards the future with great expectations.

Having stated the reasons for researching this subject in the introduction, in what now follows, I wish to articulate the possible achievements of the research; namely how the resultant ideas may influence or rather say, improve ecclesial and pastoral praxis, promotion of liturgical renewal and the social political ethos; that is, the Christological implications for human welfare in modern Africa. In other words, the spirit of self-reliance and purposeful leadership which one can elicit from Christ's humble Kingship according to gospel witness impels me into having the precolonial African kingship systems unearthed and exposed for the benefit of my christological proposal. At the end, contemporary historical facts will be viewed with the lens of my christology in order to point up abiding messages to the Africa of our present, as of our tomorrow.

10.2   ECCELSIAL IMPLICATIONS

My King-Christology does not represent an authoritarian and triumphalistic imaging of Christ which manufactures religious symbols favoured and acceptable to those who wield ruthless power in the church and state establishments or to those who would absolutize the structures in the church to the detriment of the *Ecclesia* as *communio*. King-Christology has an affability comparable to the person of Christ himself. Its value for ecclesial and pastoral issues is as much limitless and profound as the mystery it intends to conceptualize in reality. The first christian communities knew that in the OT, kings ruled Israel as God's sons and directed the affairs of the *Qahal* or the *edah* in history and judged its members on behalf of God. The NT church knew and recognized that Caesar and other local kings such as Herod reigned and wielded authority in its stictest and hegemonic forms. In casting Jesus as the Messiah-King, the evangelists employed one of the many categories derived from the Jewish religious experience to express their communities' witness of Jesus. In such a manner, King-Christology is the product of the NT ecclesial experience. That experience involves the manner the NT communities to which the four gospels and the epistles were addressed gave meaning to their *life-situations* and activities in the light of Christ, the King-Servant and the King-Victor of evils, sins and death.

The witness of the first christian communities point up other ecclesial attitudes discernible from their own stuations and praxis. While traditional African kingship systems survived on the support rendered by councils, the Prime Ministers and the King-makers which, no doubt, reflect the hierarchical structure in our present-day ecclesial communities in Africa, the Servant-Kingship of Christ the Lord of the Church must be allowed to shine as an important pole of reference to African ecclesial praxis. Besides, the patriarchal character of African kingship sytems accords with the explicit will of the King-Saviour to confer upon men of good moral standing the sacerdotal authority of governing, teaching and sanctifying the members of the ecclesial community.

The African personality shares life in a collegial context. He is a bunch of interpersonal relationships which finds its survival and meaning in community. Thus, African sociology reveals that the *homo Africanus* is welded into a human community. Here is an ideal soil from where *sensus Ecclesiae* emerges as a singular quality and consequence of my King-Christology.[1] In the sense of the Church as communion with God through Jesus Christ, leadership in our parishes should become more participative and co-responsible.[2] King-Christology stands to prosper our programmes of inculturation, and especially as it highlights the New Testament theology of the Small Christian Communities (SCCs) and the need for community up-building and support. The SCCs should be allowed to emerge and to flourish as new models of the Church in Africa. The interdisciplinary approach adopted in this study uncovers, among other things, that Africans of the early states efficiently organized and cultivated their own affairs in clans and kin-groups such as was known among the Yoruba, the Ganda and the Zulu and so on. New Testament exegesis reveals the faces of many small and disperate groups of people who, notwithstanding their differences of opinion, found meaning in keeping company with Jesus.[3] Besides, the earliest New Testament Churches accepted Jesus as the *Christos*, the Anointed One, the son of David, Son of God. The SCCs should, in their basic orientations, be allowed to be African. It was in such settings that the leadership of the African kings were recognized, experienced and followed. Thus, the SCCs must be seen as formative ground where the *Goodnews* of the Messiah-King takes flesh in the African soil and sense of community: *ebi* (Yoruba), *kika* (Ganda), and *umunna* (Igbo)-systems.[4] There are values in churches patterned and structured in small communities. It is in such communities that ecclesial presence based and rooted in the traditional African communities; and which draws from the African communitarian sense of sharing can be

---

[1] On the origin of the concept, see, Paul VI, The Encyclical Letter, *"Ecclesiam Suam"* AAS 56(1964)609-659.

[2] Cf. Seventh General Assembly of the Synod of Bishops, *Propositio 10*.

[3] F. Wilfred, "Towards an Anthropologicall and Culturally Founded Ecclesiology: Reflections from and Asian Perspective", *VJTR* 54(1990)501-511; especially pp. 506-508.

[4] C. U. Manus, "The Community of Love in Luke's Acts: A Sociological Exegesis of Acts 2:41-47 in the African Context" *WAJES* 2(1990)11-37, esp. pp. 24-27.

realized par excellence.[5] As we build and fortify our churches in the structure of the SCCs, we build resistance to the unchecked desertions of members of our large-size parishes and out-stations into all kinds of indigenous christian churches mush-rooming up in virtually all African cities and villages. As in the traditional kingdoms, it shall be in the SCCs that meaningful social activities towards the wellbeing of the members become realistic and the person-to-person relationship better achieved. Thus, the SCCs can be seen as Africa's new clan of the People of God under the the leadership of *Obakarenko*, Christ. As a christo-logical programme, King-Christology is capable of shedding light on the significance of faithful discipleship and follwership; and of providing the models which promote African forms of power-sharing and role-play in pastoral councils, parochial structures, the organization and management of pious societies in the Churches.[6] The communtarian life of the Africans, a value which has received international appreciation in recent times, therefore calls for an ecclesiology which is Small Christian community-oriented in which the Kingship of Christ is at best encountered and worshipped.[7] King-Christology, a neo-logism devised for my current research work is ecclesial Christology. Its ecclesiality consists in the fact that its content is congruent with Conciliar and Papal pronoucements.[8] Finally, Jesus' eternal Kingship implies that in his humility and life-style, he is continuously building up the kingdom of disciples, witnesses and followers in Africa and the world and shepherding them in his living community, the Church.

---

[5] See, P. Kasenene, "Natural Communities in Ecumenical Activity", *AFER* 33(1991)150-159.

[6] Here, let me draw the attention of the reader to the practical suggestions made in the study of J. Kelly, "The Evolution of Small Christian Communities", *AFER* 33(1991)108-120.

[7] C. U. Manus, "'King-Christology': The result of a critical study of Matt 28:16-20", p. 42

[8] See Pope Pius XI's Encyclical, *Quas Primas* of December 11, 1925.

10.3   LITURGICAL IMPLICATIONS

King-Christology has cause to influence the promotion of African Christian liturgical rites and worship. African kingship rituals of installation contain essential ingredients of African worship such as prayers, music, drumming, anointing, cleansing and the 'almighty' *eating* just to name a few. The bodily gestures which accompany the ritual performances on such occasions indicate the deep sense of ritual feelings Africans have as well as their sense of divine mystery and transcendence. This communal sense of the sacred becons African liturgists to explore the rites, reach out to the African spiritual heritage, analyse the data and purify their findings of all traces of unpalatable trado-religious elements and integrate their sacramental features to constitute a renewed African Christian Liturgical corpus.[9] This is a proposal that must be speedly heeded, after all,

> ... in the liturgy the Church does not wish to impose a rigid uniformoty in matters which do not involve the faith or the good of the whole community. Rather does she respect and foster the qualities and talents of the various races and nations. Anything in these people's way of life which is not indissolubly bound up with superstition and error she studies with sympathy, and, if possible, preserves intact. She sometimes even admits such things into the liturgy itself, provided they harmonize with its true and authentic spirit.[10]

Christ's incarnation should not be conceived only as the in-breaking of the divine *Logos* in human history but also as the mystery of the advent of the Royal Prince of David born in Bethlehem (Mt 2,5-6). The incarnation of Christ presupposes the incarnation of the gospel in African cultures. His incarnation is his humanization.[11] Like the Magi, what counts so

---

[9] These anthropological insights complement the biblical and the theological arguments to give worship in Africa its distinctive character. On the scientific rationale for the place of liturgy as an academic study in Africa, see J. Ndyabahika, "Worship in African Christianity", *ATJ* 20(1991)54-62.

[10] "The Constitution on the Sacred Liturgy", art. 37, in A. Flannery, Vatican Council II. The Conciliar and Post Conciliar Documents, New York, Costello, 1975, p. 13.

[11] Here is a nuanced view of the statement in The Lineamenta. Synod of Bishops: Special Assembly for Africa. The Church in Africa and her Evangelising Mission Towards the Year 2000, "You Shall be my Witnesses" (Acts 1:8), Libreria Editrice Vaticana, Vatican City, 1990, p. 48, No. 48.

much for us in Africa is the encounter with the *Christ*. The question of the non-Jewish strangers: "Where is he who has been born king of the Jews?" (Mt 2,2), in many respects, reflects those asked by our forebears.The *pou* (where) question remains significant for our contextual purposes. It is where Jesus is as King that a royal community of interpersonal relationships is constituted. There he is worshipped. His risen status and his presence in the African community of christians bolsters our sense of the transcendence and the grip of the Ultimate Reality. He can be nothing else than our King, our *Obakarenko*.

Thus, the Mass and the liturgical services for the Feast of Christ, the King, the consecration of bishops, parts of the Liturgy for the ordination of priests and the enthronement of African Christian kings and the title-taking ceremonies of Chiefs shall become ritually indigenized with the aid of African ritual forms. The Eucharist could be partaken in in a much nuanced formula of *eating* and *drinking* expressive of the minds and bodies of African participants at the rituals they are familiar with on such occasions. Such will demonstrate how Africans share and celebrate the unique biblical story of the coming of the King of kings into their world. In such celebrations, we, as Africans, shall be articulating our own identity, our communality, and our catholicity in such a manner that it transcends the traditional ritual ceremonies of Africa. In the same light, we shall be celebrating the Christian story and the goodnews in public and thus be showing our non-christian brothers and sisters the gospels' superiority over our own "graphies". We shall then not only be celebrating the "Christ of culture" with our cultures but also the "Christ against culture" and the "Christ transforming culture".[12] By so doing, King-Christology will enrich our encounter expressed in the regular worshipping and witnessing patterns of life of African Christian congregations. Already, among some Africans, like the Luba in the Roman Catholic Diocese of Mbujimayi in Zaire, Christ is conceived and presented in their liturgy with the paraphernalia of a great King (Chief). For the Luba Church, Christ is *Ntita*, King of kings, *Luaba*, one chosen to rule and *Cilobo*, the Hero who, like the Zulu *Nkosi*, leads his warriors and never runs back from the enemy.[13]

---

[12] R. H. Niebuhr, Christ and Culture, London, Faber & Faber, 1951.

[13] N. A. *Didia Mfumu* (Meal of the Lord, Circle C) in The Missal of the Mbujimayi Diocese, Kinshasa, 1980, p. 87 especially the Entrance hymn and pp. 123, 160 the Offertory Song.

10.4   THE SOCIAL POLITICAL IMPLICATIONS

One of the distinctive findings arising from this study on the nature of the Reign of God and the Kingship of Christ is God's will that man and woman everywhere should attain the fullness of life. But the living conditions and the social political climate of todays' Africa negate the realization of the Creator's good intentions. The story of Christ-King is a story of "Jesus, Son of the Most High God" (Mk 5,7 par). It is a story with a difference; a story of a man who is inviting, yet with a personality that shatters strongholds and principalities. *His-story* , among other things, addresses itself to the philosophies of the junta regimes, one-party systems and the mode of sharing power in a continent blessed with robust health in human and material resources. As *goodnews, King-Christology* invites us to invest our talents in the re-structuration and re-organization of Africa's body politic. Certainly, a critical hermeneutic is required to address the urgent issues. Firstly, let us appraise ourselves of the current state of affairs.

To start with, the perceptive analysis of Paul Harrison in his book, *The Greening of Africa*, discussed by Gerard Whelan in his article, *Facing the African Economic Crisis* provides a good and clear window on the African world:

> In 1983-85 thirty African countries were affected with severe drought. The rains have been better since then but, as one commentator puts it, "The famines were ... not a sudden isolated disaster but rather the visible symtoms of a deeper illness". Average population growth in the continent is 3.2% per capita, food production declined 12% between 1960-82. In 1971, 81 million people were starving; by 1981 this figure had risen to 91 million. A further 260 million were considered "absolutely poor" in 1981 and the same number again judged not to be receiving the full working persons diet of 2660 calories per day.[14]

Inspite however of the alarming figures Harrison offers on the situation of a continent whose population is currently estimated as 553 million (1985); it is, for me, his unqualified "deeper

---

[14] P. Harrison, The Greening of Africa, Paladin, London, 1987, p. 19 cited by G. Whelan, "Facing the African Economic Crisis", *African Christian Studies* 5(1989)43-63, p. 44; cf. also T. Falola, "Economic and social development in contemporary Africa" in Olaniyan (ed.), *op. cit.,* pp. 111-126.

illness"; namely bad government and lack of purposeful direction that is most disturbing as it is the root cause of the instability in most of Black Africa.

In 1990, some African leaders of the former British and French colonies such as Nigeria, Zambia, Benin, Gabon and Cote d'Ivoire began the efforts to introduce multi-party democracies in its various forms in their countries. Some of the leaders were forced to change their patterns of government as pressures from mass riotings in the capitals could no longer be contained, and other some, military in administration, in the wake of the astronomical rise in the prices of basic foodstuffs, have proved themselves incapable of salvaging their nations' economic problems. While the former was the situation in Zambia, the later reflected events in Nigeria until late last year. In Nigeria, Local Councils, Governroship and States parliament elections in 1991 have taken place as steps in the right direction towards party politics in 1992. The state of affairs in Ghana, though the economy is said to be picking up, still remains unprdictable. The year 1990 (March) saw the fall of Mali's seventeen-year-old military regime as a result of popular unrest. Popular demand for National Conferences have become the strong weapons against unpopular regimes in many regions of Black Africa. It had been fiercely demanded in Cameroun and Zaire in 1991 and even much earlier in Nigeria by some critics and journalists. In February 1990, President Mathieu Kerekou was forced to abdicate and the Prime Minister, Nicephore Sogolo won the elections beating him in a landslide victory. In Gabon and Cote d'Ivoire, elections were organized but so orchestrated that the ruling parties were returned to power. In the case of Cote d'Ivoire, due to popular street demonstrations in the months of February and May 1990, President Houphouet-Boigny accepted to allow opposition parties to be established. In the elections that followed after, he and his party defeated the opposition. In 1991, the wind of such popular uprisings spread over to Zaire, Kenya, Togo and even most recently to Congo Brasaville. The rulers of these African countries have come under serious challenges as they are pressed upon to set up opposition parties. Street demonstrations have replaced law and order. The short-term arrangements which have been concluded with the opposition movements such as in Zaire still appear crisis-ridden. Chaos and anarchy still prevail and the weak in the society suffers. Kenyan and Zimbabwean leaderships, though ideologically opposed, consider a one-party system as an "insurer of a stable democracy".[15] Constant

---

[15] "Democracy in Africa: African Arguments for and against", *Africa Bulletin* 21(1991)3.

strikes my Malian workers in favour of a multi-party government has forced President Ali Saibou to promise the establishment of the first ever democratic governemnt since France checked out in 1960.

In the former Portuguese colonies, the situation is worth nothing to write home about. The ruling parties who wielded ruthless and high-handed forms of administration in Cape Verde, Sao Tome and Principe were thrown out in recent general elections. Mozambique has relatively known few years of peace since 1975 she gained independence from Portugal. The right-wing rebel group, The Mozambican National Resistance (Renamo), has for 15 years opposed the ruling Frelimo Party. Over 900.000 Africans have been killed in the ensuing war and over two million people who have been rendered homeless depend on emergency food aid for their survival.[16] Renamo has forced the Central Government to declare that the nation's first ever democratic elections would be held in June and September, 1991. In Angola, The Popular Movement for the Liberation of Angola, (MPLA), has for over 15 years ruled the people through a one-party government.[17] The National Union for the Total Independence of Angola, (UNITA), has, since 1975, been warring against MPLA in order to participate in the rulership of their nation.

In the Horn of Africa it is sordid. The horrendous situations in Ethiopia and its neigbhours are quite fresh in our minds. For some 30 years, The Eritrean Peoples Liberation Front (EPLF) has actively been engaged in a fight against Ethiopia for independence for her 20 million people. Hope of peace in that region is still fragile. For some eight years now, Sudan's war pits rebels of the Christian and the Traditional Religionists of the south against the army of the mostly Arab and Muslim north. The Islamic Government that came into power since 1989 in Sudan has damaged the nation beyond repair and in its ignorance, or arrogance remains unwilling to acknowledge the reality of the devastating famine sweeping through the Sudan.[18] Besides, this northern backed Government has been providing the Baggara tribes with modern weapons to raid and attack the Dinka who live in the south with the Shilluk whose kingship we have studied here because of their leadership of the Sudanese People's Liberation Army.

---

[16] Cf. J. Contreras, "A Man-Made Calamity", *Newsweek* May 20, 1991, p. 18.

[17] See, *Africa Research Bulletin,* December, 1990, pp. 1-31.

[18] Cf. J. Bartholet, "The Silent Dying", *Newsweek* May 20, 1991, p. 15.

248

The consequences of Black Africa's inability to rule herself well is immense. The civil uprisings against Central Governments' undemocratic policies have ruined agriculture in Liberia, Angola and Mozambique. Hunger has become the order of the day. In Sudan, Somalia, especially in and around Mogadishu, the civil wars have led to severe food shortages. Conscriptions of able-bodied youth into the army has left Ethiopia grossly impoverished. As one author put it, the waste in human resources in the region "have become the superstructure of famine in Africa".[19] Part of the disasterous consequences of repressive leadership and bad economic policies in modern Africa are wars, distress and the polarizations into ethnic and religious identities. In other words, these wars deepen the socio-economic disabilities of contemporary African nations.

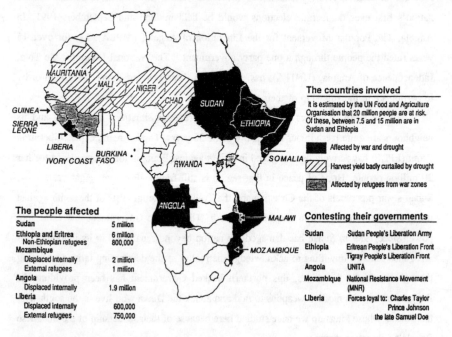

The countries involved

It is estimated by the UN Food and Agriculture Organisation that 20 million people are at risk. Of these, between 7.5 and 15 million are in Sudan and Ethiopia

■ Affected by war and drought

▨ Harvest yield badly curtailed by drought

▧ Affected by refugees from war zones

The people affected

Sudan	5 million
Ethiopia and Eritrea	6 million
Non-Ethiopian refugees	800,000
Mozambique	
Displaced internally	2 million
External refugees	1 million
Angola	
Displaced internally	1.9 million
Liberia	
Displaced internally	600,000
External refugees	750,000

Contesting their governments

Sudan	Sudan People's Liberation Army
Ethiopia	Eritrean People's Liberation Front / Tigray People's Liberation Front
Angola	UNITA
Mozambique	National Resistance Movement (MNR)
Liberia	Forces loyal to: Charles Taylor / Prince Johnson / the late Samuel Doe

War and drought bring famine to Black Africa.

Source: The Guradian International, Wednesday January 2, 1991 p.4.

---

[19] V. Brittain, "Fighting brings grim harvest of despair", *The Guardian International*, Wednesday, January 2, 1991, p. 4.

Beside the pollution of arable lands and the rich and lush environment of Africa, V. Brittain is correct in his remark that, "education and health - the keys to any escape from poverty are eluding more Africans every year".[20]

Having listened to stories of the precolonial African kings; the appalling socio-political state of affairs in contemporary Africa and the story of the Christ-King in the gospels, one cannot but be critical of the role of the potentates, the apparent deifications of the powers that be and the stultifying overlordism and undemocratic systems in Black Africa. The insight gained from the "stories" compels me to devise a critique on the *status quo* in order to sound a clarion call for a *change of heart* in disfavour of the myth of the untouchable "sacred" one-partyism in most of Black Africa and their "misguided government policies" which continue to "jeopardize millions of lives".[21] The ideas that will prosper the critique must spring from the texts from which King-Christology issues out. The texts of the Anointing (Lk 7,36-50 par); the Transfiguration; the Triumphal Entry and the Trial Scene in John 18,33ff, all show that the followers of Jesus held him as the King of the Davidic Royal House. Even though the texts are often silent about Jesus' approval of their opinion, the fact remains that Jesus saw his kingship as service to the needy, the oppressed and to the dispossessed. This is that great paradox of Jesus' kingship which contrasts with the ancient African kingships but provides a model and inspiration for contemporary leadership. It is Jesus' style of kingship which makes Africans regard him as the "greatest" of the kings; and the King with whom even the kingless societies in Africa readily identify. In the OT, it was on the grounds of the liberation or the salvific acts of God which Israel experienced that caused the people to acknowledge him as their King and the Lord who had dominion over them and other nations. It was similarly on the basis of the protectorate roles of many African kings to their subjects that they were loyally followed, obeyed and maintained in office as the *Oba*, the *Kabaka* etc. It was much more on the evidence of the healing acts and authority Jesus exhibited as the spokesman of God that his immediate followers honoured and feted his entry into the Holy City as King. This is a powerful message for Africa today. The question for the generality of our leaders is: despite the enormous wealth of their states and their natural resources, what have some of the leaders accomplished for human promotion

---

[20] *Ibid.*

[21] E. Dickinson, "Disaster Fatigue", *Newsweek* May 20, 1991, pp. 10-13, p. 12.

since independence? Our question supposes that we can only trust, choose and honour leaders who recognize the human worth; who have braced themselves up to serve, to eliminate Africa's socio-economic disparities, curb the tentacles of their acolytes who engage in illicit hoarding of wealth under the mask of single partyisms. The ideals which shine from Jesus' Servant-Kingship behest the African electorate to elect leaders who have as ever top on their agebda Africa's socio-political and economic problems and those who are ready to tackle the urgent problems of reconcilaition, underdevelopemnt, hunger and malnutrition, poverty, joblessness, ethnicity; and the leaders who show no partiality to any religion in a multi-religious Africa; name them all - the malaise of our time. Such are the leaders we shall follow. Such leaders are the persons who have or shall have our mandates. Those leaders who initiate and execute good responsible government are the leaders who re-create the kingdom of men and women into the Kingdom of God.

The presence of the Reign of God means nothing if not seen in the works Jesus performed for the physical and spiritual salvation of people. Jesus is King for the African Christians who live their lives under oppression, poverty, hunger and even political exploitation by local overlords and domestic rulers who flaunt the principles of democracy everyday in their rulership and with their "yes-men" wallow in the midstream of corruption and affluence in the midst of teeming poverty-striken peasants. Jesus' whole life and work and his royalty speak to the leaders of African and Third World peoples. His lifestyle as King shows the need for the emergence of a society where *mutual service* even unto death is the crown of leadership. The gospel of the Christ-King, therefore, invites African leaders to recognize the need to institute multi-party democratic forms of governance in which the full participation of people in government serves "as a means of liberating their creativity and industry".[22] They are called upon to combine selflessness and efficiency in the spirit of service in order "to work for the happiness, the freedom and the prosperity of all their citizens without any distinction".[23] The Regin of God which Jesus preaches is a rule of peace, love and justice. Africa of the present yearns for these values. Jesus accepts and tolerates all classes of people and different movements with their different shades of opinion.

---

[22] See, "Democracy in Africa", p. 1.

[23] N. A. The Right Time for Change: What Hope for a Crisis-Striken Africa. A Proposal Reflection, AACC General Secretariat, Nairobi, October, 1990, p. 18.

In the Reign of God, no one individual lives his life under any form of intimidation, cruelty and oppression nor under any inhuman acts of man toward fellow man or woman. He condemns whoever lets fundamental human rights be down-drodden. Jesus' spirit of tolerance should inspire our leaders to become broad minded and to accept political opponents as partners in nation building.

The demise of communism in Eastern Europe and the turbulence of capitalism in Africa remain visible signs of the times for African leadership to review Africa's political history and development. Neither, at least, has proved successfully relevant to the African social-political realities. Do these changes not spell a *kairos*, a moment of decision for Africa? Do we not perceive the possibility for the dawn of a genuine opportunity for the formation of purely African political options where our strengths and energies can fully be tapped and harnessed "to serve each and every one's welfare?" and "in a form of democracy based on justice and the participation of all ..."[24] typical of our traditional spirit of communalism? Kingship is one of the three offices of Christ. This study has made Christ's office of kingship become much more realistic to our faith and cognitive faculties. Faith in Jesus Christ and his message about the Reign of God enables African Christians to share in His role as King. As kings, the African Christians have inalienable leadership roles to exercise in both the society and in the Church of Christ. To my mind, Africa's hope for survival lies in an Associative Democracy (AD). The Christ-King is a ruler to whom all persons are priceworth. Those systems which diminish African peoples' wellbeing and keep Africa continually impoverished , marginalized and exploited whether locally or in collusion with the trans-national corporations and financial institutions are demonic and anti-Christ. At this point, the *Lineamenta* has this well-knit advice:

> A new stage has arrived in the evangelisation of African societies, in the area of the promotion of humanity, and justice and peace. The Second Vatican Council has contributed to a better perception of the close link between the announcement of the Gospel and the concerete actions done on behalf of humanity.
> In questioning Herself on the mission of evangelisation towards the year 2000, the Church in Africa cannot avoid the question of Her involvement

---

[24] *Ibid.*, pp. 3, 21.

in activities to benefit humanity in Africa. In many ways, Africa today presents some worrying economic, social and political situations.[25]

To close the entire reflections, I humbly wish to state: since Christian missionaries had baptised individuals in Africa and had failed to baptize the African cultures,[26] even though they were leaders in the education and "civilizing" programmes of the colonists, this study represents one of the ongoing efforts to complement the conversion of Africa in its totality. This has to be appreciated in view of the fact that the Messiah-King

> emptied himself, taking the form of a servant, being born in the likeness of men. And being found in the human form he humbled himself and became obedient unto death, even death on a cross (Phil 2,7-8).

By his incarnation, Jesus settled in a people's culture. The Christ event happened in a Hebrew and Jewish cultural context. But many of the missionaries failed to empty themselves as the Christ-King did of himself. While we do not denigrate their efforts, we believe that the Kingship of Christ empowers African Christians to encounter the *Christ* in all our native ways of life so that he can judge and tabernacle in our midst.

---

[25] Synod of Bishops, *The Lineamenta*, p. 77, No. 85.

[26] J. Aguwa, "Christianity and the Development of Igbo culture Today" *Bigard Theological Studies* 10(1990)26-37; also J. O. Egbulefu, "The Church in Africa towards the third Millennium. The present problems of the young African Church as the occasion for the Synod", *Omnis Terra* 211(1990)413-424; p. 417, also C. G. Baeta "The engagement of Christianity with African concepts and way of life", in *idem*. (ed.), Christianity in Tropical Africa, London, Oxford University Press, 1966, p. 128.

BIBLIOGRAPHY

A.   DICTIONARIES, ENCYCLOPEDIAE AND COMMENTARIES

BARRET, D. B.   1982.   World Christian Encyclopedia. A Comparative Survey
                              of Churches and Religions in the Modern World - AD
                              1900-2000, Oxford University Press.

BAUER, J. B.   1976.   Encyclopedia of Biblical Theology, London.

BROWN, R. E.   1970.   The Gospel According to John (XII-XXI), AB 29A,
                              New York, Doubleday.

----------.   1979.   The Birth of the Messiah. A Commentary on the
                              Infancy Narratives in Matthew and Luke, Garden City,
                              New York, Image Books.

BUTTRICK, G. A.   1955.   The Interpretater's Dictionary of the Bible, New York,
                              Abingdon Press.

ELIADE, M. et
al. eds.   1987.   The Encyclopedia of Religion, Vol. 8, New York,
                              London, Macmillan.

FORD, J. M.   1975.   Revelation, Introduction Translation and Commentary,
                              AB, New York, Doubleday.

GNILKA, J.   1990.   Jesus von Nazaret. Botschaft und Geschichte. Herders
                              Theologischer Kommentar zum Neuen Testament,
                              Supplementband 3, Freiburg-Basel-Wien.

GUNDRY, R. H.   1982.   Matthew. A Commentary on His Literary and
                              Theological Art, Grand Rapids, Eerdmans.

HENDRIKSEN, W.   1954.   New Testament Commentary. Exposition of the Gospel
                              According to John, Vol. II, Michigan, Grand Rapids,
                              Baker.

HOSKYNS, E. C.   1947.   The Fourth Gospel. London, Faber

HUNTER, A.M.   1963.   The Gospel According to John, The CBC, Cambridge,
                              CUP.

HURTADO, L. W.   1989.   Mark, NIBC, Peabody, Massachussetts, Hendrickson.

KITTEL, G. (ed.).   1964.   Theological Dictionary of the New Testament, Grand Rapids, Eerdmans.

KYSAR, R.   1986.   John. ACNT, Minneapolis, Augusburg Publishing House.

MOUNCE, R. H.   1977.   The Book of Revelation, Michigan, Eerdmans.

N. A.   1967.   The Catholic Encyclopedia, Vol.III, New York, McGraw-Hill.

PLUMMER, A.   1982.   The Gospel According to St. Mark, Thornapple Commentaries, Grand Rapids, Michigan, Baker (The 1914 Reprint).

RAHNER, K.   1970.   Encyclopedia of Theology, London, Burns and Oates.

ROGERSON, J. W. &
MCKAY, J. W.   1977.   Psalms 51 - 100. The CBC, London, CUP.

SANDERS, J. N. &
MASTIN, B. A.   1968.   A Commentary on the Gospel According to St John, London, Adams & Charles Black.

SCHERMAN, N. &
ZLOTOWITZ,
M. eds.   1985.   Psalms 73 - 150 (Tehillim). A Traditional Commentary on the Books of the Bible, Art Scroll Tanach Series, Mesorah.

TAYLOR, V.   1966.   The Gospel According to Mark: The Greek Text with Introduction, Notes and Indexes, 2nd Edition, New York, St. Martins Press.

B. AFRICAN CULTURES AND KINGSHIPS

Books

ABIMBOLA, W. 1976. Ifá: An Exposition of Ifá Literary Corpus, Ibadan, Oxford University Press.

AFIGBO, A. E. 1981. Ropes of Sand. Studies of Igbo History and Culture, Nsukka, University Press Ltd with Oxford University Press.

ANTON, F. et al. eds. 1978. Primitive Art, New York, H.N. Abrams.

ARINZE, F. A. 1970. Sacrifice in Ibo Religion, Ibadan, Ibadan University Press.

ASHE, R. P. 1889. Two Kings of Uganda, London, Sampson-Low.

AWOLALU, J. O. 1979. Yoruba Beliefs and Sacrificial Rites, London, Longman.

BASCOM, W. 1969. Ifá Divination: Communication Between Gods and Man in West Africa, Bloomington, Indiana University Press.

BINNS, C. T. 1963. The Last Zulu King. The Life and Death of Cetashwayo, London, Longmans.

BRYANT, A. T. 1929. Olden Times in Zululand and Natal, London, Longmans.

----------. 1949. The Zulu People As They Were Before The White Man Came, Pietermaritzburg, Shuter & Shooter (1967 Repr.)

BUCHER, H. 1980. Spirits and Power: An Analysis of Shona Cosmology, London, Oxford University Press.

BUJO, B. 1986. Afrikanische Theologie in ihrem gesellschaftlichen Kontext, Theologie Interkulturell, Band 1, Düsseldorf, Patmos Verlag.

CALLAWAY, H. 1870. Divination Among the Amazulu in their own Words with English Translation, Natal, Blair.

----------. 1970. The Religious System of the Amazulu, Cape Town, Struik (Reprint).

CHINWEIZU. 1978. The West and the Rest of Us, London, Lagos NOK Publishers.

COLPE, C. 1961. Die religionsgeschichtliche Schule, Göttingen, Vandenhoeck und Ruprecht.

DAVIDSON, B. 1967. The Growth of African Civilization. East and CentralAfrica to the Late Nineteenth Century, London, Longman.

----------. 1968. Africa in History: Themes and Outlines, London, Weidenfeld and Nicolson.

DICKSON, K. A. 1984. Theology in Africa, New York, Maryknoll, Orbis.

DREWAL, H. J.
et al eds. 1989. Yoruba: Nine Centuries of African Art and Thought, New York, Center for African Art with H.N. Abrams.

EJIOFOR, L. U. 1982. Igbo Kingdoms. Power and Control, Onitsha (Nigeria), Africana Publishers.

ENGNELL, I. 1945. Studies in Divine Kingship in the Ancient Near East,Uppsala, Almqvist.

EQUIANO, O. 1794. The Interesting Narrative of the Life of Olaudah Equiano or Gustavus Vasa The African, 8th Edition, Norwich.

FRANKFORT, H. 1965. Kingship and the Gods, Chicago, The University of Chicago Press.

FRAZER, J. G. 1922. The Golden Bough. A Study in Magic and Religion, London, Macmillan.

FROBENIUS, L. 1913. The Voice of Africa, Vol. 1, New York, Benjamin Blom.

GEERTZ, C. 1973. The Interpretation of Cultures. Selected Essays, New York, Basic Books.

GIBSON, J. Y. 1911. The Story of the Zulus, London, Longmans (1970 Repr. at New York, Negro Universities Press).

257

GLEASON, Judith.   1973.   A Recitation of Ifá. Oracle of the Yoruba, New York, Grossmann Publishers.

GOODY, J. ed.   1966.   Succession to High Office, Cambridge, CUP.

HOCART, A. M.   1941.   Kingship, London, Watts Press.

IDOWU, E. B.   1966.   *Olodumare*. God in Yoruba Belief, London, Longmans.

JOHNSON, S.   1921.   The History of the Yorubas, CMS Bookshops, Lagos (1926 Repr.).

KABASELE, F. et al.
(eds.)   1986.   Chemins de la christologie africaine, Enraciner l'évangile, initiations africaines et pedagogie de la foi, Paris.

KAGAWA, A.   1934.   The Customs of the Baganda. Columbia University Contributions to Anthropology 22, Columbia University Press.

KRIGE, E. J.   1936.   The Social System of the Zulus, London, Longmans (3rd Edition, Pietermaritzburg, Shuter and Shooter, 1957).

LAITIN, D. D.   1986.   Hegemony and Culture: Politics and Religious Change among the Yoruba, The University of Chicago Press.

LEGUM, C.   1966.   Africa. A Handbook to the Continent, New York.

LIENHARDT,
R. G.   1966.   Divinity and Experience. The Religion of the Dinka, London, Oxford University Press.

MBITI, J. S.   1970.   Concepts of God in Africa, London, SPCK.

----------.   1971.   New Testament Eschatology in an African Background. A Study of the Encounter between New Testament Theology and African Traditional Concepts, Oxford Univeristy Press, London, (SCM Press, 1978).

MCCLELLAND,
E. M.   1982.   The Cult of Ifá Among the Yoruba, Vol. 1, London, Ethnographica.

MEEK, C. K.   1931.   A Sudanese Kingdom. An Ethnographical Study of the Jukan Peoples of Nigeria, London, Paul Kegan.

258

METUH, E. I.   1981.   God and Man in African Religion: A Case Study of the Igbo of Nigeria, London, Chapman.

MIDDLETON, J.   1960.   Lugbara Religion. Ritual and Authority among an East African People, London, Oxford Universty Press.

MILLINGO, E.   1984.   The World in - Between. Christian Healing and Struggle for Spiritual Survival, London, Hurst.

MOFOKENG,
T. A.   1983.   The Crucified Among the Crossbearers. Towards a Black Christology, Kampen.

MOLEMA, S. M.   1963.   The Bantu. Past and Present, Cape Town, Struik.

MUZOREWA,
G. H.   1985.   The Origins And Development of African Theology, New York, Maryknoll, Orbis.

NZIMIRO, I.   1972.   Studies in Ibo Political Systems: Chieftaincy and Politics in Four Niger States, London, Frank Cass.

OJO, G. J. A.   1966.   Yoruba Palaces, London, Oxford University Press.

OLANIYAN, R. ed. 1982.   African History and Culture, Lagos, Longman.

ONWUEJEOGWU,
M. A.   1981.   An Igbo Civilization. Nri Kingdom and Hegemony, London, Ethnographica.

PALAU-
MARTI, M.   1974.   Roi-Dieu au Benin, Sud-Togo, Dahomey, Nigéria Occidentale, Paris, Collection Mondes d'Outre Mer.

PEEK, P. M.   1991.   African Divination Systems: Ways of Knowing, Bloomington/Indianapolis, Indiana University Press.

POBEE, J. S.   1979.   Toward an African Theology, Nashville, Abingdon.

PRITCHARD,
Evans E. E.   1948.   The Divine Kingship of the Shilluk of the Nilothic Sudan. The Frazer Lecture for 1948, Cambridge.

----------.   1956.   Nuer Religion, Oxford University Press.

RAU, B.   (N.D).   Feast to Famine. The Cause of Africa's Underdevelopment. A Document of the African Faith and Justice Network, Washington, DC.

ROSCOE, J.   1911.   The Baganda. An Account of their Native Customs and
                              Beliefs, London, Macmillan.

SELIGMAN, C. G.   1934.   Egypt and Negro-Africa. A Study in Divine Kingship.
                              The Frazer Lecture for 1933, London.

SHORTER, A.   1978.   African Christian Spirituality, New York, Maryknoll,
                              Orbis.

SMITH, E. W.   1950.   African Ideas of God, Edinburgh, House Press.

SMITH, R. S.   1988.   Kingdoms of the Yoruba, London, James Currey, 3rd
                              Edition.

SPEKE, J. H.   1863.   Journal of the Discovery of the Source of the Nile,
                              Edinburgh, Blackwood.

STRIDE, G. &
IFEKA, Caroline   1971.   Peoples and Empires of West Africa. West Africa in
                              History 1000 - 1800, Lagos, Nelson.

UDOH, E. B.   1983.   Guest Christology. An Interpretative View of the
                              Christological Problem in Africa, Ph.D Dissertation,
                              Princeton University, Princeton; also Frankfurt/Main,
                              Peter Lang, Studies in Intercultural History of
                              Christianity, No 59.

WESSELS, A.   1990.   Images of Jesus. How Jesus is Perceived and Portrayed
                              in Non-European Cultures, London, SCM Press.

Articles

ABE, G. O.   1990.   "Theological Concepts of Jewish and AfricanNames of
                              God", *AJT* Vol. 4, pp. 424-429.

ABELES, M.   1981.   "Sacred Kingship and the Formation of the State" in
                              H.J.M. Claessen & P. Skalník (eds.), The Study of the
                              State, NB SS 35, The Hague, Mouton, pp. 1-14.

ABIMBOLA, W.   1973.   "The Literature of Ifá Cult" in S.O. Biobauk (ed.),
                              Sources of Yoruba History, Clarendon, Oxford, pp. 41-
                              45.

ABOGURIN, S. O.   1980.   "La recherche moderne du Jésus historique et le
                              christianisme en Afrique", Journal Théologique de
                              l'Afrique Vol. 1, pp. 36ff.

260

ADEDIRAN, 'B.   1986.   "Politics and Religion in Yorubaland: A Case Study of Ile-Ife c. 1850-1930" in *Islam and the Modern Age* November, pp. 217-240; also published in *Afrika Zamani*, Vol. 16-17, pp. 129-144.

ADELOWO, E. D. 1990.   "Rituals, Symbolism and Symbols in Yoruba Traditional Religious Thought" *AJT* Vol 4, pp. 162-173.

ARENS, W.   1979.   "The Divine Kingship of the Shilluk. A Contemporary Re-evaluation", *Ethnos*, Vol 14, pp. 167-181.

ASIWAJU, A. I. 1976.   "Political Motivation and Oral Historical Traditions in Africa: The Case of Yoruba Crowns, 1900-1960", *Africa* Vol 46, pp. 113-127.

BABALOLA, E. O. 1991.   "The Reality of African Traditional Religion: A Yoruba Case Study", *NJTh* Vol 1, pp. 50-63.

BEDIAKO, K.   1983.   "Biblical Christologies in the Context of African Religions" in V.Samuel & C. Sugden (eds.), Sharing Jesus in the Two Thirds World, Bangalore, Brilliant Printers, pp. 115-175.

BUJO, B.   1981.   "Pour une ethique africano-christocentrique", *BTA* Vol 3, pp. 41-52.

-------.   1982.   A Christocentric ethic for black Africa", *TD* Vol 3, pp. 82-84.

CARVALHO,
E. de.   1981.   "What do the Africans say that Jesus is?",*ATJ* Vol 10, Nos 1 & 2, pp. 17-25.

CLAESSEN,
H.J.M.   1978.   "The Early State. A Structural Approach" in H.J.M. Claessen & P. Skalník (eds.), The Ealy State, *op. cit.* pp. 533-596.

----------.   1981.   "The Early African State" in Classen & Skalník (eds.), The Study of the State, NBS SS 35, The Hague, Mouton, pp. 66ff.

----------.   1986.   "Kingship in the Early State", *Bijdragen TLV*, Vol 142, pp. 113-129.

CZAJKOWSKI, M. 1988. "Die Inkulturation des Evangeliums im Neuen Testament und Heute", *Collectinea Theologica*, Vol 58, pp. 29-38.

DIATTA, N. 1989. "Jésus, le maitre dínitiation initié" *Telema* Vol 57, pp. 49-72.

DUPUIS, J. 1988. "On Some Recent Christological Literature", *Gregorianum* Vol 69, pp. 713-740.

EDWARDS, P.&
SHAW Rosalind. 1989. "The Invisible *Chi* in Equiano's *Interesting Narrative*", *JRA* Vol 19, pp. 146-156.

EJIZU, C. I. 1991. "Religion and Politics in Nigeria: The Perspective of the Indegenous Religion", *NJTh* Vol 1, pp. 72-86.

EZEANYA, S. N. 1969. "God, Spirits and the Spirit World. With Special Reference to the Igbo-speaking people of Southern Nigeria", in K. A. Dickson and P. Ellingworth (eds.), Biblical Revelation and African Beliefs, London, Lutterworth, pp. 30-46.

FALK, Nancy E. 1974. "Wilderness and Kingship in Ancient South Asia" *HR* Vol 13, pp. 1-15.

FORDE, D. 1965. "Tropical African Studies", *Africa* Vol 35, pp. 30-104.

FORTES, M. 1969. "Of Installation Ceremonies: Presidential Address 1967" in Proceedings of the Royal Anthropological Institute, London, pp. 5-20.

GBADEGESIN, O. 1984. "Destiny, Personality and Ultimate Reality of Human Existence: A Yoruba Perspective" *URAM* Vol 7, pp. 173-188.

GLUCKMANN, M. 1970. "The Kingdom of the Zulu of South Africa" in M. Fortes & E.E. Evans Pritchard eds. African Political Systems, London, Oxford University Press.

GODELIER, M. 1977. "Economy and Religion, an evolutionary Optical Illusion" in J. Friedman & M.J. Rowlands eds., The Evolution of Social Systems, London, Duckworth, pp. 3-12.

GOTTANELLI, C. 1987. "Kingship" in M. Eliade et al eds., The Encyclopedia of Religion, Vol 8, New York, London, Macmillan

262

HORTON, R.   1962.   "The Kalabari World-view: An Outline and Interpretation", *Africa* Vol 32, pp. 197-219.

----------.   1969.   "Types of Spirit Possession in Kalabari Religion" in J. Beattie, J. Middleton eds., Spirit Mediumship and Society of Africa, London, Routeledge and Paul Kegan.

----------.   1971.   "African Conversion", *Africa* Vol 41, pp. 85-108.

KABASELE, F.   1986.   "Le Christ comme Ancestre et Ainé" in *idem et al eds.*, Chemins, *op.cit.*, pp. 127-143.

KANDUSI, E.   1991.   "Justice, Peace and the Intergrity of Creation: A Perspective from Third World Theologians" *Scriptura*, Vol 39, pp. 52-57.

KRIGE, E. J.   1968.   "Girls' Puberty Songs and their Relation to Fertility, Health, Morality and Religion Among the Zulu", *Africa* Vol 38, pp. 173-185.

----------.   1975.   "Divine Kingship, change and development" in M. Fortes and Sheila Paterson eds., Studies in African Social Anthropology, London, Academic, pp. 55-74.

LIENHARDT, R. G.   1954.   "The Shilluk of the Upper Nile" in C.D Forde ed., African Worlds, London, Oxford University Press, pp. 138-163.

--------------.   1955.   "Nilothic Kings and their Mothers' Kin", *Africa* Vol 25, pp. 25-42.

LLOYD, P. C.   1960.   "Sacred Kingship and Government Among the Yoruba" *Africa* Vol 30, pp. 221-237.

----------.   1967.   "The Traditional Political System of the Yoruba" in R, Cohen and J. Middleton, eds., Comparative Political Systems, Garden City, Natural History Press, pp. 270-292.

----------.   1968.   "Conflict Theory and Yoruba kingdom" in I.M. Lewis ed., History and Social Anthropology, ASA M 7, London, Tavistock Publications, pp. 25-62.

MAIR, Lucy.   1977.   African Kingdoms, Oxford, Clarendon Press.

MBITI, J. S.   1968.   "Afrikanische Beiträge zur Christologie" in P. Beyerhaus et al (Hrsg), Theologische Stimmen aus Asien, Afrika und Lateinamerika, Vol 3, München, pp. 78-85.

----------.   1972.   "Some African Concepts of Christology" in G.F. Vicedom ed., Christ and Younger Churches, London, SPCK, pp. 51-62.

----------.   1982.   "Some African Concepts of the Universe" in R. Olaniyan ed., African History and Culture, op.cit., pp. 193-199.

MELLOR, W. F.   1932.   "Bead Embroidery of Remo", Nigeria Vol 14, pp. 154-155.

METUH, E. I.   1985.   "Ritual Dirt and Purification among the Igbo" JRA Vol 15, pp. 3-23.

MIDDLETON, J.   1954.   "Some Social Aspects of Lugbara Myth" Africa Vol 24, pp. 189-198.

MORTON, W. P.   1967.   "The Yoruba Kingdom of Oyo" in D. Forde, P. Kaberry eds., West African Kingdoms in the nineteenth century, London, OUP. pp. 50-54ff.

M'TIMKULU, D.   1977.   "Some Aspects of Zulu Religion" in N.S. Booth ed., African Religions: A Symposium, New York, London, Lagos, NOK Publishers, pp. 13-20.

MUGAMBI,
J. N. K.   1989.   "Christological Paradigms in African Christianity" in J.N.K. Mugambi and L. Magesa eds., Jesus in African Christianity. Experimentation and Diversity in African Christology, Nairobi, Initiatives Publishers.

MULLER, J.-C.   1986.   "'Divine Kingship' in Chiefdoms and States. A Single Ideological Model" in Claessen and Skalník, op.cit., pp. 239-330.

MURDOCK, G. P. 1959.   Africa. Its Peoples and their Culture History, New York, McGraw-Hill.

NKWOKA, A. O.   1991.   "Jesus As Eldest Brother (Okpara): An Igbo Paradigm for Christianity in the African Context", AJT Vol 5, pp. 87-103.

264

NYAMITI, C.   1989.   "A Critical Assessment on Some Issues in Today's
                          African Theology", *African Christian Studies* Vol 5,
                          pp. 5-18.

----------.   1989.   "African Christologies Today" in J.N.K. Mgambi & L.
                          Magesa eds., Jesus in African Christianity, *op.cit.*, 18-
                          39.

NZOMIWU,
J. P. C.   1989.   "Inculturation: Its Meaning and Implications for the
                          Nigerian Church", *Africana Marburgensia* Vol 13, pp.
                          11-23.

OKERE, T.   1986.   "A Review Article on Nyamiti's Christ As Our
                          Ancestor", *NJTh* Vol 1, pp. 68-90.

ONAIYEKAN, J.   1991.   "Christological Trends in Contemporary African
                          Theology. A Challenge to Nigerian Theologians", *NJTh*
                          Vol 1, pp. 11-27.

ONUNWA, U.   1989.   "The Concept of Secularization and the study of West
                          African Traditional Religion", *Africana Marburgensia*
                          Vol 13, pp. 3-10.

OYEDIRAN, O.   1973.   "The Position of the *Oni* in the Changing Political
                          System of the Ile-Ife", *JHSN* Vol 6, pp. 376-396.

PARRINDER, E.   1956.   "Divine Kingship in West Africa", *Numen*
                          Vol 3, pp. 111-121.

RAY, B. C.   1972.   "Royal Shrines and Ceremonies of Buganda", *The
                          Uganda Journal* Vol 36, pp. 35-48.

--------.   1976.   African Religions, Englewood Cliffs, New Jersey,
                          Prentice Hall.

--------.   1977.   "Sacred Space and Royal Shrines in Buganda", *HR* Vol
                          16, pp. 363-373.

--------.   1980.   "The Story of Kintu: Myth, Death and Ontology in
                          Baganda" in Ivan Karp and Charles S. Bird eds.,
                          Explorations in African Systems of Thought,
                          Bloomington, Indiana University Press, pp. 60-79.

--------.   1990.   "The Kabaka as the Symbolic Center of Buganda".
                          Unpublished Paper, Charlottenville, pp. 1-12.

RIAD, M. 1959. "The Divine Kingship of the Shilluk and its Origin", *Archiv für Völkerkunde*, Vol 14, pp. 141-284.

RICHARDS, A. I. 1961. "African Kings and their Royal relatives", *Journal of the Royal Anthropological Institute*, Vol 91, pp. 136-148.

SCHNEPEL, B. 1987. "Max Weber's Theory of Charisma and its Applicability to Anthropological Research" *JASO* Vol 17, pp. 26-48.

----------. 1988. "Shilluk Royal Ceremonies of Death and Installation", *Anthropos* Vol 83, pp. 433-452.

SCHOFFELEERS, J. M. 1982. "Christ as the Medicine-man and the medicine-man as Christ. A Tentative History of African Christological Thought", *Man and Life Journal of the Institute of Social Research and Applied Anthropology*, Vol 8, pp. 11-28.

----------. 1985. "Oral History and the Retrieval of the Distant Past: On the Legendary Chronicles as Sources of Historical Information" in W.van Binsbergen and J.M Schoffeleers eds., Theoretical Explorations in African Religion, London, KPI, pp. 164-188.

----------. 1989. "Folk Christology in Africa: The Dialectics of the Nganga Paradigm", *JRA* Vol 19, pp. 157-183.

SETILOANE, G. 1975. "Confessing Christ Today. From One African Perspective: Man and Community", *JTSA* Vol 12, pp. 29-38.

----------. 1979. "Où est la theologie africaine?" in K. Appiah-Kubi et al. eds., Liberation ou adaptation? La theologie africaine s'interroge. Le Colloque d'Accra, Paris, L'Hamattan, pp. 81ff.

TENGAN, E. B. 1990. "The Sisala Universe: Its Composition and Structure. (An Essay in Cosmology)", *JRa* Vol 20, pp. 2-11.

THOMPSON, R. F. 1969/70 "The Sign of the Divine King: An Essay on Yoruba Bead-Embroidered Crowns with Veil and Bird Decorations", Vol *African Arts* Vol 3, pp. 8-17; 74-80.

266

UZUKWU, E. E.   1982.   "Igbo World and Ultimate Reality and Meaning" *URAM*
Vol 5, pp. 188-209.

VANSINA, J.   1962.   "A Comparison of African Kingdoms" *Africa* Vol 32,
pp. 324-333.

WALL, L.   1976.   "Anuak Politics. Ecology and the Origins of Shilluk
Kingship ", *Ethnology* Vol 15, pp. 151-162.

WARUTA, D. W.   1989.   "Who is Jesus for Africans Today? Prophet, Priest,
Potentate" in Mugambi & Magesa eds., Jesus in
African Christianity, pp. 43-44.

D. BIBLICAL: THE OLD AND THE NEW TESTAMENTS

Books

AMBROZIC, A. 1972. The Hidden Kingdom: A Redaction-Critical Study of the References to the Kingdom in Mark's Gospel. The CBQ Monograph Series 2, CBAA, Washington.

BEUTLER, J. 1991/92. Das Markusevangelium (Kap. 8,27-13,37). Vorlesungen Phil.-Theol. Hochschule Sankt Georgen, Frankfurt/Main.

----------. & FORTNA, R. T. 1991. The Shepherd Discourse of John 10 in its Context, SNTS MS 67, Cambridge, CUP.

BORG, M. J. 1984. Conflict, Holiness and Politics in the Teachings of Jesus, New York, E. Mellen.

----------. 1988. Jesus; A New Vision, San Francisco, Harper & Row.

BUBER, M. 1932. Königtum Gottes, Berlin Schcken Verlag.

BUCHANAN, G. W. 1970. The Consequences of the Covenant, NovT Suppl. 20, Leiden, Brill.

----------. 1984. Jesus. The King and His Kingdom, Macon, Mercer University Pree.

BULTMANN, R. 1970. Die Geschichte de synoptischen Tradition, 8 Aufl., Göttingen, Vandenhoeck und Ruprecht.

CASSIDY, R. J. 1978. Jesus, Politics and Society. A Study of Luke's Gospel, New York, Maryknoll, Orbis.

CHARLESWORTH, J. H. 1988. Jesus Within Judaism. New Light from Exciting Archaelogical Discoveries, New York, Dowbleday.

DALMAN, G. 1898. Die Worte Jesu mit Berückschtigung des nachkanonischen jüdischen Schrifttums und der aramäischen Sprache, Band 1, Leipzig, ET by D.M Kay, The Words of Jesus ..., Vol 1, Edinburgh, T & T Clark 1902.

268

DEBROWSKI, E.   1933.   La Transfiguration de Jésus, Scripta Pontificii Instituti
                                Biblici 85, Rome.

DOOD, C. H.   1935.   The Parables of the Kingdom, London, Nisbet.

DUPONT-
SOMMER   1973.   The Essene Writings from Qumran, ET by G. Vermes,
                                Gloucester, Massachussetts, Smith Press.

EDWARDS, O. C.   1981.   Luke's Story of Jesus, Philadelphia, Fortress Press.

FIORENZA,
Elizabeth S.   1983.   In Memory of Her: A Feminist Theological
                                Reconstruction of Christian Origins, New York,
                                Crossroad.

FREED, E. D.   1965.   Old Testament Quotations in the Gospel of John, NovT.
                                Suppl, Leiden, Brill.

FULLER, R. H.   1954.   The Mission and Achievement of Jesus.

GALOT, J.   1989.   Who is Christ? A Theology of Incarnation, Chicago,
                                Franciscan Herald Press.

GASTON, L.   1970.   No Stone on Another: Studies in the Significance of the
                                Fall of Jerusalem in the Synoptic Gospels, NovT Suppl.
                                23, Leiden, Brill.

GERBRANDT,
G. E.   1986.   Kingship According to the Deuteronomistic History,
                                SBL DS 87, Atlanta, Scholars Press.

GERHARDSSON,
B.   1966.   The Testing of God's Son. An Analysis of the Early
                                Christian Midrash, Lund, Gleerup.

GNILKA, J.   1979.   Das Evangelium nach Markus, 2. Teilband Mk 8,17-
                                16,20, EKKNT 2, Zürich, Benzinger Verlag.

GOULDER, M. D. 1974.   Midrash and Lection in Matthew, London, SPCK.

GRAY, J.   1979.   The Biblical Doctrine of the Reign of God, Edinburgh,
                                T & T Clark.

HARTMAN, L. F. &
DI LELLA, A. A.   1978.   The Book of Daniel, AB 23, Garden City, Doubleday.

269

HORSLEY, R.	1987.	Jesus and the Spiral of violence, San Francisco, Harper & Row.
----------.	1989.	Sociology of the Jesus Movement, New York, Crossroad.
HUBAUT, M.	1976.	La parabole des vignérons homicides, Paris, Gabalda.
JEREMIAS, J.	1954.	The Parables of Jesus, London, SCM Press.
----------.	1960.	The Eucharistic Words of Jesus, London; SCM press and New York, Scribner, 1966.
----------.	1971.	New Testament Theology, Part I, The Proclamation of Jesus, Loondon, SCM Press.
JOHNSON, M. D.	1969.	The Purpose of the Biblical Genealogies, NTS MS 8, London, Cambridge, CUP.
JUEL, D.	1977.	Messiah and Temple: The Trial of Jesus in the Gospel of Mark, SBL DS 31, Missoula, Motana, Scholars Press.
JÜNGLING, H.-W.	1981.	Richter 19 - Ein Plädoyer für das Königtum. Stilistische Analyse der Tendenzerzählung Ri 19,1-30a; 21,25. AnBib 84, Rome, Biblical Institute.
JUNKER, H.	1932.	Untersuchungen über literarische und exegetische Probleme des Buches Daniel, Bonn, Haustein.
KASPER, W.	1985.	Jesus the Christ, Kent, Burns and Oates.
KELBER, W. H.	1974.	The Kingdom in Mark. A Place and a New Time, Philadelphia, Fortress Press.
----------.	1979.	Mark's Story of Jesus, Philadelphia, Fortress Press.
KIM, M.-S.	1989.	Die Trägergruppe von Q - Sozialgeschchtliche Forshung zu Q-Überlieferung in den synoptischen Evangelium, Hamburg, Verlag Peter Jensen.
KINGSBURY, J. D.	1983	The Christology of Mark's Gospel, Philadelphia, Fortress Press.
LEIVESTAD, R.	1987.	Jesus in His own Perspective. An Examination of the Sayings, Actions and Eschatological Titles, ET by David E. Aune, Augsburg.

270

LEVEY, S. H.   1974.   The Messiah: An Aramaic Interpretation. The
                                     Messianic Exegesis of the Targum, MHUC 2,
                                     Cincinnati, Hebrew Union College-Jewish Institute of
                                     Religion.

LOHSE, E.   1964.   Die Texte aus Qumran, München.

MACK, B. L.   1988.   A Myth of Innocence: Mark and Christian Origins,
                                     Philadelphia, Fortress Press.

MACKEY, J. P.   1969.   Jesus the Man and the Myth. A Contemporary
                                     Christology, London, SCM press.

MATERA, F. J.   1982.   The Kingship of Jesus. Composition and Theology in
                                     Mark 15, SBL DS 66, Chico, Scholars Press.

MCKENZIE, S. L.   1991.   The Trouble with Kings. The Composition of the Book
                                     of Kings in the Deuteronomistic History, Leiden, E.J.
                                     Brill.

MEIER, J. P.   1978.   The Vision of Matthew: Christ, Church and Morality in
                                     the First Gospel, New York, Paulist Press.

MEYER, B. F.   1979.   The Aims of Jesus, London, SCM Press.

MISHKIN, J. L.   N.D.   Elijah Transfigured: A Study of the Narrative of the
                                     Transfiguration in the Gospel of Mark, Ann Arbor,
                                     University Microfilms International Dissertations.

MOWINCKEL, S.   1962.   The Psalms in Israel's Worship, Vol 1, New York,
                                     Nashville, Abingdon, Oxford, Blackwell.

NEILL, S.   1976.   Jesus Through Many Eyes. Introduction to the
                                     Theology of the New Testament, Philadelphia, Fortress
                                     Press.

----------. &
WRIGHT, T.   1988.   The Interpretation of the New Testament 1861-1986,
                                     Oxford/New York, Oxford University Press.

NEUSNER, J.   1984.   Messiah in Context: Israel's History and Destinyin
                                     Formative Judaism, Philadelphia, Fortress Press.

OYEN, G. van.   1987.   De Summaria in Marcus en de compositie van Mc 1,
                                     14-8, 28, SNTA 12, Peeters, Leuven University Press.

PERRIN, N.   1963.   The Kingdom of God in the Teaching of Jesus,
                                     London, SCM Press.

_____.   1976.   Jesus and the Language of the Kingdom: Symbol and Metaphor in New Testament Interpretation, London, SCM Press.

POKORNY, P.   1987.   The Genesis of Christology. Foundations for a Theology of the New Testament, ET by M. Lefébure, Edinburgh, T & T Clark.

PRITCHARD,
J. B. ed.   1969.   Ancient Near Eastern Texts Relating to the Old Testament, 3rd Edition, Princeton.

RAD, G. von.   1976.   The Message of the Prophets, London, SCM Press.

RHOADS, D. M &
MICHIE, D. M.   1982.   Mark as Story. An Introduction to the Narrative of a Gospel, Philadelphia, Fortress Press.

ROBBINS, V. K.   1984.   Jesus the Teacher: A Socio-Rhetorical Interpretation of Mark, Philadelphia, Fortress Press.

ROWLEY, H. H.   1959.   Darius the Mede and the Four World Empires in the Book of Daniel, Cardiff, The University of Wales Press.

SCHILLEBEECKX,
E.   1974.   *Jesus.* An Experiment in Christology, ET by Hubert Hoskins, London, Willaims Collins, (1979).

_____.   1977.   *Christ.* The Christian Experience in the Modern World, ET by John Bowden, London SCM Press (1982).

_____.   1980.   Interim Report on the Books, *Jesus* and *Christ*, ET by John Bowden, London, SCM Press.

SCHWEITZER, A.   1954.   The Quest of the Historical Jesus, London, Adam & Charles Black.

SINGER, S.   1946.   *Alenu,* 19th Edition.

STANTON, G. N.   1974.   Jesus of Nazareth in New Testament Preaching, SNTS MS 27, Cambridge, CUP.

VERSEPUT, D.   1986.   The Rejection of the Humble Messianic King. A Study of the Composition of Matthew 11-12, EUS 291, Frankfurt/Main-Bern-New York.

WEISS, J.   1971.   Jesus' Proclamation of the Kingdom of God, ET by
                                R.H. Hiers and D.L. Holland London.

WINSTONE,
H. ed.   1985.   The Sunday Missal. Texts Approved for Use in
                                England and Wales, Scotland and Ireland, and Africa,
                                London, Collins.

Articles

AALEN, S.   1961.   "'Reign'and 'House'in the Kingdom of God in the
                                Gospel" *NTS* Vol 8, pp. 215-246.

ABEL, E. L.   1973/74.   "The Genealogies of Jesus *ho Christos*" *NTS* Vol 20,
                                pp. 205-206.

ABOGURIN, S. O.   1988.   "The Cosmic Significance of Jesus Christ in the African
                                Context. An Exegesis of Phillipians 2:5-11", *Orita,
                                Ibadan Journal of Religious Studies* Vol 20, pp. 3-14.

BARTON, S. C.   1991.   "Mark as Narrative. The Story of the Anointing
                                Woman", *ExpT* Vol 102, pp. 230-234.

BEUTLER, J.   1991.   "Response from a European Perspective" in R.A.
                                Culpepper, F.F. Segovia eds., The Fourth Gospel from
                                a Literary Perspective (Semeia 53), Atlanta, Scholars
                                Press, pp. 191-202.

BLANKINSOPP, J.   1961.   "The Oracle of Judah and the Messianic Entry" *JBL*
                                Vol 80, pp. 55-64.

BORG, M. J.   1988.   "A Renaissance in Jesus Studies", *Theology Today* Vol
                                45, pp. 280-292.

----------.   1991.   "Portraits of Jesus in Contemporary North American
                                Scholarship", *HTR* Vol 84, pp. 1-22.

BROWN, J. P.   1987.   "Kingdom of God" in Eliade et al. eds., The
                                Encyclopedia of Religion, Vol 8, pp. 304-312.

BRUCE, F. F.   1961.   "The Book of Zecharia and the Passion Narrative"
                                BJRL Vol 43, pp. 336-353.

BUCHAN, W. M.   1989.   "Research on the Lord's Prayer" *ExpT,* Vol 100, pp.
                                336-339.

BURROWS, M.   1955.   "Thy Kingdom Come", *JBL*, Vol 74, pp. 1-8.

CHARETTE, B.   1992.   "'To Proclaim Liberty to the Captives'. Matthew
                              11,28-30 in the Light of OT Prophetic Expectation",
                              NTS, Vol 38, pp. 290-297.

CHARLESWORTH,
J. H.   1986.   "From Barran Mazes to Gentle Rappings: The
                              Emergence of Jesus Research", *Princeton Seminary
                              Bulletin*, Vol 7, pp. 225-230.

COLLINS, R. F.   1976.   "Baptism or Anointing", *The Bible Today*, April, pp.
                              821-831.

-----------.   1978.   "The Search for Jesus: Reflections on the Fourth
                              Gospel", *Laval théologique et philosophique*, Vol 24,
                              pp. 27-48.

COMBRINK, B &
MÜLLER, B.   1991.   "The Gospel of Matthew in the African Context - in
                              dialogue with Chris Manus", *Scriptura*, Vol 39, pp. 43-
                              51.

CONZELMANN,
H.   1970.   "History and Theology in the Passion Narrative of the
                              Synoptic Gospels" *Interp.*, Vol 24 pp. 178-197.

DAUTZENBERG,
G.   1991.   "Jesus und die Tora",*Orientierung*, Vol 55, pp. 229-
                              232.

DELOBEL, J.   1966.   "L'Onction par la Pécheresse. La Composition litteraire
                              de Lc, VII, 36-50", *ETL*, Vol 42, pp. 415-475.

DUNCAN,
J.-M Derret.   1971.   "Law in the New Testament: The Palm Sunday Colt"
                              NovT Vol 13, pp. 241-258.

DUPONT, J.   1956/57.   "L'Arrière-fond Biblique du Recit des tentations de
                              Jésus" *NTS*, Vol 1, pp. 299-304.

ELLIOTT, J. K.   1973/74.   "The Anointing of Jesus", *ExpT* Vol 85, pp. 103-107.

FORD, J. M.   1968.   "'The Son of Man': A Euphemism?" *JBL* Vol 87, 257-
                              266.

GREEVEN, H.   1959.   "*Proskyneo*", *TWNT*, pp. 750-767.

274

HARRINGTON,
D. J.   1991.   "'Jesus, the Son of David, the Son of Abraham ...';
                         Christology and Second Temple Judaism", *ITQ*, Vol
                         57, pp. 185-195.

HOWARD, D. M.   1988.   "The Case of Kingship in the Old Testament Narrative
                         Books and the Psalms", *TrinJ* Vol 9 NS, pp. 19-35.

JENKINS, A. K.   1983.   "Young Man or Angel?", *ExpT* Vol 94, pp. 237-239.

KEALY, S. P.   1991.   "Gospel Studies Since 1970 (2)", *ITQ* Vol 57, pp. 93-
                         104.

KRAELING,
E. G. H.   1933.   "Some Babylonian and Iranian Mythology in the
                         Seventh Chapter of Daniel" in J.D.C. Pavry ed.,
                         Orental Studies, London, Oxford University Press, pp.
                         228-231.

KUHN, H.-W.   1959.   "Das Reittier Jesu in der Einzuggeschichte des
                         Markusevangeliums", *ZNW* Vol 50, pp. 80-91.

LAMBRECHT, J.   1984.   "Christus muß König sein", *Communio, Internationale
                         Katholische Zeitschrift*, Vol 13, pp. 18-26.

-----------.   1991.   "John the Baptist and Jesus in Mark 1, 1-15, Markan
                         Redaction of Q?" Paper read at the 46th General
                         Meeting of the SNTS, Bethel, Bielefeld, Germany, 29
                         July - August, pp. 1-22 + Footnotes, pp. 1-24.

LOHFINK. N.   1988.   "Der Messiaskönig und seine Armen kommen zum
                         Zion" in L. Schenke (Hrsg.), Studien zum
                         Matthäusevangelium, Fs. W. Pesch, SBS Stuttgart, pp.
                         181-200.

LOHSE, E.   1972.   "*huios David*", *TDNT*, Vol 8, pp. 478-488.

MANSON, T. W.   1950.   "The Son of Man in Daniel, Enoch and the Gospels",
                         BJRL, Vol 32 pp. 171-193.

MANUS, C. U.   1985.   "The Centurion's Confession of Faith (Mk 15,39):
                         Reflections on Mark's Christology and its Significance
                         in the Life of African Christians" *BAT*, Vol 7, pp. 261-
                         278.

----------. 1986. "The Concept of Death and the After-Life in the Old Testament and Igbo Traditional Religion: Some Reflections for Contemporary Missiology", Mission Studies, Journal of the International Association for Mission Studies, Vol 3, pp. 41-56.

----------. 1987. "The Resurrection of Jesus: Some Critical and Exegetical Considerations in the Nigerian Context", *JMB* Vol 41, pp. 30-43.

----------. 1987. "The Universalism of Luke and the Motif of Reconciliattion in Luke 23,6-12", *ATJ* Vol 16, pp. 121-135.

----------. 1988. "Miracle Workers/Healers as Divine Men: Their Role in the Nigerian Church and Society", *AJT*, Vol 32, pp. 658-669.

----------. 1989. "The Areopagus Speech (Acts 17,16-34): A Study on Luke's Approach to Evangelism and its Significance in the African Context", *RAT* Vol 13, pp.155-170.

----------. 1990. "The Community of Love in Luke's Acts: A Sociological Exegesis of Acts 2:41-47 in the african Context", *WAJES* Vol 2, pp. 11-37.

----------. 1990. "Luke's Account of Paul in Thessalonica (Acts 17,1-9)" in R.F. Collins ed., The Thessalonian Correspondence, BETL 87, Peeters, Leuven University Press, pp.27-38.

----------. 1991. "Jesus And the Jewish Authorities in the Fourth Gospel" in W. Amewowo et al. eds. Communauté Johanniques, Johannine Communities, Actes du Quartrième Congrès des Biblistes Africains, Kinshasa, Saint Paul, pp. 135-155.

----------. 1991. "*Jesu Kristi Oba*: A Christology of "Christ the King" among the Indigenous Christian Churches in Yorubaland, Nigeria", *AJT* Vol 5, pp. 311-330.

----------. 1991. "'*King- Christology*': The Result of a critical study of Matt 28:16-20 as an example of contextual exegesis in Africa", *Scriptura*, Vol 39, pp. 25-42.

----------.   1991.   "'King-Christology': Reflections on the Figure of the
                                        Endzeit Discourse Material (Mt 25,31-46) in the
                                        African Context", Acta Theologica Vol 11, pp.19-41.

----------.   1991.   "'King-Christology': The Example of Some Aladura
                                        Churches in Nigeria", forthcoming in Africana
                                        Marburgensia, Marburg University.

MARTIN, F.   1975.   "The Image of the Shepherd in the Gospel of St.
                                        Matthew", Sc.Es., Vol 27, pp. 272-274

MATERA, F. J.   1988.   "The Prologue as the Interpretative Key to Mark's
                                        Gospel", JSNT, Vol 34, pp. 3-20.

MEIER, J. P.   1990.   "The Historical Jesus: Rethinking some Concepts", TS
                                        Vol 51, pp. 3-24.

MÜNDERLEIN, G. 1961/62.   "Die Erwählung durch das Pleroma", NTS Vol 8, pp.
                                        264-276.

MICHAELS, J. R.   1990.   "John 18,31 and the Trial of Jesus", NTS Vol 36, pp.
                                        474-479.

MILAVEC, A.   1990.   "The Identity of "the son" and "the Others"": Mark's
                                        Parable of the Wicked Husbandmen Reconsidered",
                                        BTB Vol 20, pp. 30-37.

NWACHUKWU, F &
MANUS, C. U.   1992.   "Forgiveness and Non-Forgiveness in Mt 12,31-32:
                                        Exegesis against the Background of Early Jewish and
                                        African Thought-Forms", forthcoming in ATJ Vol 21.

OBIJOLE, R.   1986.   "Principalities and Powers in St. Paul's Gospel of
                                        Reconciliation", AJBS Vol 1, pp. 113-125.

----------.   1988.   "St. Paul's Concept of Principalities and Powers in
                                        African Context", ATJ Vol 17, pp. 118-129.

O'COLLINS, G.   1987.   "Jesus" in M. Eliade et al eds., The Encyclopedia of
                                        Religion, Vol 8, New York, Macmillan.

OKOLO, C. B.   1980.   "Emanuel" : An African Enquiry", RAT Vol 2, pp. 15-
                                        22.

OKURE, Teresa   1990.   "Inculturation: biblically/theological basis" in T. Okure,
                                        P.van Thiel et al. eds., 32 Articles Evaluating
                                        Inculturation of Christianity in Africa, Eldoret,

AMECEA, Gaba Publications, Spearhead Nos. 112-114, pp. 57-58.

O'NEILL, J. C.   1991.   "The Kingdom of God". A Paper read at the 46th General Meeting of the SNTS, Bethel, Bielefeld, Germany, 29 July - 2 August, pp. 1-11.

OSEI-BONSU, J.   1990.   "The Contextualization of Christianity: Some New Testament Antecedents", *IBS*, Vol 12, pp. 129-148.

-------------.   1990.   "Biblically/theologically based Inculturation", *AFER* Vol 32, pp. 346-358.

REUMANN, J.   1989.   "Jesus and Christology", in E.J. Epp and W. MacRae (eds.), The New Testament and its Modern Interpreters, Philadelphia, Fortress Press, Atlanta, Scholars Press, pp. 501-564.

ROSS, J. M.   1991.   "The Son of Man", *IBS*, Vol 13, pp. 186-198.

RUDLOFF, D.   1979.   "Die Drei Könige im Geschichte und Kunst" in *Die Christen-Gemeinschaft*, Vol 51, pp. 15-22.

SABBE, M.   1991.   "The Trial of Jesus Before Pilate in John and its Relation to the Synoptic Gospels" in *idem*, Studia Neotestamentica: Collected Essays, BETL 98, Peeters, Leuven University Press.

SANDMEL, S.   1962.   "Parallelomania", *JBL* Vol 81, pp. 1-13.

SCHLIER, H.   1964.   "*elaion*", *TDNT* Vol 2, pp. 470-473.

SCHWEIZER, E.   1972.   "*huios*", TDNT, Vol 8, pp. 363-392.

STENDAHL, K.   1960.   "Quis et Unde? An Analysis of Mt 1-2" in W. Eltester, ed., Judentum, Urchristentum, Kirche, Berlin, Töpelmann.

WILLIAMS, D. T.   1989.   "The Four-fold Office of Christ", *ExpT* Vol 100, pp. 134-136.

ZELLER, D.   1991.   "Jesu Ankündigung des Reiches Gottes, ein uneingelöster Scheck auf Zukunft" in H. Wißmann Hrsg., Zur Erschließung von Zukunft in den Religionen, Zukunftserwartung und Gegenwartsbewältigung in der Religionsgeschichte, Würzburg, Königshausen & Neumann.

278

D. GENERAL WORKS

AGUWA, J. 1990. "Christianity and the Development of Igbo culture Today", *Bigard Theological Studies* 10(1990)26-37.

BAETA, C. G. 1966. "The engagement of Christianity with African Concepts and way of life", in *idem*. (ed), Chrsitianity in Tropical Africa, London, Oxford University Press.

BATHOLET, J. 1991. "The Silent Dying", *Newsweek* May 20, p. 15.

BOESAK, A. A. 1977. Farewell to Innocence: A Socio-ethical Study on Black Theology and Power, New York, Maryknoll, Orbis.

BRAYBROKE, M. 1991. Time to Meet. Part One. London, SCM Press.

BRITTAIN, V. 1991. "Fighting brings grim harvest of despair, *The Guardian International*, Wednesday, January 2, p. 4.

CONTRERAS, J. 1991. "A Man-Made Calamity", *Newsweek* May 20, p. 18.

N. A. 1991. "Democracy in Africa. Arguments for and against", *Africa Bulletin*, Vol 21, p. 1-3.

DICKINSON, E. 1991. "Disaster Fatigue", *Newsweek* May 20, pp. 10-13.

N. A. 1980. *Didia Mfumu* (Meal of the Lord, Circle C), in The Missal of the Mbujimayi Diocese, Kinshasa.

EGBULEFU, J. O. 1990. "The Church in Africa towards the third Millennium. The present problems of the young African Church as the occasion for the Synod", *Omnis Terra* 211(1990)413-424.

FALOLA, T. 1982. "Economic and social development in cotemporary Africa" in Olaniyan ed., African History and Culture, pp. 111-126.

FLANNERY, A. ed. 1975. Vatican Council II: The Conciliar and Post Conciliar Documents, New York, Costello, pp. 818-820; 958-968, esp.: *Ad Gentes Divinitus* No. 6; *Gaudium et Spes* Nos. 53; 58-59; *The Constitution on the Sacred Liturgy*, art. 37.

HARRISON, P. 1987. The Greening of Africa, London, Paladin.

279

JOHN PAUL II.   1980.   "Address to the Bishops of Zaire", Kinshasa, 3 May, in *AFER*, Vol 22, pp. 223-224.

------------.   1980.   Africa. Apostolic Pilgrimage, Boston, St Paul's Editions.

------------.   *Evangelii Nuntiandi*, No. 20.

KASENENE, P.   1991.   "Natural Communities in Ecumenical Activity", *AFER* Vol 33, pp.150-159.

KELLY, J.   1991.   "The Evolution of Small Christian Communities", *AFER* Vol 33, pp.108-120.

MOLONEY, R.   1987.   "African Christology", *TS* Vol 48, pp. 505-515.

N. A.   1990.   *The Lineamenta*. Synod of Bishopy: Special Assembly for Africa. The Church in Africa and Her Evangelising Mission Towards the Year 2000. "You shall be my Witnesses" (Acts 1:8), Libreria Editrice Vaticana, Vatican City.

NYAMITI, C.   1984.   Christ as Our Ancestor. Christology from the African Perspective, Gweru, Mambo Press.

NDYABAHIKA, J.   1991.   "Worship in African Christianity", *ATJ* Vol 20, pp.54-62.

NIEBUHR, R. H.   1951.   Christ and Culture, London, Faber and Faber.

O'SHEA, W. J.   1967.   "Feast of Christ the King" in NCE, Vol 3, New York, McGraw-Hill, pp. 627-628.

PAUL VI.   1964.   *Ecclesiam Suam*. The Ecyclical Letter, *AAS* Vol 56, pp. 609-659.

PIUS XI.   1925.   *Quas Primas*. The Encyclical Letter, *AAS* Vol 17, pp. 593-610.

RAHNER, K.   1954.   "Chalkedon - Ende oder Anfang?" in A. Grillmeier and H. Bacht, Hrsg., Das Konzil von Chalkedon, Vol 3, Würzburg, pp. 5-49.

---------.   1966.   Theological Investigations, Vol 1, London, Burns and Oates.

N. A.   1990.   The Right Time to Change: What Hope for a Crisis-Striken Africa?. A Proposal Reflection, AACC General Secretariat, Nairobi, October, p. 18.

SEGUNDO, J. L.   1976.   The Liberation of Theology, ET by John Drury, New York, Maryknoll, Orbis.

SHORTER, A.   1982.   "Folk Christianity and Functional Christology" AFER Vol 24, pp. 133-137.

SMITH, W. C.   1991.   "Christian-Muslim Relations: The Theological Dimension". Studies in Interreligious Dialogue, Vol 1, pp. 8-24.

SHREITER, R. J.   1985.   Constructing Local Theologies, New York, Marknoll, Orbis.

SOBRINO, J.   1985.   Christology at the Crossroads. A Latin American Perspective, ET by John Drury, New York, Maryknoll, Orbis, 8th Edition.

TABER, C.   1978.   "Is there One Way to Do Theology?", Gospel in Context Vol 1, pp. 2-10.

TAYLOR, J. V.   1963.   The Primal Vision, London, SCM Press.

WEBER, M.   1968.   Economy and Society. An Outline of Interpretative Sociology, eds. G.Roth & C. Wittich, (1921), New York, Bedminster Press.

WHELAN, G.   1989.   "Facing the African Economic Crisis", African Christian Studies, Vol 5, pp. 43-63.

WILFRED, F.   1990.   "Towards an Anthropologically and Culturally Founded Ecclesiology: Reflections from an Asian Perspective", VJTR, Vol 54, pp. 501-511.

UZUKWU, E. E.   1991.   "Evangelization in Context: Human Promotion and Liberation", AJT Vol 5, pp. 274-285.

STUDIEN ZUR INTERKULTURELLEN GESCHICHTE DES CHRISTENTUMS
ETUDES D'HISTOIRE INTERCULTURELLE DU CHRISTIANISME
STUDIES IN THE INTERCULTURAL HISTORY OF CHRISTIANITY

Begründet von/fondé par/founded by
Hans Jochen Margull †, Hamburg

Herausgegeben von/edité par/edited by

Richard Friedli   Walter J. Hollenweger   Theo Sundermeier
Université de Fribourg   University of Birmingham   Universität Heidelberg

Jan A.B. Jongeneel
Rijksuniversiteit Utrecht